THE LIONS FINALLY ROAR

THE FORD FAMILY, THE DETROIT LIONS, AND THE ROAD TO REDEMPTION IN THE NFL

BILL MORRIS

PEGASUS BOOKS

NEW YORK LONDON

ALSO BY BILL MORRIS

NOVELS

Motor City Burning

All Souls' Day

Motor City

NONFICTION

*The Age of Astonishment: John Morris in the Miracle Century,
From the Civil War to the Cold War*

American Berserk: A Cub Reporter, a Small-Town Daily, the Schizo '70s

THE LIONS FINALLY ROAR

Pegasus Books, Ltd.
148 West 37th Street, 13th Floor
New York, NY 10018

Copyright © 2024 by Bill Morris

First Pegasus Books cloth edition September 2024

Interior design by Maria Fernandez

Library of Congress Cataloging-in-Publication Data is available.

ISBN: 978-1-63936-718-4

10 9 8 7 6 5 4 3 2 1

Printed in the United States of America
Distributed by Simon & Schuster
www.pegasusbooks.com

For the people of Detroit, who survive everything America can dish out.

CONTENTS

PREGAME

This book is a mongrel. It's nonfiction, but it's a mix of numerous breeds, including biography, history, reportage, memoir, and, when the record runs thin, informed speculation. The book is based on interviews (by the author and others) and such published sources as books, newspaper and magazine articles, web postings, podcasts, media guides, videos, newsreels, and scholarly articles. In the Notes section at the end of the book, the reader will find the sources of all quoted remarks and most statements of fact. When I've engaged in speculation I've announced it by such markers as "it's likely" or "here's a theory." I have done my best to stick to the facts in my pursuit of the truth. Any errors are entirely the fault of the author.

FIRST QUARTER

GOING DOWN

(1957–1973)

THE LAST HURRAH

It's noon on Sunday, Dec. 29, 1957. Briggs Stadium, the big sooty iceberg at the corner of Michigan and Trumbull just west of downtown Detroit, is already buzzing even though kickoff is still an hour away. The teams have just come out of their locker rooms to warm up—the hometown Lions in their Honolulu-blue jerseys and unadorned silver helmets and pants, the visiting Cleveland Browns all in white except for the orange globes of their helmets, an incongruous suggestion of sunshine and citrus on a team from that gray factory town where the combustible Cuyahoga River discharges its toxins into Lake Erie.

The winner of today's game will be champions of the National Football League.

The two teams are old familiars. The Lions beat the Browns to win championships in 1952 and '53 before losing to them, badly, in '54. Now, as the players do calisthenics and run pass routes and boot balls high into the sky, puffs of steam shoot from their mouths. The temperature is hovering above freezing—nearly balmy by end-of-year Midwestern standards, when football games are often played on fields that have turned to viscous soup or frozen solid as a sidewalk. Today there will be no rain or sleet or snow. The field is dry, the winter grass patchy in spots, and the sun keeps peeking through a tattered cover of clouds. Even so, this is one of the shortest days of the year, and the banks of blazing lights that rim the stadium have already been turned on.

Among the 55,263 fans squeezed into the stadium on this day is a dapper man who prowls the press box like a caged puma. This is a roofed aerie atop the second deck that curls around the corner of the stadium where home plate stands in the summertime, a reminder that Briggs Stadium was built for baseball, not football—for Tigers, not Lions. From up here you look almost straight down at the field, a dizzying bird's-eye view. The man pacing the press box stands apart from the blue-collar fans packing the seats beneath him. Instead of a nylon parka he wears a sleek camel hair overcoat and a cashmere scarf. There is no grease on the fingernails inside his leather gloves. A fedora rests atop his perfectly watered dark hair. He has been a Lions fan since he was a boy, and a year ago he bought into the 144-member syndicate that owns the team. Today, for the first time, he'll find out how it feels to have skin in the game when a championship is on the line.

This is thirty-two-year-old William Clay Ford, the youngest grandson of auto pioneer Henry Ford, a man who was minted a multimillionaire the day he was born and has become richer, almost effortlessly, every day of his life. Now his personal wealth is beyond imagining, a hundred million dollars—a billion in today's money—maybe more, maybe much more.

Ford stops pacing the press box and picks up a pair of binoculars so he can get a closer look at the activity on the field. His gaze lands on a man with a shock of yellow hair who's dressed in street clothes and sitting on a bench beside a pair of crutches. The man's right ankle is encased in a plaster cast. This is Bobby Layne, the Lions' star quarterback, a hell-raising Texan whose ankle was shattered during a late-season win over these same Cleveland Browns. Losing Layne was typical of the adversity that has dogged this team since training camp. Buddy Parker, the coach who led the team to those back-to-back championships in 1952 and '53, walked off the job in disgust just before the '57 season began. "This," he declared, "is the worst team in training camp I have ever seen—no life, no go. It's a completely dead team." One of Parker's assistants, mild-mannered, untested George Wilson, had stepped into the coaching vacancy.

Then, during training camp, Layne got charged with drunken driving. He got off because the arresting officer, suddenly finding himself in an uncomfortably hot spotlight, decided that, well yes, come to think of it, he might have confused Layne's Texas drawl with the slurred speech of a man who'd had a few too many—a suggestion put forward by Layne's inventive defense lawyer. After the charges were dropped, the team's trainer posted a sign in the locker room: "Ah ain't drunk. Ah'm from Texas." Everyone thought that was very funny.

Including Bill Ford, who is no stranger to sliding behind the wheel of a car after a few pops. He finds himself drawn to these rowdy, rough, nearly unmanageable football players, especially Layne. Their go-to-hell attitude is so refreshing compared to the bean counters and brown-nosers you run into in the shiny new headquarters of Ford Motor Company, that icy palace known as the Glass House.

Now Ford's binoculars come to rest on Tobin Rote, Layne's backup, who's firing warm-up passes, grinning, chattering with coaches. Rote, another Texan, is a guy with a rifle arm who loves to run over defenders, and he looks relaxed out there, confident, almost cocky. Rote's aura chases away some of Ford's anxiety over Layne's injury. The Lions acquired Rote from the Green Bay Packers before the season in case something happened to Layne, and Rote has proved to be an invaluable insurance policy. After Layne's injury, Rote came off the bench and cemented the victory over the Browns, then he brought the team back from a ten-point halftime deficit to beat the Chicago Bears in the regular season finale, followed by another comeback win over the San Francisco 49ers in the Western Conference playoff, a game made necessary by the two teams' identical 8–4 records in the regular season. And so here the Lions are in the league championship game, riding a four-game winning streak, but battered, tired, and stretched thin, clear underdogs to the well-rested and dangerous Browns.

Watching Tobin Rote throw his warm-up tosses gives Bill Ford a warm feeling. The warmth increases when he notices his wife Martha—Martha

Firestone, the rubber heiress from Akron—sitting there in her mink coat with the other Grosse Pointe wives, sipping a cup of hot chocolate, trying to get their daughters, nine-year-old Muffy and six-year-old Sheila, to quit darting around like a couple of deranged minnows. Infant son Billy is at home, but soon enough he'll join these Sunday family pilgrimages. Bill Ford feels lucky. Martha married him for love not for money. Martha is in his corner, and she isn't coming out.

It's time, at last, for the kickoff. The Lions' kicker blasts the ball through the Cleveland end zone for a touchback, an omen of things to come. From there the game unfolds like a waking dream. The Lions score the first three times they touch the ball, and by the end of the first quarter they hold a 17–0 lead. It doesn't seem quite real to Bill Ford and a lot of other people in the stadium. After Cleveland's Jim Brown, the Rookie of the Year, runs for a touchdown to keep the game within reach, the Lions fake a field goal and Rote lofts a touchdown pass to a wide-open receiver. The Browns are stunned. Then comes the backbreaker.

Just before halftime, Detroit's defensive back Terry Barr snatches an interception at the Cleveland nineteen-yard line and scampers untouched into the end zone for a touchdown—a dagger that makes the score 31–7. After he crosses the goal line, Barr simply flips the ball to the referee and jogs back to the bench, tapping hands with teammates coming onto the field for the extra-point kick. Barr doesn't slam the ball into the turf, or do a dance, or run toward the nearest camera, or leap into the air while bumping his teammates' helmets and chests. Why would he? He has simply done what he's expected to do, what he's paid to do. The message behind the subdued behavior of Barr and his teammates is clear: in 1957, sports have not yet devolved into just another branch of American showbiz.

Late in the fourth quarter, with dusk descending and the outcome decided, Bill Ford scans the crowd. He's hoarse from yelling. For the first time he tastes the iron in the breeze coming off the nearby river. As the clock ticks down, he realizes that everyone is standing, bouncing up and down—the whole building is shaking. A couple of jokers in the faraway centerfield bleachers have stripped off their shirts and they're dancing in the aisles, no doubt fueled by repeat doses of Stroh's beer and some antifreeze with a stronger kick. Bill Ford realizes he is witnessing delirium.

The final score is an astonishment: Lions 59, Browns 14. Tobin Rote has passed for four touchdowns and run for another. Though no one knows it, Rote's performance will stand as the pinnacle of his seventeen-year career, much as this day will stand as the last hurrah for the Detroit Lions, who are about to embark on six and half decades of unrelenting futility. But that's the future. Now fans are streaming onto the field as the players carry around Joe Schmidt, Detroit's star linebacker and cocaptain, on their shoulders. Fans join in the scrum. A city's delirium is turning into pandemonium.

It has seeped into the locker room by the time Bill Ford pushes his way through the cigar smoke and champagne spray and bear hugs. He'd gotten word that Joe Schmidt and his roommate, the defensive lineman Gene Cronin, planned to throw a postgame party, win or lose. After congratulating Cronin, Ford says, "I hear you and Joe are having a party."

"Yeah," Cronin says uneasily, not sure where this is going.

Ford surprises him. "Can Martha and I come?"

Cronin is in just his second season in Detroit, but that's long enough to figure out that you don't say no to a member of the syndicate that owns the team, especially if his name is Ford. Cronin gives him directions.

Driving to the party in his Continental Mark II with the heater roaring to chase away Martha's chill, Bill Ford realizes that what he loves about this day—what he loves about this game and this team and its fans—is that it all happens inside the chalked lines of the playing field, an orderly, violent, thrilling world that exists outside the suffocating world he grew up in and is expected to remain in forever, playing by its rigid rules, locked inside the walls of the Ford family fortune and the Ford Motor Company but relegated now to a decorative role, a man without real power, an afterthought just like his father. But what Bill Ford witnessed inside Briggs Stadium today might be a chance to step away from the family and the company, a chance to be emperor of his own world. As he pulls up in front of Schmidt and Cronin's apartment, the idea might come to Bill Ford almost as an epiphany, unassailable, the perfect way out of his cage: *I should buy the Detroit Lions.*

The party is already at full roar, and Bill Ford dives right in. "So he and Martha showed up," Cronin said later, "and at the end of the night they had to carry him out."

It isn't the last time Bill Ford will celebrate a little too much after a Detroit Lions game. But it is the last time in his long life he will celebrate them winning a championship.

BIRTH OF THE CURSE

Bill Ford didn't act on his urge to buy the Lions right after their 1957 championship win. He decided to sit back and study the team's ownership syndicate, the front office and the coaching staff, how they operated, how they related to the players.

He didn't like what he saw. With Layne and Rote platooning at quarterback, the team got whipped in the 1958 season opener by the Baltimore Colts, 28–15—no cause for alarm since the Colts, led by their rising star quarterback Johnny Unitas, were favorites to win the Western Division. But the next Sunday the Lions played to an uninspired 13–13 tie with the lowly Green Bay Packers, who were on their way to a one-win season. Coach George Wilson criticized both of his quarterbacks for their play calling, and the *Detroit News* later reported that Layne had showed up tipsy for a team meeting the day before the Green Bay game.

The Monday morning after that game, Wilson's telephone rang. The caller was Buddy Parker, his predecessor in Detroit, now head coach of the Pittsburgh Steelers. Parker, known as a wheeler-dealer, had engineered the savvy trade for Tobin Rote while he was in Detroit, but on this morning he was on a routine mission to ask if Wilson could send him some game film. Wilson's mind was elsewhere. Ever since training camp he'd been thinking that Layne would soon turn thirty-two, getting old by NFL standards, and that he had ended the past two seasons on the bench—with the broken ankle in '57 and with a concussion the year before. As his injuries piled up, Layne had begun to change. When he was in his prime, Wilson recalled, Layne didn't chew out a lineman for missing a block, even if the quarterback got flattened as a result of the miscue. Layne would give the lineman a wink and tell him to forget it, and the lineman would make sure he didn't miss the block next time. But when the hits—and the injuries—kept coming, Wilson noticed that Layne began to cuss out his teammates, and they began to lose respect for him. To top it off, there was Layne's carousing and a growing chorus of whispers that his love of gambling didn't stop at the poker table—that he gambled on NFL games, possibly on Lions games. As brilliant as he still was at times, Layne had become a distraction. Platooning quarterbacks was obviously not working, and so, Walker decided, something had to give. He surprised Parker with a question that had nothing to do with game film: "Would you like to trade for a quarterback?"

"Who?" Parker asked.

"Bobby Layne."

There was silence on the Pittsburgh end of the line. When Parker got hold of himself, he said that yes, he would indeed like to talk about trading for Bobby Layne. By the time the phone call ended, the deal was done. Detroit would ship Layne to Pittsburgh in exchange for Earl Morrall, a promising young quarterback who'd been the second pick in the 1956 draft, plus two future draft picks. With Tobin Rote as his starter and Morrall serving as backup—and with the headache of Bobby Layne forever gone—George Wilson felt it had been a productive morning.

Now he had to break the news to Layne. Wilson had expected Layne to drop by the team's office to pick up his paycheck, but Layne had gone out to Metro Airport to meet his wife, Carol, who was flying in from their home in Lubbock, Texas. Worried that news of the trade would reach Layne, Wilson frantically called the airport and had him paged.

As the couple was leaving the airport, they heard the page. When Layne picked up the phone he heard Wilson blurt it out: "I've got to tell you something I don't want to." The bottom fell out for Layne. He knew instantly that he'd been traded. When the call ended, a stricken Layne turned to his wife and said, "It seems to me he could've sat down across a desk and looked at me and told me—long as I've been here."

Carol tried to soothe him. "He probably wanted to make sure you knew it before you heard it on the radio or read it in the paper."

"Maybe," Layne replied, not sounding convinced. "But you can't tell me it happened that sudden. I don't believe they had a meetin' and everybody said, 'Aye' or raised their hands just like that. It wasn't just one day. There had to have been some talk before."

By the time Layne arrived at Briggs Stadium to clean out his locker, the news was on the street and a posse of reporters was waiting for him. Ever ready with a colorful quote, Layne on that day produced no dazzlers, delivering instead a litany of platitudes mixed with expressions of bruised feelings. "It's just one of those things, I guess they always work out for the best," he began, before veering into more personal territory. "It hurts quite a bit. . . . I haven't got a lot to complain about, I guess . . . but regardless of what people think of me, I gave my heart and soul to play football. I really tried to play my best. I've got an awful lot of friends here, and I hate to leave."

Many of Layne's teammates—and virtually all of the team's fans—hated to see him leave. "It makes me sick," said the Lions' popular linebacker Joe Schmidt, a future Hall of Famer. "I think it's a big mistake. He's still a damned good quarterback." Rookie defensive lineman Alex Karras, also destined for the Hall of Fame, chimed in: "My reaction, like everyone else, was 'Why?' No one could give us a real good explanation, and that disturbed a lot of us. Once he was gone the team just wasn't what it used to be." As for the why, Karras speculated: "It must have been something he must have done that wasn't good for the NFL."

Something like gambling on games, possibly shaving points?

On his way out the door, Layne may or may not have uttered words that were destined to become an urban legend in Detroit: *This team will not win for another fifty years.*

◆

And so was born the Curse of Bobby Layne. Real or imagined, it was destined to have a long life in Detroit, beginning the very next morning when the newspapers hit the street. LAYNE TRADED TO THE STEELERS shouted the *Detroit Free Press* headline at the top of the front page, above the paper's name and stories about the fading health of Pope Pius XII and the ongoing walkout by autoworkers at GM and Chrysler—two major stories in a city with a large Catholic population and a thriving auto industry. The paper's play of the three stories made it clear: Bobby Layne's departure was bigger news in Detroit than a dying pope or another UAW strike.

The Pittsburgh papers were a bit more restrained in their coverage. The *Post-Gazette* played the story on the front page, but below a banner headline about the pope's health and a story about a riot in a London theater during a showing of the new Elvis Presley movie, *King Creole*. The *Pittsburgh Press*, meanwhile, welcomed "the swashbuckling roustabout" who would now lead the Steelers' offense.

The day after the trade, Tobin Rote pulled a muscle in his right leg during practice, and the *Free Press* ran two stories, the first drumbeats in a coming string of stories implying that the team was cursed. WHAT A MESS! ROTE HURT DURING LION DRILL read one headline. The other was a bit mistier: LION MORALE HITS BOTTOM AFTER TRADE. The writer of the latter story, George Puscas, quoted an unnamed Lion player uttering a complaint that sounded suspiciously like a product of sportswriter's license: "Did you ever see a team with Morrall and no morale?" Whether the quote was fabricated or not, Rote and Morrall both played in the next game, an unimpressive 42–28 loss to the Los Angeles Rams. The team would stumble to a 4–7–1 season and a fifth-place finish. Behind Layne, meanwhile, the Steelers clawed their way to a 7–4–1 record, their best mark in more than a decade. Curse or no curse, the twin foundation stones had been set in place for the Lions' coming decades of futility: quarterback controversies and a revolving door in the head coach's office.

◆

Bill Ford took note of all this, especially the fact that George Wilson had been free to make a blockbuster trade on the spur of the moment, without consulting Ford or the other members of the team's board of directors. Ford did not see this as an organizational flaw. After watching his big brother Henry II transform Ford Motor Company from a chaotic mess into a humming profit machine over the past dozen years, Bill Ford must have seen the loose structure of the Detroit Lions as enticing. The team had no executive committee or policy committee, no bean counters to thwart a man's dreams. If the coach was free to engineer a major trade without consulting any higher-ups, imagine the power a sole owner would have! He could dictate the hiring and firing of coaches and general managers, the drafting and trading of specific players, even the price of tickets. . .

The gears were turning, but Bill Ford was not ready to pounce just yet. First he needed to sort out the palace intrigues that were poisoning the atmosphere on the board of directors and seeping into the team's performance on the field. After their championship season and the Bobby Layne trade, the Lions would stumble through two losing seasons and back-to-back fifth-place finishes. Where others saw failure, Bill Ford saw opportunity.

BORN UNDER A BAD SIGN

One source of the palace intrigues poisoning the team's ownership syndicate was that time-tested soap opera staple: a romance between a middle-aged man and a much younger woman. The star of this particular soap opera was D. Lyle Fife, owner of an electrical supply company and one of the seven wealthy businessmen who had bought the last-place, money-losing Detroit Lions in 1948 for the fire-sale price of $165,000. The team's presidency, an unpaid post, was awarded to Fife, the vice presidency to fellow co-owner Edwin J. Anderson, head of the local Goebel's brewery, a natty dresser with furry eyebrows and a fondness for feathered Alpine hats. At the time of the sale, according to the *New York Times*, the owners planned to expand the seven-man syndicate to fifty members or more, a group that would eventually grow to 144 and come to include William Clay Ford.

In the middle of the 1949 season, Fife had filed for divorce from his wife of thirty-three years so he could marry his secretary, Judy Hohnstine. Hell hath no fury—another soap opera staple—and Fife's wife had promptly filed a countersuit, charging that her husband "had fled to Europe with another woman." As conservative as they were, men in the upper echelons of Detroit society—which generally meant the upper echelons of the auto industry—were no strangers to mistresses and prostitutes, or to adoptions and abortions that quietly dealt with unwanted consequences of those adventures. The unwritten code was that such matters were to be kept quiet and, above all, must never be allowed to interfere with a decades-old marriage. Detroit has always been a provincial town where appearances matter, and the Lions' board of directors was very much a product of that time and place. Its members, like Mrs. Fife, were not pleased with this unseemly breach of the code. It was Anderson who'd suggested that Fife slip away to Europe with his young bride until the dust settled in Detroit.

Anderson had kept in touch with Fife during his European exile/ honeymoon. One day Anderson cabled: "Things are tight, suggest you resign." Fife obliged. Anderson replaced him as president, and Fife was reduced to watching from the sidelines as the Lions entered their glory phase, winning four division titles and three NFL championships in the next eight seasons. Fife may have been the forgotten co-owner, but he was not yet gone.

◆

Fast forward almost a decade later to the summer of 1958, months before the Bobby Layne trade. Anderson got bounced from his job as president of the Goebel's brewery, and the Lions' directors, including newcomer Bill Ford, were convinced that Anderson had gotten sacked because he had devoted so much time and energy to turning the team into champions. As a reward for his devotion, the board named Anderson general manager and gave him a handsome salary of $40,000 a year.

But the palace intrigues continued to fester, and by 1961 the Lions were embroiled in a bare-knuckled proxy fight for control of the team. Fife wanted his old post back, but Bill Ford, after his years of watching and waiting, had replaced Anderson as president and was solidly in favor of keeping him on as general manager. Fife tried to convince his fellow shareholders that Anderson, as president and general manager, had "mismanaged" the team to three championships, had negotiated an "unsatisfactory" television contract that was the third most lucrative in the league, and had let Tobin Rote play out his option and walk away to the Canadian Football League.

"Regardless of this," *Sports Illustrated* reported in early 1961, "Anderson has been a good manager and, more important, he has William Ford on his side. Ford . . . issued a statement in full support of Anderson." Ford also gave a clunky quote to the *New York Times*, saying the proxy fight "comes at a time when we should be able to devote full efforts to the difficult task of signing recent draft choices and is ill-timed."

When the stockholders voted on Feb. 23, the Ford-Anderson faction won handily. In the heat of battle before the vote, Henry II had offered his youngest brother a typically blunt suggestion: "Why don't you just take over, Bill?"

He was working on it.

◆

Since taking over the unpaid post of team president in 1961, Bill Ford had grown close to many of the players. He attended all games, home and away, and became a fixture in the locker room after games, offering congratulations or condolences. He once flew from London to Baltimore to watch the Lions play the Colts, then promptly flew back to London after the game. When flights out of Detroit were grounded by inclement weather on the day the Lions were in Chicago playing the Bears late in the 1961 season, Ford was reduced to watching the game at home on TV. With the Lions trailing 15–9 late in the fourth quarter, Ford became so incensed by a Lions miscue that, in an Elvisoidal outburst, he kicked a hole in the TV screen. Realizing the game wasn't over yet, Ford rushed to the servants' quarters and found a radio just in time to hear the announcer describe Terry Barr catching the game-tying touchdown pass. The extra point kick sealed a 16–15 victory. A sheepish Ford vowed that his days of kicking holes in TV screens were over. At home games, Ford screamed himself hoarse in the press box, as he had been doing at least since that championship game in 1957. No one doubted that Bill Ford cared deeply about the team.

Occasionally Ford took select players on duck-hunting trips at a private reserve in Canada, where they stayed in a plush log cabin and ate catered meals and drank booze like it was tap water. "It was such a good time," recalled linebacker Wayne Walker. "[Ford] was just, in those situations, one of the guys. It was truly great."

Early in the decade Ford took the players to a Ford factory and let them pick out any car they wanted. He even paid the insurance. For a player making $6,000 or less a year—about $60,000 in today's money—a free car was a spectacular perk. But the largesse lasted just one year because most of the players crashed their cars.

After victories, players gathered at Joe Schmidt's Golden Lion restaurant in Grosse Pointe, and Bill and Martha Ford sometimes stopped by to take part in what one player called "spirit parties." Pat Studstill, a flanker and punter, recalled, "We had a real close team at that time. This was '62, and we kind of thought he was looking to buy the club. I'm pretty sure he kind of put out a 'Should I buy the club?'"

Apparently the answer from the players was yes, because by mid-October 1963 Ford was finally ready to drop what he called his "bombshell." At the Detroit Lions' annual board of directors meeting, he made a $6 million offer to buy out his 143 fellow shareholders. If the deal went through, it would be the most money ever paid for an American sports franchise at that time, and it represented a handsome return for every member of the syndicate. After minimal debate, the board of directors voted to accept the offer. Now the deal would be put to a vote of the entire syndicate.*

---

* Ford's historic offer must be seen in perspective. In today's dollars it amounts to about $59 million, which has led many people to think of Bill Ford as a savvy investor—since the team is now worth $3 billion, based on such factors as stadium deal, revenue, operating income, and debt. But there is only one team in the thirty-two-team league today that's worth less: the small-market Cincinnati Bengals. The most valuable franchise, the expansion Dallas Cowboys, which has branded itself as "America's Team," is worth nearly three times as much as the Lions. Yes, Bill Ford did well with his investment, but other owners have done far, far better.

When the Lions' co-owners gathered at the Statler Hilton Hotel in downtown Detroit on Nov. 22 for a formal vote, 94 percent of the shares were in favor of the sale. Bill Ford was now sole owner of the Detroit Lions, subject to approval by the rest of the NFL owners, which was seen as a formality. After the vote, an ebullient Ford and a handful of friends and supporters moved to the hotel dining room for a celebratory luncheon. On the way, Ford turned to his executive assistant Dick Morris and said, "I tell you what, we're not going to have great big tables with twenty guys sitting around for board meetings." With a triumphant laugh, he added: "I'm going to hold my board meetings in a phone booth!" The die of sole ownership was already cast.

As the men were studying their menus, a waitress approached the table with a stricken look on her face and asked if they had heard about President Kennedy. Bill Ford's first reaction was to wait for the punch line. John F. Kennedy had once enjoyed the highest approval ratings of any postwar president. Even after the embarrassing Bay of Pigs fiasco during the early months of his presidency, Kennedy got a counterintuitive *rise* in approval—to a stratospheric 83 percent. He got another bounce from his cool-headed handling of the Cuban Missile Crisis in October 1962, just in time for the midterm elections. But by the fall of 1963 his approval rating had plummeted to a dismal 56 percent, the lowest of his presidency, which meant that barely half of the American electorate felt he was doing a good job. People were beginning to make jokes about the poor little rich boy from Massachusetts—"sick" jokes, in the opinion of Bill Ford, a poor little rich boy from Michigan—and with the 1964 election just twelve months away, Democratic party higher-ups were beginning to fret that the incumbent might not win reelection.

Instead of delivering a punch line, the waitress told the men at the table that the president had been shot dead in Dallas.

"It turned into a sad, terrible day," Ford would muse years later. "It's a terrible coincidence that both of these things would occur around the same time. But there were a couple of times over the years when some things happened to us that you just couldn't figure out why or how it happened, and you'd briefly think if there's some kind of stigma attached to anything else that may have taken place that awful day."

Fifty years after that awful day, a team historian would write: "For those who believe in omens, it seems fitting that the William Clay Ford era—an ongoing half-century span of controversy, turmoil, and tragedy on and off the field—began on the auspicious date of Nov. 22, 1963."

Omen, stigma, curse. Call it what you will, the Ford family's ownership of the Detroit Lions was born under the very worst kind of bad sign.

A DEGAS BRONZE
AND A JOB OFFER

A few days before Christmas 1963, Bill Ford checked into a suite in the Plaza Hotel overlooking New York's Central Park. The Lions had just completed a losing season, and Ford was not happy with his expensive new toy. He burned with a desire to return the team to its glory years of the 1950s, when it won four Western Conference titles and three NFL championships. Bill Ford had always followed his instincts—a luxury available to the very rich—and now his gut was telling him that if he wanted to make the Lions his own and turn them back into champions, he would have to make changes at the top. He had an idea where to begin.

Traveling with Ford was his executive assistant Dick Morris, who Ford referred to as "my PR guy." Morris had been working as a reporter at the *Washington Post* a dozen years earlier when Ford Motor Company recruiters wooed him to Detroit to join their expanding public relations staff on the eve of the company's fiftieth anniversary in 1953. After writing speeches and press releases and performing assorted duties for Bill Ford's eldest brother, Henry Ford II, Morris was tasked with promoting Bill Ford's dream car, the elegant but ill-fated Continental Mark II. Bill Ford and Dick Morris were unalike in many ways: Motor City royalty vs. the son of a Southern college professor; Yale vs. the University of Georgia; a wiry, nearly fragile man vs. a big solid guy who, at 6'2" and 225 pounds, looked like he could hold his own in a scrape; a resident of gilded Grosse Pointe vs. a mid-level executive who had just moved his growing family from an apartment on the West Side of Detroit into a modest frame house in the northern suburb of Birmingham, a rung below posh Bloomfield Hills, the other Grosse Pointe.

Yet these two men found that they had things in common that transcended their divergent backgrounds and the usual protocols that separate employer and employee. For one thing, they were always impeccably groomed and dressed, a couple of clothes horses in the thoroughbred class. For another, they both loved to play golf, they both loved to watch the Detroit Lions play football, and they were both avid participants in the car world's rococo drinking culture. After working and traveling and drinking together for ten years, they had moved beyond the standard boss-employee arrangement and had arrived at something very much like a friendship. They made each other laugh, which proved to be no small thing. Whenever Bill Ford said something funny, which he seemed to do a lot, Dick Morris did a tightly choreographed little dance—he would bend forward at the waist and one knee would kick upward like a piston as he unleashed a belly laugh. Morris was a flesh-and-blood laugh track. He was Ed McMahon to Ford's Johnny Carson.

After the men had finished unpacking their bags, Ford announced that he needed to run a little errand. "I've got to go shopping for My Relative," he said. "She's got something at some art gallery she wants for Christmas."

The Fords, like many wealthy families, were big on pet names. Bill Ford's grandmother Clara was Callie. His sister Josephine was Dodie. His eldest daughter Martha was Muffy. But Bill went beyond these family-wide terms of endearment and created droll monikers of his own that tended to have an edge. His wife Martha, as Dick Morris knew, was My Relative. Van Patrick, the stentorian announcer of Lions games on radio and TV, was The Voice. Tex Schramm, the general manager of the Dallas Cowboys known for his liberal reading of league rules, was Loophole. Big brother Henry II's second wife, the beautiful Italian divorcée Cristina Vettore Austin, would be known as The Pizza Queen. (Henry II's daughters by his first marriage took the barb a step further and called this usurper The Dago.) Bill Ford's mother-in-law, Martha Parke Firestone, owned a museum-worthy collection of couture clothing that led Bill to dub her The Living Doll. And in Bill's eyes, his eldest brother Henry II was, always and forever, Lard Ass.

Bill Ford and Dick Morris walked the two blocks down Fifth Avenue to the art gallery on 57th Street. The nation was still numb from the assassination of President John F. Kennedy a month earlier. Did the two men talk about the assassination as they walked? Or did they talk about something closer to home: last week's death of Dinah Washington, the famous singer and wife of the Lions' star defensive back Dick "Night Train" Lane, who died in her bed at the age of thirty-nine, a vial of sedatives on the night table beside her?

Ford and Morris probably steered clear of such topics. They were out on the town yet again, far from home and wives and kids, a moment of escape when weighty matters were not on the menu. As soon as they entered the art gallery, a woman came sweeping toward them. "Oh, Mr. Ford, I'm so delighted to *see* you again!"

She led the men to a private viewing room at the rear of the gallery where a shrouded object stood on a table. With a flourish the woman removed the covering to reveal a sculpture: a gorgeous bronze schoolgirl by Edgar Degas.

The two men circled the sculpture for a long moment without speaking while the art dealer prattled on about how Mrs. Ford had absolutely fallen in love with the little schoolgirl the instant she'd laid eyes on her. Bill Ford, who had grown up in a mansion filled with artistic masterpieces, cut the woman off. "Well," he said, "if that's what Martha wants, I guess that's what I'm going to get her." Then he made arrangements to have the sculpture shipped to Grosse Pointe in time for Christmas.

On the way back to the hotel, Morris was in a daze, trying to sort out what he'd just witnessed. He was no appraiser of fine art, but he had a keen sense of the value of things, and he was guessing that the sculpture had to be worth at least $100,000, probably more. Easily enough to put all four of his children through college, with plenty to spare. (Today such Degas bronzes fetch about $20 million at auction.) Finally he managed to say, "That's a beautiful piece, Bill. Martha will be thrilled with it."

Ford didn't respond.

"I listened to the transaction back there pretty closely," Morris went on, "and I never heard anyone mention the price of the thing."

"I don't know what the price was."

"Weren't you curious?"

"No, I wasn't curious. If she wants it, she gets it."

Morris had a pair of reactions to this astonishing nonchalance. F. Scott Fitzgerald was right, he was thinking, the rich really are different from the rest of us; and the old cliché is true—if you have to ask the price of something, you can't afford it. Those reactions, while not inaccurate, missed a subtle point. Nelson W. Aldrich Jr., an insightful chronicler of American wealth, noted that people of Bill Ford's class neglect to ask the price of a Degas bronze not only because they know they can afford it but because any mention of money would tarnish the experience of acquiring it. Rich people don't *buy* things, Aldrich wrote: "They 'discover' their treasures in antique stores or 'find' them in galleries. The process is one of ingestion, not purchase. . . . The whole point of inculcating the peculiar aesthetic of the class is to lift its habit above the quick and nasty transactions of the cash nexus to the exalted plane of disinterested delight."

When they got back to their suite at the Plaza at dusk, Bill Ford didn't exhibit any visible delight, disinterested or otherwise, at having ingested a Degas bronze. With the Christmas lights of Central Park beginning to sparkle down below, Ford cracked open a fifth of Jack Daniel's and got ready to ingest some bourbon. The men needed to get warmed up for the long night ahead. After pouring a couple of drinks, Ford launched into a familiar rant about his displeasure with the Lions' general manager, Edwin Anderson. In those premerger years, the National Football League and the rival American Football League held separate drafts, which resulted in some sharp competition for the top college talent. During the 1964 drafts, held just a few weeks earlier, Anderson had persuaded the team's front office, including Ford, to use their first-round pick to draft Pete Beathard, a highly prized quarterback out of Southern Cal. The Kansas City Chiefs of the AFL also drafted Beathard—then made an eye-popping offer: a $15,000 signing bonus, a two-year no-cut contract at $20,000 a year, a new car, a free apartment, and shares of a pay-TV company. The maraschino atop that frothy sundae was a paid-up life insurance policy.

"That kind of money is ridiculous," Ford said when the details of the contract hit the papers. "If we gave that sort of offer, it would wreck our whole ball club. It would have been the most damaging thing possible for team morale. No one rookie can be worth that much. It's good riddance for me at those prices."

This from a man who had just bought a Degas sculpture without bothering to ask the price.

Beathard wound up signing with Kansas City—and the Lions wound up getting nothing with their precious first-round pick. It was not the first time a Lions draft pick had been plucked away by the upstart AFL. In fact, it was the third time in the past four years it had happened, which gave the Lions the distinction of being the worst losers in the accelerating money war between the rival leagues. It also gave the organization an unshakeable reputation for being cheap. Bill Ford laid the blame on Edwin Anderson, and now he reminded Morris that he wasn't the only one who was fed up with the general manager. The players had hanged Anderson in effigy from a goal post a few years earlier, and a macabre photograph had gone out on the national wire services.

His tirade over, Ford refilled the two glasses and lit a fresh cigarette. "I've got the Lions now and I'm putting together an organization," he said to Morris. After a long pause he added, "I'd like for you to be my general manager."

Morris coughed on his bourbon, though this wasn't the first time Ford had made an outlandish offer. During the recent drafts, the Green Bay Packers of the NFL took a center out of Holy Cross named Jon Morris with the twenty-seventh overall pick, while the Boston Patriots of the AFL took him with the league's twenty-ninth pick. Morris, worried that he might not be able to cut it with the powerful Packers, opted to sign with the Patriots.

Shortly after the draft, Dick Morris had mentioned to Bill Ford in passing that a nephew of his named Jon Morris had just signed a contract with Boston that paid him a $10,000 signing bonus, $13,000 for his first season and a guaranteed $17,000 for his second. And, Morris added with a chuckle, his nephew didn't know what to do with all that money, so he went out and paid cash for a candy-apple-red Pontiac convertible.

"Why didn't you say something?" Ford had said at the time. "We could have drafted him!"

Dick Morris was flabbergasted. Ford had not asked, "What does the scouting report say on Jon Morris?" Or even: "Have you seen him play? Is he any good?" In that moment, Morris realized that Ford would have drafted a player, sight unseen, simply because he was a relative of someone in his inner circle. And now, even though he was unwilling to match Kansas City's offer for Pete Beathard, he was blaming Edwin Anderson for letting another top prospect slip away.

Morris asked himself: *What are the chances of success in an organization that's run like that?*

If Morris had been flabbergasted by Ford's offer to draft a player sight unseen, this job offer knocked him flat. Coinciding with Ford's recent takeover of the Lions, CBS had signed a two-year, $28 million contract to televise NFL games, which added $1 million a year to each team's bottom line and made Ford look like a genius investor. Pro football was now a big and growing industry, and Dick Morris, a former newspaperman who'd spent the past dozen years promoting cars he didn't know or care much about, was being invited to take on a job he knew precisely nothing about.

That job involved a set of specific skills—understanding the game of football, for starters, plus scouting college players, deciding on draft picks, engineering trades, and negotiating contracts while, above all, keeping the fans and a demanding, hands-on owner happy. Aside from his immaculate lack of qualifications, Morris had another reason for demurring.

"Bill," he said, "that's a very fine compliment, but I don't know that I'd be your man. I have some serious doubts."

"Oh, you can handle it with your left hand," Ford retorted.

It was a characteristic thing for a person of Ford's class to say—this sense, born of privilege, that brains and class and a little effort could overcome any challenge and that success, like money, just fell out of the sky.

Sipping his drink, Dick Morris came to a decision. It was time to let Bill Ford know the deeper reason for his demurral. "I'll seriously consider taking the GM job," he said, "if you'll do something about that guy sitting on that table there"—he pointed at the bottle—"Mr. Jack Daniel from Lynchburg, Tennessee."

Now it was Ford's turn to be flabbergasted. "You've got to be kidding."

"I'm not kidding. I'm worried about it. We're both doing it too much, and I think you're getting to the point where it's serious and I want to tell you that as both a friend and an employee. And I'm not going to undertake the responsibility of running your football team if the drinking continues at the level it's now going."

"Well, maybe you've got a point," Ford conceded. But he quickly came back to himself. He was not a man accustomed to getting lectured by an employee or hearing no for an answer. There was a hint of acid in his next question: "Are you turning me down?"

"No, but I don't think it's going to work without your help."

They dropped the conversation, finished their drinks, then hit the town.

That job offer set the tone for everything that was to come.

THE LONG LOST WEEKEND

Dick Morris was not imagining things. By all accounts, Bill Ford's drinking had become excessive even by the elastic standards of the Motor City. The Lions provided a perfect pretext for Ford to get loaded: if the team won, he had a cause for celebration; if they lost, he had an excuse for drowning his sorrows. Unlike big brother Henry II, who could pound down the scotch and Pommard wine and raise hell and then show up early for work the next morning, ready to go—he claimed he didn't get hangovers— Bill's drinking was becoming dark and debilitating. And he would drink anything—an icy double martini, a goblet of room-temperature gin, Bacardi rum disguised in a bottle of Pepsi, a nip of nice bourbon.

He started staying up late and showing up at his Design Center office late, if he showed up at all. The joke went like this: "Where can you always park at the Design Center? In Bill Ford's space. He's never here." His wife Martha learned to feed the children a predinner snack to tide them over until their father got home from work, usually late and usually with more than a few drinks humming in his bloodstream. And his appearance was beginning to suffer. The sharp good looks he'd inherited from his father were giving way to bloat. His eyes wore a permanent glaze.

Dick Morris understood as well as anyone why Bill Ford had taken off on his long lost weekend with no indication when, or if, Monday would arrive. It all went back to that spring day in 1956 when Bill Ford, swaddled in a hip cast after tearing an Achilles tendon, hobbled on crutches into the room where Ford Motor Company's executive committee was going to determine the fate of Bill's baby, the elegant Continental Mark II, arguably the most beautiful car the company had ever produced.

Operating on a wing and a prayer, as he put it, Bill Ford had cobbled together a dedicated team of stylists, engineers, body designers, and publicists, and they set about producing a new luxury car from scratch. These were young men, thirtyish like Bill Ford, driven, passionate, willing to work seven days a week. They sweated over every detail—the hood ornament, door handles, ashtrays, the thickness of the needles on the instrument gauges, the best way to announce the car to the public, and the best way to promote it.

"There was more attention paid to detail in that car than anything I've ever been exposed to before or since," Ford stated years later.

The quality of the workmanship and materials were sacrosanct to Bill Ford, and he resisted all attempts to cut corners. When Lewis Crusoe, who now ran Ford Division, suggested replacing the distinctive star hood ornament with a cheap plastic one, Bill Ford fought him off like an alley cat. He reminded Crusoe—who he derided as "a farmer"—that the purpose of the Mark II was to rekindle memories of the original Continental, the pet project of Bill and Henry II's father, Edsel, a design so classic that it had been displayed recently at the Museum of Modern Art in New York. The Mark II was a worthy successor with its clean lines, long hood, and short trunk deck with a trademark bulge for the spare tire. In an age when Detroit stylists were laying on the chrome and gewgaws, the car was a masterpiece of restraint, a testament to Bill Ford's refined taste. He had big plans to add a four-door model to the original two-door offering. It would break Cadillac's monopoly on the luxury market and, for good measure, help Ford take a major step toward a divisional structure like the one that had made General Motors into a colossus. The car was, in Bill Ford's eyes, a sophisticated form of advertising. Its prestige would rub off on all other Ford products.

Before the car debuted in October 1955, Dick Morris helped put together a promotional tour, a "dog and pony show" in Bill Ford's words, that traveled across the country, from New York to Chicago, Dallas, Los Angeles, and San Francisco, where they showed roped-off models to enthusiastic crowds. In L.A., Frank Sinatra insisted on being the first owner of a Mark II. Elvis Presley and Liz Taylor were also early buyers. The car buff magazines anointed the car an instant classic.

But Bill Ford was laid up in his hip cast shortly after the car's stellar debut, and he missed the chance to defend his pet project against the machinations of backstabbing Lewis Crusoe, who regarded the car as a costly vanity project for the founder's youngest grandson. Crusoe was determined to kill it.

Ernie Breech, the chairman, a man Bill Ford viewed as a bean-counting Ozark hillbilly, opened the executive committee meeting by reminding the room that the company had just gone public and now they all had to answer to stockholders, and he was not going to go to his first annual meeting and admit that he'd approved building a car that lost a thousand dollars per unit, no matter how pretty it was.

And there sat Bill Ford's eldest brother, Henry II—Bill still called Henry Lard Ass and Henry still called Bill the Kid, boyhood invective that would follow both men to their graves—and Bill could see that Henry II, now president of the company and an ardent acolyte of Ernie Breech, was just sitting there drinking in his mentor's little sermon, not a word of support for his kid brother.

After a fast start with the 1956 models, sales of the $10,000 car had dropped off—dropped off a cliff, Bill Ford had to admit—and suddenly Ernie Breech, Lewis Crusoe, Bob McNamara, and the rest of the bean counters were yammering about the unprofitability of a car that was never intended to be a money-maker. *The sonsabitches were moving the goal posts in the middle of the game!* These were the cost-conscious geniuses who were about to roll the dice on a $350 million gamble called the Edsel. After

Breech had finished his sermon, McNamara, king of the bean counters, had rattled off the statistics that proved beyond a doubt, at least to his steel-trap mind, that the car should be allowed to die in its crib. When it had come time to vote on a motion to discontinue the Mark II after just two years of production, everyone on the committee voted "aye"—everyone except Bill Ford, who was sitting in the back of the room with his plaster-encased leg resting on a chair. Henry II turned to see who had delivered the sole "nay" vote. "Oh," he said dismissively, "that's Bill."

"Yes, it's me," Bill snapped at his brother. Then, struggling to his feet and limping toward the door on his crutches, he barked at the secretary, "And I want that duly recorded that's there's a 'nay' vote on this." His fury was pathetic, Bill Ford had realized even then, the yelp of a beaten man. In that moment, he said later, "I felt I'd had the heart cut out of me." Soon after that day, as Dick Morris had witnessed firsthand, Bill Ford started in on the suicidal drinking.

◆

Dick Morris was my father. He never lost the honeyed drawl from his native Georgia—back home he would always be known as *Rich*-it—but among the car guys in Detroit, all the Jacks and Bills and Genes and Bobs, he soon became Dick Morris.

My mother was pregnant with me in the summer of 1952 when my father agreed to leave his reporter's job at the *Washington Post* and take the PR job with Ford. In my preteen years, I remember occasions when Bill Ford dropped by our house in Birmingham, possibly on his way home from the Lions' training camp on the campus of Cranbrook School in nearby Bloomfield Hills. He and my father would settle in the living room, working on tumblers of bourbon, listening to jazz records, smoking, chatting and laughing, always laughing. I can still hear it: male laughter, the tinkle of ice cubes, Ella Fitzgerald singing "Mack the Knife."

Another detail I recall is that my father had his initials monogrammed on the pocket of his dress shirts—a simple *RM* because he had no middle name. But Bill Ford had his initials—the imperial *WCF*—monogrammed on the door of his Continental Mark II parked in our driveway, a dreamboat painted Honolulu blue to match the Lions' home jerseys. Even at the age of ten, that difference spoke to me. So did the similarities between the two men. They both parted their hair with a straight rule and kept it perfectly combed. They wore exquisitely tailored suits, fastened little garters below the knee to hold up their socks, and when they traveled they slipped each shoe into its own felt pouch before packing. I'm guessing Bill Ford's inner clothes horse was foaled during his years at Yale. The Ivy League Look, declared *National Review*, created "signifiers that would identify in-group from interloper," adding that "the style became so smart that periodicals such as *Esquire* kept their eye on the college men of Yale and Princeton as closely as they did the matinee idols of Hollywood."

New Haven had its own little Savile Row when Bill Ford was an undergraduate at Yale—J. Press, Chipp, Fenn-Feinstein. Bill Ford, who became a regular on "best dressed" lists, favored Fenn-Feinstein suits, as did his brother Henry II, Dick Morris, and John F. Kennedy. Bean counters bought their suits off the rack at Brooks Brothers.

◆

Drinking rituals evolved. Most days at quitting time, Bill Ford and a rotating cast of his inner circle, usually including Dick Morris and Gene Bordinat, whom Bill Ford had put in charge of the styling studio, would stop by the Dearborn Inn to unwind and talk shop. This ritual became so predictable that the waiters had their drinks on the table before the men sat down.

"A couple of things always impressed me," Bordinat would recall. "Bill was always in a hurry because he always had to get home"—the kids were waiting for their supper—"but he had four double-martinis before he would leave the table. The fact that he was in a hurry didn't keep him from having four. So he would just quaff 'em down faster."

Another thing that impressed Bordinat was the etiquette surrounding the check. "Bill always got out before the bill came," Bordinat said. "Bill never, ever picked up a bill. At one time I thought, well, you know, if you've got that much money, you just don't think about those things. He thinks about those things! When it came to big stuff, man, he was generous. And that little piddling stuff, you know, 'I'm paying these guys enough. Let them pick it up.'"

Which is to say Bill Ford wasn't cheap, like some rich people. And he wasn't oblivious to money. He thought about money a lot—but he thought about it in ways that bewildered his less affluent employees. He may have never picked up a bar check, but he didn't think twice about paying a stratospheric sum for a football team or an unknown sum for a sculpture by Edgar Degas.

People were starting to notice his drinking. One day Gene Bordinat got a call from Henry Ford II. "Gene," the boss said, "I want you to take my brother Bill's car keys away from him."

"Which car?" Bordinat asked.

"All of them."

This was bad news. Getting dragged into a cross fire between two of the Ford brothers was guaranteed career suicide. "Well, Mr. Ford," Bordinat said, "I'll do this because you asked me to do it, but I sure as hell would like to know why I'm doing it because I might be asked, you know."

Henry II launched into a litany of recent episodes. Seems Bill had sideswiped half a dozen parked cars on East Jefferson on his way home from the Dearborn Inn a few weeks ago. "Well, that wasn't so bad," Henry II said, "but he did it again last night. Of course, we know the police and all that, but Bill's been drinking a little. We've got to get on top of this, and I don't want him to have any keys."

Bordinat said, "Okay." But the man was not stupid and he certainly was not suicidal, so he approached Ed Polley, a longtime Ford family retainer who was in charge of the company garage, and asked him to pick up all of Bill Ford's car keys and make them disappear. Polley obliged since the order came directly from Henry II. Which saved Bordinat's neck.

Dick Morris traveled widely with Bill Ford in those years—always first class—on the promotional tour for the Mark II, to the Paris Auto Show, to dealer and press events and major car races. The booze was always flowing when car guys were far from home, and there were added temptations. When Henry II traveled to Paris on business, as the family biographers Peter Collier and David Horowitz recounted, he liked to visit high-class bordellos, especially one on Rue Paul Valéry. When friends in Grosse Pointe asked Henry what he planned to do for fun in Paris, he would reply, "I'm going to visit Paul Valéry." Which mystified them because Henry II was rarely seen reading a book, and it was highly unlikely he was a fan of the French symbolists. Besides, a visit with Paul Valéry would have required a séance since the poet had died in 1945. In his biography of Henry II, Victor Lasky quotes an unnamed source as saying, "Henry was always supplied with hookers whenever he came to Las Vegas. And he could get pretty rough with the girls. Yes, he was that kind of guy. But, Henry being Henry, such episodes were usually hushed up."

Of course we know the police and all that . . .

Dick Morris was no stranger to hushed-up episodes. In the early 1960s, he had accompanied Bill Ford to San Francisco for a press event to introduce the new lineup of Ford models. They stayed at the elegant Mark Hopkins Hotel—nothing but the very best for Bill Ford—and on the night before the big press luncheon they hit the town hard, which had become standard procedure. They finally made it to bed around four in the morning, and when Morris got up after a few hours of sleep to make final preparations for the luncheon, there was no sign of Bill Ford. Morris pounded on Ford's bedroom door. Nothing. Morris began to sweat.

"So the time comes for the luncheon," he recalled, "with our regional public relations people having brought all the newspaper and television people in to meet William Clay Ford, the scion. And Bill's not there. He was supposed to make a little talk, which he hated pathologically—he absolutely had the worst case of stage fright of any man I ever knew. So I tell the crowd, 'Mr. Ford had some business to cover.' And I make some chitchat and show them a film, and meanwhile I'm running back and forth trying to get him out of the damn bed. And then I wonder: if I pour cold water on him and manage to get him out of bed, do I want him to show up at this thing looking like the wrath of God?"

Bill Ford finally showed up around two o'clock, freshly showered and shaved. After he shook hands all around and said he didn't have any announcement to make, the disappointed newspaper and TV and radio people packed up and melted away. "And of course the regional PR people were out of their minds," Morris said, "because they had built that luncheon up."

Just another day in the life of the hard-drinking scion and his hard-drinking PR guy.

◆

A plump target for the laughter at the nightly Dearborn Inn cocktail sessions was George Walker, the freelance designer who'd overseen the styling of the 1949 Ford—the car that just might have saved the company—and the equally smashing Thunderbird. Back in 1955 Walker had been anointed a vice president and put in charge of the 650 people who worked in the styling department, and two years later his blazing salesman's smile had adorned the cover of *Time* magazine. Everyone around the table at the Dearborn Inn got a kick out of the article's headline, THE CELLINI OF CHROME, a not-too-subtle way of linking Walker, who had a reputation for being as horny as a billy goat, to Benvenuto Cellini, one of the legendary lotharios of the Italian Renaissance. The *Time* article included George Walker's description of his "finest moment," which took place while he was vacationing in Florida: "I was terrific. There I was in my white Continental, and I was wearing a pure-silk, pure-white, embroidered cowboy shirt, and black gabardine trousers. Beside me in the car was my jet-black Great Dane, imported from Europe, named Dana von Krupp. You just can't do any better than that."

You just can't do any more *pathetic* than that, as far as Bill Ford was concerned. Pathetic was a shibboleth used by people of Bill Ford's class to describe someone who had to try too hard to be attractive, which was supposed to look effortless. To top it off, Walker slapped on so much Fabergé cologne that his office smelled like a four-story whorehouse, and on more than one occasion it had gotten back to Bill Ford that Walker referred to him as "the fucking kid." For such a skillful self-promoter and social climber, Walker could be a tone-deaf dumbass. Bill Ford decided he had to go. And so in 1961, as he was maneuvering to buy the Lions, Ford worked behind the scenes to line up support so he could install his own choice to replace Walker: effortlessly stylish Gene Bordinat. Bill Ford had not been stripped of all power inside Ford Motor Company after the death of the Mark II. He'd sat on the board of directors since 1948, he was a vice president and, after a recent stock split, he personally owned 12 percent of the Class B voting stock, which made him the company's single largest stockholder. If he wasn't a force in the day-to-day running of the company, he was still a member of the Ford family, and he still had enough clout to pull levers behind the curtain.

Ford worked the levers right down to the wire. On the night before the executive committee meeting in 1961, the conclave where the deck of plum assignments was shuffled and careers and fortunes were made or broken, Bill Ford asked his PR guy to stay late at the office to take part in a cloak-and-dagger operation. At about eight o'clock, the phone rang in Bordinat's home.

He heard Dick Morris's familiar southern drawl coming over the line: "Mistuh Bordinat, are you going to be there for a moment?" Bordinat was mystified by the formality of the question. *Mr.* Bordinat? It was coming from the easygoing Southern boy who had never uttered a serious word in Bordinat's presence. Bordinat liked Morris but regarded him as nothing more than Bill Ford's bag carrier. Bordinat replied that he had no plans to go out that evening.

"Mistuh William Clay Ford will be calling in about four minutes."

"Well, Mr. Morris," Bordinat said, mimicking the formal tone, "I'll be here."

Five minutes later, Bordinat's phone rang again. "Gene," Bill Ford said, getting straight to the point, "I just wanted you to know that tomorrow I'm putting your name up to become the director of styling and a vice president of the corporation. I hope you'll accept this."

Bordinat didn't need time to think it over. "Bill," he said, "I sure as hell will."

"I don't anticipate any difficulty at all," Ford said, mentioning that he had quietly run the plan by his brothers and "all the guys."

And so it was done. The next day, the executive committee elevated Bordinat and effectively shuttled Walker into limbo, where he would spend the next four years before retiring as a very rich and very bitter man. That evening at the Dearborn Inn, Bill Ford recounted how Walker had reacted when he got the news that he was being bypassed by Bordinat. "I thought George was going to die from apoplexy," Ford told the gang with unconcealed glee. "I went into his office and told him, and he slumped back in his chair and I thought he was going to buy it. For a brief moment, all the air went out of him."

Listening to this story, Bordinat was thinking that people don't really understand Bill Ford. They underestimate him, take him for a lightweight, a playboy. They don't realize that when he really wants something, he knows how to fight for it. That genteel veneer fools a lot of people.

This episode revealed that Bill Ford's instincts and personal preferences, coupled with his willingness to work diligently behind the scenes, were all he needed to make changes at the highest levels of an organization. In this case, it worked out. Bordinat would have a sterling twenty-year run at the helm of Ford styling. But instincts and personal preferences would not serve Bill Ford so well in the handling of his football team. In fact, quite the opposite.

SPORTSMAN OF THE YEAR

After that ominous day at the Statler Hilton Hotel in late November and that unsatisfying trip to New York in late December, the New Year opened on an upbeat note for the new owner of the Detroit Lions. On Jan. 10, 1964, the Detroit Football Company ceased to exist and was replaced by the Detroit Lions, Inc. It was official: Bill Ford was now sole owner of the team.

Two months later, the first iteration of a sporty new car called the Mustang rolled off the assembly line at Ford's River Rouge plant. Detroit automakers were awakening to the potential of the youth market, and this car had everything young buyers wanted: it was unfussy, fast, light, affordable. And *fun*. That first Mustang, a Caspian Blue hardtop, was one of 22,000 snapped up on the first day the car officially went on sale. By the end of the year nearly a quarter of a million Mustangs were on the road. An American icon was born, and Bill Ford, the single largest holder of Ford Motor Company stock, kept getting richer by the day without lifting a finger.

Meanwhile, in an unassuming house known as Hitsville U.S.A., just west of General Motors headquarters, homegrown Motown Records was pumping out the finger-popping hits as fast as the Big Three could pump out the fire-breathing cars. Radios in car dashboards and living rooms and bedrooms across the city—across the country, around the world—were buzzing with the latest hits from Martha and the Vandellas, Stevie Wonder, the Temptations, the Miracles, the Supremes. When the Mustang debuted, Motown's Mary Wells was on top of the R&B charts with "My Guy," while the No. 1 pop song was "I Want to Hold Your Hand," an infectious confection by four shaggy-haired rockers from Liverpool who called themselves the Beatles. The British Invasion had begun.

A week after the first Mustang came into the world, Bill Ford got more good news. NFL commissioner Pete Rozelle announced that the league was reinstating the Lions' star defensive lineman Alex Karras and the Green Bay Packers' star running back Paul Hornung after they'd served eleven-month suspensions, without pay, for gambling on NFL games. The suspensions had rocked the league—and revealed the very different personalities of two very different men who played for two very different teams in two very different towns.

Hornung, with his blond hair and chiseled good looks, was football's "golden boy." After he'd won the Heisman Trophy while playing college ball at Notre Dame in 1956, the lowly Packers made him the top draft pick, but he struggled. When the team hired Vince Lombardi as coach in 1959, Hornung began to blossom, leading the league in scoring the next three seasons (he was also a deadly accurate field goal kicker). He was named the league's Most Valuable Player in 1961, the year Bill Ford became president of the Lions, just as the Packers were beginning a decade of dominance and the Lions were entering a decade of decline. In his pursuit of nocturnal amusements, Hornung was in a league with Bobby Layne. "Everything was tied together," Hornung wrote in his autobiography, "the drinking, the womanizing, the partying, the traveling, the gambling. And, of course, football made it all possible."

Alex Karras was the opposite of Hornung's glitz and glamor. He was the son of a Greek immigrant, a scowling, irascible trench warrior who'd grown up in the steel town of Gary, Indiana, where he learned to play a vicious brand of football and developed a disdain for all authority figures—and also for Notre Dame and its plush campus, located just sixty miles but a

whole world away from gritty Gary. While playing at the University of
Iowa, Karras became so displeased with his lack of playing time that in
a fit of rage he threw a cleated shoe at his coach, Forest Evashevski, then
quit the team. He was eventually reinstated, but he and Evashevski never
spoke again off the field.

The Lions drafted him with the tenth pick in 1958, and at 6'2" and
250 pounds he quickly asserted himself as a premier defensive lineman, a
gifted pass rusher—and a hothead. The Lions opened the 1962 season with
three straight wins and were finally poised to overtake the Packers. Late
in the fourth game of the season, in Green Bay, the Lions were leading
the Packers 7–6 and simply had to run out the clock to seal the win. But
Lions quarterback Milt Plum attempted a pass to Terry Barr, who slipped
and fell, and the Packers' Herb Adderley intercepted the pass to set up Paul
Hornung's winning field goal kick in the closing seconds. In the locker
room after the game, Karras didn't throw a shoe. He hurled his helmet at
Plum's head. The missile, which could have caused serious harm, missed
its target by inches.

There's compelling evidence that Plum did not deserve Karras's fury.
Bob Whitlow, the Lions' center that year, still carried vivid memories of
that interception forty years later. "I was in the huddle," he recalled for the
historian Bill Dow. "George [Wilson] sent in the play. We had already
called a running play—thirty-six slant for [Nick] Pietrosante. Third and
seven at our own forty-eight, a minute-eighteen to go. I can still remember
everything about it."

The players in the huddle were stunned that the coach had called for a
risky pass, according to Whitlow: "One of the guys said, 'Bullshit—don't
throw the ball, run the ball.' Milt said, 'George sent it in. We better do it.'
Terry would have caught it. He slipped, you know, it was raining, misting-
rain a little bit. There the ball was, and Adderley just intercepted it. It wasn't
Milt's fault. Hell, the ball was *right there*. That cost us the championship."

That loss was a watershed moment. It split the team into rival factions, defense against offense, each side quick to point fingers at the shortcomings of the other side. The bitter aftertaste of that loss in Green Bay would linger for years. The Lions got a small helping of revenge on Thanksgiving Day in Detroit, crushing the Packers and handing them their only loss of the season in front of a full house and a record TV audience of 12 million. Despite the Thanksgiving Day Massacre, the Lions finished in second place behind the Packers and missed a shot at the title. Again.

◆

As different as they were, Karras and Hornung had one thing in common: a penchant for gambling on NFL games, which was explicitly forbidden by their contracts. When whispers of gambling reached Pete Rozelle shortly after he was named commissioner in 1960, he saw both a dangerous cancer and a tantalizing opportunity.

With notable exceptions, commissioners of big-league sports in America tend to be lap dogs of the team owners who appoint them, but Rozelle, just thirty-three years old and relatively unknown when he got the top NFL job, had different ideas. He was aware that his predecessor, Bert Bell, had been popular with the owners because he envisioned a league where all teams were competitive and all shared equally in the bounty. Bell didn't want a few big-city powerhouses with a bunch of small-market also-rans orbiting around them. "On any given Sunday," Bell's mantra went, "any team can beat any other team." To this end he instituted the draft, which gave the worst teams the highest picks, he developed a balanced scheduling system and became attuned to the immense potential of television money. After Bell suffered a fatal heart attack during an Eagles-Steelers game in 1959, the owners were divided on who should succeed him. They engaged in an ugly slugfest and cast twenty-three ballots before grudgingly awarding the job to Rozelle. Three of the twelve teams abstained from the final vote. Detroit was one of them. Hardly a ringing vote of confidence.

Unfazed, Rozelle, who saw himself as the new sheriff in town, hit the ground running. He brought in sixteen former FBI agents to launch a gambling investigation, interviewing fifty-two players on eight teams and sifting through intelligence from an ongoing probe of local mob activity by the Detroit police, who claimed the Lindell AC, a popular bar in downtown Detroit, was a hangout not only of sports stars and their fans but also of "known hoodlums." (AC stood for Athletic Club, a wry nod to the tony Detroit Athletic Club, which stood nearby.) The Lindell happened to be owned by the Greek brothers Johnny and Jimmy Butsicaris and their buddy Alex Karras. That connection gnawed at the new commissioner.

In a striking show of independence, Rozelle did not confer with team owners during his investigation, and he kept them in the dark about his planned course of action until shortly before he dropped the hammer. In announcing the suspensions on April 17, 1963, Rozelle stressed that there was no evidence of criminal activity, bribes, or point shaving, but he pointed out that Hornung's and Karras's gambling was "continuing, flagrant, and increasing"—and it violated their contracts. The suspensions were "indefinite" but would last at least through the 1963 season, and in addition to forfeiting their pay both players were fined $2,000. Rozelle wasn't finished. He fined the Lions $4,000, and he fined five Lions players—Joe Schmidt, Wayne Walker, John Gordy, Sam Williams, and Gary Lowe—$2,000 apiece for betting $50 on the Packers-Giants NFL championship game of 1962. Rozelle explained that the fine against the Lions' management was for a twofold offense: ignoring the reports from the Detroit police and allowing "undesirable" personnel on the sidelines during games, a clear reference to the Butsicaris brothers.

The suspensions may have been sensational—they were front-page news across the country—but the fines were far from equitable. For the Lions' ownership syndicate, $4,000 was pocket change, while $2,000 was about one-sixth of a professional football player's annual salary at that time. Once again, the working stiffs got the short end of the stick, and the rich guys got the sweetheart deal. As if to underscore the point, Karras arranged to wrestle Dick the Bruiser at Detroit's Olympia Stadium during his suspension—and loudly announced that he was getting paid $17,000 for one night's work, about $4,000 more than he earned playing a whole season for the Lions.

Advance ticket sales for the big bout were sluggish, so Dick the Bruiser, a 260-pound mayhem artist who'd played for the Green Bay Packers in the '50s, got together with the Lindell staff and concocted a publicity stunt. Dick would stroll into the bar and get in Karras's face, and since newspaper reporters were among the bar's more ardent regulars, there was hope the fake fracas would generate some ink. The bar was full of the usual suspects that night. In addition to newspaper regulars there were some bleacher creatures who'd come to watch the Tigers-A's game on TV, a few sharp-looking women hoping to meet a pro ballplayer, pimps in fur coats, bookies, hillbillies fresh from second-shift factory jobs. But when Dick the Bruiser yanked a TV off the wall, the Butsicaris's seventy-year-old Uncle Charlie, who was not in on the prank, whacked the Bruiser under the eye with a pool cue. Stunned, the Bruiser flew into a genuine rage and soon the place was engulfed in an epic brawl that left him, half a dozen Detroit cops, and the entire saloon in tatters. You can't buy that kind of publicity.

The Lions' training camp that summer offered another odd sight: the team agreed to let a gangly New York writer named George Plimpton try out at quarterback. Plimpton, a participatory journalist, was gathering yarn for a humorous inside-the-huddle book he would call *Paper Lion*. It was destined to become a bestseller.

While Plimpton was busy throwing interceptions and fumbling handoffs, Karras and Hornung were busy exhibiting very different reactions to their suspensions. Karras called Rozelle a "buzzard" and grumbled, "I haven't done anything wrong, and I'm not guilty of anything."

Hornung, on the other hand, was choirboy-contrite. The day after the suspensions were announced, Hornung said, "I made a terrible mistake. I realize that now. I am truly sorry." Vince Lombardi, the Packers' coach, was so distraught by Hornung's suspension that he considered resigning. But he stayed on after conceding to Rozelle, "You've got to do what you've got to do."

The rest of the football world seemed to agree. *Sports Illustrated* anointed Rozelle its Sportsman of the Year for 1963. "In that decision of wise severity," the magazine wrote about the suspensions, "Rozelle demonstrated strength, courage and his belief that the league's integrity was first among its possessions."

Bill Ford's reaction to the suspensions was revealing. While both teams announced that they would comply with Rozelle's edict—what choice did they have?—Bill Ford, unlike Vince Lombardi, made it clear that he had misgivings. "Compliance," he said, "does not mean that we agree with the nature or extent of the penalties imposed. The decision was extremely severe." *Sports Illustrated* reported that Ford continued to "smolder" over the suspensions. Ford also held half a dozen clandestine meetings with Rozelle in out-of-the-way saloons, hoping to hasten Karras's reinstatement.

When Ford paid off Karras's fine and Rozelle objected, Ford shot back: "He wasn't fined—he was put out of a job. All I know is he was broke and I helped him. I read the [NFL] constitution and bylaws and so did my attorney and I'm in violation of nothing."

Strong words. Even more telling, Ford remained loyal to Karras as the Lions stumbled to a 5–8–1 record and a fourth-place finish in 1963. Loyalty had become a lodestar in Bill Ford's world. He demanded it from subordinates and bestowed it without reservation on loyalists he liked and trusted. This virtue, if that's the word, would prove to be his Achilles heel.

Like Bill Ford, Karras never stopped smoldering. One December night in 1963, as the first season of his indefinite exile was winding down, Karras was in the Lindell toting up the day's receipts when the door squealed open. In walked portly Joe Louisell, a criminal defense lawyer of such legendary skill that he was known as the Perry Mason of Detroit. Louisell had defended assorted mobsters, killers, and hit men, and he'd cooked up the "Texas drawl" defense that had won Bobby Layne acquittal on the drunken driving charge back in 1958.

After ordering a triple bourbon, Louisell joined Karras and informed him that the NFL owners were meeting in Miami in January and now was the time to start pushing Rozelle to reinstate him. When Karras said he couldn't afford Louisell's fee, the lawyer offered to take on the case pro bono. Then he got to the point. "Here's my argument," he said. "Were you to sell your interest in the bar business, you can't get another liquor license for three years. We can sue them for lost wages if they force you to sell your share in the Lindell and don't reinstate you."

Since this was Joe Louisell talking, Karras paid close attention as the lawyer advised him to quit working in the bar and go spend the rest of the winter with his wife's parents in pristine Clinton, Iowa, far from the "undesirable" characters and "hoodlums" who frequented the Lindell. And above all, Louisell commanded, don't say another word to another reporter.

Karras, for once, did as he was told. He spent the rest of that winter teaching his four-year-old son to swim in the pool at the Clinton YMCA. Louisell, meanwhile, was pulling strings, and in early March he and his client were granted an audience in Rozelle's twenty-third-floor corner office at Rockefeller Center in New York. The commissioner kept them waiting for an hour, which got Karras so steamed he threatened to walk out. Louisell talked him down. When they were finally ushered into the inner sanctum, Rozelle was on the phone. He kept chattering away, ignoring his visitors. Karras noticed that Rozelle sported a mahogany suntan. There was still snow on the ground in Iowa and Michigan, and this joker had a tan.

When Rozelle kept talking on the phone, Louisell lost patience and ordered him to hang up. "This man's life is important!" he snapped.

"Okay, Mr. Louisell," Rozelle said, finally ending the call after establishing who was in charge here. "I'm listening."

Louisell laid out his plan to sue the league for lost wages if Karras was forced out of the Lindell but not reinstated by the NFL. "You've unjustly punished Alex Karras for a year," Louisell said in closing. "My advice to you is to make a decision within a week. If it's negative, I will tear the NFL apart."

A week later, Rozelle reinstated Karras and Hornung, stressing that neither player had bet against his own team or given less than his best effort on the field. A month after the reinstatements, Bill Ford proved his loyalty by awarding Karras a new two-year contract at more than $20,000 a year.

With Karras back at defensive left tackle alongside 300-pound Roger Brown, the Lions' defense returned to form and the team returned to winning. But their 1964 record of 7–5–2 was only good enough for a middling fourth-place finish in the Western Division. After his frustrating freshman season, the sole owner of the Lions decided it was time to put his stamp on the team.

His deft maneuvering of Gene Bordinat into the top styling job in 1961 had convinced Ford he could trust his instincts, and now his gut was telling him to make changes in the coaching staff. He didn't want to fire genial George Wilson, who was respected by the players and popular with the fans, but maybe he could get rid of Wilson by inducing Wilson to get rid of himself—and then bring in a handpicked successor. If he could pull that off, Ford told himself, he would be on the way to making the Detroit Lions *his* team.

Four days before Christmas, he made his first move. Ford ordered a reluctant Wilson to announce that he was firing all five of his assistant coaches, a tight-knit group that worked well together. *Merry Christmas!* When asked why the team was making such a radical change after a winning season, Ford replied with that most shopworn of sports clichés: he said he wanted to make a "fresh start."

Now the spotlight swung toward George Wilson, but he didn't let it shine for long. There had been reports in the papers that Wilson was unhappy with the way his wings had been trimmed after Ford bought the team. Gone were the days when Wilson could get rid of a troublesome quarterback with a simple phone call, or dictate draft picks, or even choose his own assistant coaches. Now everything had to go through hands-on Bill Ford. So two days after he was ordered to fire his staff, an angry Wilson announced that he was resigning. "I can't live with myself under these conditions," he said. Ford had succeeded at making his wish come true, and he did what rich people do in such circumstances: he paid off the last year of Wilson's $47,000 contract without blinking, then showed him the door. Getting rid of George Wilson proved to be Bill Ford's first major misstep. Far worse ones were on the way.

THE SNOWBALL SENDOFF

Russ Thomas, the Lions' new director of player personnel, was one of the three men tasked with compiling a list of head coach candidates after the 1964 season. A 235-pound bear of a lineman out of West Virginia, Thomas had played for the Lions for four seasons, until a knee injury cut his career short and left him with a permanent limp. Since his playing days he had worked for the team as an assistant coach, broadcaster, and scout, and his elevation to the player personnel job was the first indication that this loyal water carrier, a man who had literally given his body to the team, was developing a bond with the new owner. Their bond was destined to grow deep, and deeply damaging, in the coming decades.

As Thomas, general manager Edwin Anderson and the assistant GM Bud Erickson worked up their list of candidates, no one bothered to ask why the director of *player* personnel was involved in the hunt for a new head coach, just as no one was aware that Ford had secretly offered the general manager's job to his unqualified PR guy a year earlier, only to get turned down. What everyone did know was that the final decision on hiring a new head coach would belong entirely to Bill Ford.

It was Erickson who suggested adding Harry Gilmer to the list of candidates. On paper, Gilmer was a plausible choice to lead the team. He'd been a star quarterback at the University of Alabama, and he'd ended his professional career playing for the Lions in 1955 and '56, then spent four seasons as an assistant coach with the Pittsburgh Steelers and another four with the Minnesota Vikings. So he had experience as both a player and a coach, and to top it off he had a little Detroit in his DNA.

Ford, following his gut, decided to go after just one of the two dozen candidates on the list: Harry Gilmer. In keeping with league protocol, Ford got clearance from Minnesota management before approaching Gilmer. Poaching coaches went against the rules—and against Bill Ford's courtly nature.

After the Vikings' brass gave Ford the green light, Gilmer was invited to Detroit to discuss the job offer. For two and a half hours, in his own telling, he met with Ford and Thomas—but not Anderson or Erickson. When the meeting was over, Gilmer had agreed to a three-year contract at $35,000 a year—a 25 percent discount from George Wilson's salary and the first evidence of what would become Russ Thomas's trademarks at the bargaining table: a hard nose and tight fists. Bill Ford, who dreaded being seen as a deep-pocketed pushover, was pleased.

In announcing the hiring, the papers noted that Gilmer's two biggest challenges would be settling the quarterback question—Milt Plum or Earl Morrall?—and taming players who were "known for their dissension." One reporter added: "Gilmer explained that he would have a free hand in negotiating trades, but all proposed trades would be subject to approval of Thomas and Ford." In other words, the new coach would be kept on a short leash, and the team's new owner had a new right-hand man. And that right-hand man had the owner's ear.

◆

After the press conference announcing the hiring of Harry Gilmer, Bill Ford led Dick Morris into the barroom at the Book Cadillac Hotel and ordered a couple of stingers. Dismayed by the lack of change in their routines since the trip to New York, Morris said, "Bill, I don't know what I'm going to do about this business of drinking this stuff at this time of day."

"Hell," Ford said, glancing at his watch, "it's after five o'clock."

"I'm going to have to let up on it."

And he did—not for the last time. After drying out for a week and feeling that his head was screwed on tight, Morris decided to act on his misgivings. While Gene Bordinat had had the good sense to run away and hide when he was in danger of getting drawn into a cross fire between two of the Ford brothers, Dick Morris decided to jump into the breach. Aware that he could be making a fatal mistake, he called Henry II's office and asked if it would be possible to see Mr. Ford. "Sure," Ford's secretary said, "come on up."

When Morris entered the inner sanctum on the twelfth floor of the Glass House, Henry II was sitting at his desk with his arms crossed and his half-moon reading glasses perched on the end of his nose. Late afternoon sunlight slanted into the room, backlighting the smoke that rose from the sprawling River Rouge plant, that monstrous monument to old Henry's genius. Motioning toward a chair, Henry II said, "What can I do for you?"

"Well, Mr. Ford," Morris said, taking a seat, "I want to have a serious conversation with you about your brother Bill." Morris felt the temperature in the room drop, and it was not hard to read the expression on Henry II's face. It said, *What's this guy doing talking about the family?* Nobody outside the Ford family talked about the Ford family, especially in a presence of a member of the family. Morris took a deep breath and launched into his prepared spiel. "Your brother has a serious drinking problem and he's going to kill himself—"

"I agree with that," Henry II cut in. "I think Bill has a deep-seated *psychological* problem."

Breathing a little easier, Morris continued, "I wanted you to know it, and I want to tell you it's affecting me. I'm being selfish because I think I'm dead around here. Working for Bill is not doing anything for me."

As soon as he said the words, Morris knew he was, indeed, dead. Henry II gave him the lizard-eyed stare he had given to hundreds of men before ordering one of his minions to cut the man off at the knees. When Henry II didn't speak, Morris pushed ahead, citing recent episodes with Bill Ford, including the disastrous press luncheon in San Francisco and a few others. Morris sensed that the longer he talked, the deader he was. Finally he fell silent, waiting. Henry II didn't react to what he'd just heard. Instead he thanked Morris for his concern, which Morris understood to mean *The door's over there. Use it.*

Riding the elevator down from the twelfth floor, Morris realized he hadn't merely shot himself in the foot, he'd blown his foot clean off. Instead of expressing concern for his own career, he should have stressed his concern for Bill Ford's health, indeed his survival. He should have stressed that Bill had a potentially fatal disease that needed to be treated by medical professionals. Morris realized he'd failed on every count. Henry II was obviously offended by this invasion of family privacy, and Bill would regard the meeting as a betrayal when word of it got back to him, as it inevitably would. Worst of all, this feeble attempt at an intervention was unlikely to change Bill Ford's habits. If you ever want to dig your own grave, Morris told himself as he left the Glass House, you just got through putting the shovel in the ground. By the time he reached his car, Morris was convinced his career at Ford Motor Company was as good as over.

◆

Dick Morris was right about one thing: Bill Ford's habits did not change. If anything, his drinking grew even darker as the Lions' fortunes began to sour. The league's newest owner was learning a harsh lesson: Harry Gilmer might have looked good on paper, but NFL games are not played on paper. On the field the Lions under Gilmer went from mediocre to bad. The only good thing, from Bill Ford's perspective, was that the coach, and not the owner who hired him, became the scapegoat for this regression—unpopular with the players, reviled by the fans, needled mercilessly by the press. In the punishing Michigan weather, Gilmer wore a *cowboy hat*, for chrissakes, which led many people to assume he was from Texas. Wherever the guy was from, he was clearly a fish out of water in the Motor City.

Before Gilmer's first season, the Lions traded Earl Morrall to the New York Giants. With Milt Plum starting at quarterback, the team opened with three straight wins, then sputtered. In fairness, there were numerous problems that went beyond the coach and the quarterback, most notably a loose cannon of a running back with the fitting name of Joe Don Looney. An All-American at Oklahoma—before he got kicked off the team for insubordination—Looney was a barroom brawler who bulked up on a regimen of vitamins, weightlifting, and then-legal steroids. Despite his checkered college career, the New York Giants drafted him in the first round in 1964. He promptly ignored the team's dress code, shunned the press, and skipped practices. In less than a month he was gone, shipped to Baltimore, where he would become the headache of coach Don Shula, the former Lions assistant coach now on his way to a Hall of Fame career. After getting into a political argument with a couple in Baltimore, Looney broke down the door to their apartment and assaulted them. A judge gave Looney one year of probation, a $100 fine for assault, and a $50 fine for malicious mischief.

Malicious mischief—it had become Looney's brand. Russ Thomas, showing early signs of his gift for assessing talent and character, persuaded Bill Ford that Looney would give the Lions' anemic offense the spark it needed. Not for the first time, nor the last, Bill Ford heeded Thomas's advice and approved the trade in the summer of 1965. Looney appeared in nine games for the Lions that season, rushing for 356 yards and five touchdowns—nothing spectacular, and not nearly enough to reverse the team's decline. The popular linebacker Joe Schmidt, worn out by injuries and losing, retired at the end of the season and was promptly hired to coach the team's linebackers. He did his best to reform Looney, admonishing him that skipping practices was not an option, that keeping a job in the NFL required hard work. Schmidt pointed out that in his thirteen seasons as a player he never missed a single practice. "Joe," Looney said, "you should take a day off once in a while."

The team was headed to a 6–7–1 record and a sixth-place finish in the seven-team Western Conference, a pronounced step backward. As the losses piled up, Bill Ford's drinking went from dark all the way to black. Like most alcoholics, he now existed inside an impenetrable bubble of self-absorption. No one could get in and he couldn't, or wouldn't, come out. Bill Ford was in a permanent fog, and he was killing himself—the very outcome Dick Morris had warned about during his visit to Henry II's office—but he didn't care. As Bill Ford saw it, he was free to live, and die, as he pleased.

The turning point came in late 1965. The Lions had suffered back-to-back losses and were getting ready to host the powerful Baltimore Colts in their traditional Thanksgiving Day game. When Bill Ford's seventeen-year-old daughter Muffy, his eldest child, came home from her Connecticut boarding school for the holidays, she was so shocked by her father's condition and appearance that she announced she was going to withdraw from school so she could stay home and take care of him. Her concern shook him awake. Someone had finally pierced the bubble.

Years later, Bill Ford recounted his moment of reckoning: "I'd always thought, 'Oh, what the hell, it's my privilege to wreck myself if I want to, especially if I'm not hurting other people in the process.' My wife never mentioned the alcoholism to me. But then there was this confrontation with my daughter, and I thought, 'God, if it's getting to the kids I've got to do something about it.'"

And he did. He checked himself into the Donwood Clinic, a new state-of-the-art rehab facility in Toronto, where the bushes around the parking lot glittered with empty bottles discarded by incoming patients who'd taken one final nip before checking in. Ford, with the help of the drug Antabuse, sweated through the horrors of cold-turkey withdrawal after a decade of herculean drinking. Martha, as always, was at his side. When he returned home to Grosse Pointe a month later, he had gone from bloated to gaunt, his youthful good looks lost forever. He became active in Alcoholics Anonymous and never took another drink. Monday morning had come at last. The long lost weekend was over.

◆

Gilmer's—and Looney's—second season was even worse than their first. In the third game, against Atlanta, Looney had been instrumental in a long drive, and he was furious when Gilmer pulled him out of the game with the ball just short of the goal line. Looney felt he'd earned the inevitable touchdown. Later in the game, when Gilmer ordered Looney to go back in and relay a play to quarterback Milt Plum, Looney refused to budge from the sideline. "You want a messenger boy," he told Gilmer, "call Western Union."

That did it. Looney was off-loaded to the Washington Redskins. Amid all the turmoil and the losing there was a welcome ray of comic relief. Russ Thomas decided to take a chance on a left-footed, soccer-style place-kicker named Garo Yepremian, a balding, pot-bellied elf who'd grown up in Cyprus and played semipro soccer in London but knew nothing about American football. "I never saw a game until I was playing in one," he said. "I had no idea how to put my uniform on." When Gilmer informed him the Lions had lost the coin toss before his first game, Yepremian rushed to midfield, got down on his knees and started searching in the grass for the lost coin. People stopped laughing when Yepremian kicked an NFL record six field goals in a 32–31 road win over Minnesota.

Though Yepremian's left foot contributed fifty points in his rookie year, the Lions went into free fall after Looney's departure and closed out the season with an ignominious 28–16 loss at home to Minnesota on a raw snowy day that dragged them into a last-place tie with the Vikings. I was in the stands that day—Briggs Stadium had been renamed Tiger

Stadium—and for those late-season games we always dressed as though we were going on an expedition to the Arctic: long underwear, sweaters, and ski parkas, three pairs of socks and heavy boots, mittens, wool hats, scarves. And we never sat down because the seats had turned to blocks of ice and, far more important, we needed to bounce up and down to keep our blood moving and ward off frostbite. Never in my life have I been so cold.

As I watched Gilmer and his muddy players trudge toward the locker room after the game, serenaded by "Goodbye, Harry, we hate to see you go" and a lusty chorus of boos, my eye caught the arc of a snowball sailing down from the upper deck. It splashed on the field at Gilmer's feet. Two more followed, then a dozen, then it turned into a blurry barrage. As players hustled to hold protective parkas over their coach, a photographer caught the moment when one of the missiles scored a direct hit, nearly knocking Gilmer's Stetson off his head. The picture would appear in the *Free Press* the next morning, a vivid snapshot of how the Detroit fans felt about Harry Gilmer.

In the locker room, Gilmer managed to retain his sense of humor about the humiliating sendoff. "At least they didn't put rocks in the snowballs," he quipped.

Wit could not save Harry Gilmer. The team's record after his two seasons was 10–16–2, and everyone in the stadium that day knew he was doomed—including Bill Ford, who was about to follow his first two personnel missteps with a truly disastrous one. This was the beginning of a string of bad decisions that would stretch on for decades, and it's safe to say they all sprang from the same source: the history of the Ford family.

A COCOON OF PRIVILEGE

If we are all to some extent captives of our family's history, Bill Ford was a prisoner of his. And his sentence was for life, with no possibility of parole.

The darkest hour of the Ford family's history came on the morning of May 26, 1943, when Henry II and Bill's father, Edsel, died at home shortly before his fiftieth birthday, his stomach riddled with ulcers and cancer, his spirit broken by a lifetime of abuse from a domineering, erratic father who was convinced that his artistically inclined son lacked the "iron" to run the family business.

Old Henry's treatment of his only son went beyond pathological, all the way to filicidal. A typically vicious rebuke came when Edsel tried to convince Henry that sticking with the outdated Model T and offering it only in black was a senseless drag on sales. He pointed out that other manufacturers, most notably General Motors, were pummeling Ford by introducing mechanical and stylistic innovations. Henry wouldn't hear it. So while Henry was on a trip abroad in 1924, Edsel and some engineers gave a Model T a facelift, producing a prototype that was less boxy, more sculptural, more *stylish*—and lipstick red. When Henry returned from his trip, he happened upon the car before Edsel had a chance to prepare him for the big surprise. Henry circled the car three or four times, studying it closely, not saying a word. Then he exploded, ripping off the doors, shattering the windshield, tearing up the upholstery, just "kicking the car all to pieces," as one stunned onlooker put it. Henry was like a child throwing a tantrum. For Edsel, this and countless other humiliations added up to death by a thousand cuts. It was an excruciatingly slow and painful way to die, and Edsel's children were convinced that their grandfather had killed their father.

Now, with old Henry back in full control of the company after Edsel's death, there was panic in Washington that this anti-Semitic, megalomaniacal food crank was about to ruin a vital source of war matériel—producer of everything from bullets to bombers—at the peak of the Second World War. There was even talk of nationalizing this cornerstone of the Arsenal of Democracy.

Instead, strings were pulled in Washington and three months after their father's death, Bill's eldest sibling, Henry II, was given an early release from the navy in the hope he could return to Detroit and steady the sinking ship. After Henry's wife and Edsel's widow exerted fierce, behind-the-scenes pressure on the old man to step aside—Eleanor threatened to sell her 41 percent share of the company stock she'd inherited after Edsel's death—a frail and fading Henry, now eighty years old, finally agreed to relinquish control of the company as the only way to keep it in the family. And so at the age of twenty-five, untested and unsure of himself, Henry II was named vice president and thrown to the wolves.

It's worth noting that both Henry II and Bill carried fond memories of their wartime military service. Bill was a naval cadet, and part of the graduation from preflight school was a rigorous competition that involved boxing, swimming, running, and mastering an obstacle course. Of the hundreds of cadets in his class, Bill Ford, a gifted athlete, finished first. He was elated. "Without anyone knowing my name or who I was or whether I had a dime, I did it on my own," he said, adding, "I always liked sports because they involved a democracy of talent." At the age of nineteen, he was getting his first taste of being judged purely on his merits, an experience most children have before they enter kindergarten.

That's what tends to happen to people who grow up in a cocoon of privilege, and Henry Ford's grandchildren grew up in a cocoon like few others. After old Henry came into the money early in the twentieth century, Edsel had set about acquiring a veneer of polish. By the time he was a teenager he dressed well and knew his forks and drove customized "speedsters" across town every morning to attend prep school at Detroit University School. He was everything his cornpone father was not—handsome, stylish, charming, a connoisseur of fine art and fine things. He loved to draw and he loved jazz, and one of the places he went to bring up his polish was Miss Annie Ward-Foster's dance class in downtown Detroit, where he met a vivacious, dark-haired young lady with an appetite for sports and charity work. Her name was Eleanor Clay. After her father's death she'd been raised in high style by an uncle, Joseph L. Hudson, owner of the city's largest department store. Eleanor Clay was no farm girl like Edsel's mother. She had recently graduated from the exclusive Liggett School in Grosse Pointe, she was sophisticated, witty and self-confident, and, like Edsel, she loved art and music and a good time. The two fell instantly in love and were married at Hudson's mansion in Detroit on Nov. 1, 1916. The groom was twenty-two, the bride just twenty. After honeymooning in Hawaii and western Canada, the newlyweds settled into a grand home in Detroit's Indian Village. It was time to start a family, which meant it was time to start creating a cocoon of their own.

They called it Gaukler Pointe. Designed by the famed Detroit architect Albert Kahn, it is a sprawling, sixty-room mansion inspired by the stone houses in England's Cotswold district and perched on fifty-five acres (purchased from old Henry) on the shores of Lake St. Clair. Edsel and Eleanor scoured Europe buying up fireplaces and staircases and wainscoting, which they shipped across the ocean and reassembled, as well as antique furniture and artworks by Titian, Raphael, Matisse, Cézanne, and Van Gogh. Gaukler Pointe, despite its size, has the feel of an intricate, intimate cottage. It had another virtue: its remote location northeast of Detroit was a world away from old Henry's castle at Fair Lane in the western suburb of Dearborn. When he was at home with his family, Edsel was safely insulated from his toxic father and the pressures of that madhouse known as Ford Motor Company.

Edsel and Eleanor and the children moved into Gaukler Pointe in 1929, when Bill was four years old. The family now existed in a fantasyland maintained by a staff of fifty, surrounded by priceless art and antiques, with manicured grounds that featured a lagoon for Edsel's various boats. The Great Depression might as well have been unfolding on another planet. Bill and his sister Josephine, the two youngest, were free to bomb around the hallways on their tricycles, whizzing past Jacobean chairs and Tudor tables and thirteenth-century marble sculptures. When they outgrew the tricycles, they raced around the grounds in miniature motorized cars built by their grandfather. For Josephine, the only girl, Kahn built a $15,000 playhouse.

There was never any doubt about the pecking order among Edsel and Eleanor's four children. As the eldest, Henry II was the unquestioned alpha dog, a chubby kid whose head seemed to be too big for his body—in more ways than one. His sense of entitlement and imperious manner led his playmates to call him "Chief." Benson, born two years after Henry II, was nearly blind in his left eye due to a botched delivery, and he was a shy and unassertive boy who never presented a threat to his big brother's supremacy. A second son born two years after the first, I can attest from personal experience, quickly learns that he will forever be at a physical disadvantage and therefore must learn to adapt, think fast, roll with the punches. But Henry II pressed his ample advantages over Benson in ways that were both unnecessary and cruel. One incident says it all. In 1933, shortly before FBI chief J. Edgar Hoover was scheduled to visit Gaukler Pointe, Henry II contracted diphtheria and was confined to a cottage on the estate. Furious with disappointment that he would not get to meet the legendary G-man, Henry II slipped into the main house and breathed on the clothes in Benson's closet, hoping his brother would contract the disease and be forced to join him in quarantine.

"Young Henry was like a hyena," a Ford employee told the family biographers Peter Collier and David Horowitz. "He ate all he could and peed on the rest. Ben wasn't like that. He was a good and trusting boy."

The children were sent off on weekend pilgrimages to Fair Lane to visit their grandparents: Henry II and Benson making the trip one weekend, Dodie and Bill the next. Old Henry taught his grandsons how to shoot a gun and drive a car, and there were tree forts and Shetland pony rides at Fair Lane, plus an elaborate doll collection for Josephine. But these were largely joyless excursions for the children because their grandfather was so distant. "He was hard to talk to," Dodie said. "He always seemed to be thinking about something else."

Meanwhile, twenty miles to the east, Edsel and Eleanor were transforming Gaukler Pointe into a glittering social and cultural hub. They entertained lavishly, bringing in Tommy Dorsey and Frank Sinatra to perform at parties. In addition to J. Edgar Hoover and the Prince of Wales, guests included a lively array of artists and architects and writers who outshone the one-note dullards from the auto world. To his lifelong passion for drawing Edsel now added painting and photography, and he hosted seminars at which William Valentiner, the German-born art historian who was director of the Detroit Institute of Arts, gave Edsel and his friends illustrated lectures on the masters of Western art. The sight of these wealthy provincials toiling to acquire some culture was "touching and a little pathetic," according to one of Valentiner's friends, but it was a major improvement over the anti-intellectual yahoo rusticity of old Henry. And it led directly to Edsel becoming president of the DIA and commissioning the Mexican muralist Diego Rivera to cover the walls of the museum's Garden Court with the controversial Detroit Industry Murals, which depicted workers inside Ford's sprawling River Rouge factory as well as scientists producing vaccines and poison gas. The work enraged many Detroiters, including the Catholic Church and the local press, who derided the murals as "Marxist," "vulgar," and "un-American." Edsel firmly resisted calls to destroy them. Lured by the controversy, 10,000 visitors showed up to view the murals when they were unveiled. Today they are, without question, one of the city's shiniest cultural jewels.

Edsel and Eleanor also maintained vacation homes: a winter place at Hobe Sound in Florida, where Edsel kept his 125-foot yacht the *Onika*, with its opulent Chippendale living room and French Provincial state-rooms; a summer place at Seal Harbor in Maine, where the family mingled with Rockefellers and other members of the Eastern elite; and Haven Hill, a weekend getaway in the woods northwest of Detroit that Edsel referred to as his "nerve retreat." The children grew up on a diet of swimming, tennis, horseback riding, skiing and skating, and Edsel, a sports enthusiast, regularly took the boys down to Navin Field (precursor to Briggs Stadium) to see the Tigers play, to Olympia for Red Wings hockey games, and to the University of Detroit's Dinan Field, the first home of the Lions and the place where Bill Ford fell in love with the team as a boy. Too slight to play football, he excelled at tennis and soccer and was a daredevil on the ski slopes. A competitive fire burned in him from an early age.

Cars, of course, were central to his upbringing. Edsel took the boys to races at Roosevelt Raceway on Long Island, the Indianapolis 500, and Brooklands racetrack in England, where Bill fell in love with the sporty prewar MGs. When Bill was a teenager, Edsel gave him a one-off midget racer with a spirited British engine and a body fabricated in Indianapolis. Edsel had a governor installed that kept the car under thirty miles per hour. Bill promptly disabled it. One weekend when his parents were out of town he persuaded some company men to haul his racer to Dearborn so he could take a spin around the test track. He soon got the car up to 110 miles per hour—and the throttle stuck. The only way to bring the speeding racer to a stop was to drop it into neutral and work the brakes gently without going into a spin. When he finally got the demon under control and rolled it to a stop, the track hands' faces were as white as a Michigan snowdrift. "Congratulations," one of the men managed to croak, "I think you just set the new track record."

Neither Edsel nor Eleanor had gone to college, and they decided their new station in society dictated that the boys should attend an elite Eastern prep school. They settled on Hotchkiss, a feeder school for Yale. Only Benson failed to win admission to Yale and had to settle for Princeton, where he, like Henry II at Yale, dropped out before earning a degree. After the war, Bill earned an economics degree from Yale, making him the first member of the family with a college education. He then followed his father's footsteps to an ill-fated career at the company that bore their name.

◆

There's one thing to remember about the wealth that surrounded Bill Ford all his life: it was not old money. It had not been passed down through generations of a venerable Boston or Philadelphia family, or one of the cotton, sugar, or tobacco aristocracies of the antebellum South. The Ford family fortune was, even by American standards, the newest of new money. Another thing to remember is that it sprang from the tall grass of the industrial Midwest, a provincial world far removed from the cultural capitals of the coasts. So the Ford money arrived without any traditions or established protocols—no network of schools, clubs, or charities, no customs or protocols—which meant these nouveaux riches had to improvise a sense of style as they went along. And their style would give off a strong scent of the provinces and, going back a little further, of the Irish peasantry.

Henry Ford's father, William Ford, was twenty-three years old when, at the height of the potato famine, his tenant-farmer parents were evicted from the land they worked in County Cork, in southwestern Ireland. As the eldest son, William took it upon himself to get his parents and his two brothers and four sisters down to Queenstown, where they boarded one of the dread "coffin ships" and set off on the treacherous Atlantic crossing. William's mother, Thomasina, died during the voyage and was buried at sea.

Upon arriving in America, the family pushed westward until they arrived at a frontier town near Detroit called Dearborn, where two of William's uncles had settled fifteen years earlier and were now land-rich farmers. William soon prospered as well, hiring himself out as a carpenter and eventually marrying Mary Litogot O'Hern, the adopted daughter of a childless but prosperous couple. Two years later, during the summer of the Battle of Gettysburg, the Fords' first child was born. They named the boy Henry.

The story of Henry Ford's rise has been exhaustively retold, so just a few quick brushstrokes are needed here. Young Henry became obsessed with all things mechanical, most notably gasoline-powered internal-combustion engines. Like his father, Henry married the daughter of a well-off local farmer, Clara Bryant, and the newlyweds relocated to Detroit so Henry could escape the drudgery of farm work and take a job as an engineer at the Detroit Edison Company while pursuing his mechanical experiments on the side. In 1893 their only child was born, a son they named Edsel, and three years later Henry produced his first car, a "quadricycle" perched on four bicycle tires, with a tiller for steering and a gasoline-powered engine tucked beneath the driver's seat. As he zipped around the streets of Detroit on his odd little contraption, Ford came to be known as "Crazy Henry."

Ford's first two ventures into the fledgling automobile industry ended in failure. His third was different. With Henry and the businessman Alexander Malcomson splitting 51 percent of the stock, Ford Motor Company opened for business in 1903 and began producing the original Model A. It carried a price tag of $850—about $30,000 in today's money—not cheap, and certainly not cheap enough to satisfy Henry Ford. He and Malcomson had a fundamental and fatal philosophical difference: Malcomson wanted to push the company's more expensive—and more profitable—models, while Ford stubbornly insisted they focus on producing a cheap, dependable car in high volume. Something had to give. Reluctantly, in the summer of 1906

Malcomson agreed to sell Henry his stock—and the gusher of dividends
it was producing. Suddenly Henry Ford controlled the company that bore
his name. Overnight, he'd become a rich man.

The world-changing innovations—the Model T, the moving assembly
line, the $5 day—were still to come. Soon the money raining on Henry
Ford would turn into a downpour. When his youngest grandchild, William Clay Ford, was born in 1925, the family fortune was less than two
decades old, but it was growing exponentially by the day. And so were the
privileges and peculiar perils that come when money is so new and there
is so much of it.

◆

As Henry II quickly learned after his release from the navy in 1943, the
wolf with the sharpest fangs inside Ford Motor Company was a compact
street brawler named Harry Bennett, who old Henry had installed as
head of his all-powerful Service Department, an in-house Gestapo that
policed the Ford empire with iron fists. Bennett was the son old Henry
wished he'd had, a scrapper who would take on any enemy perceived or real,
from factory idlers to union sympathizers to potential kidnappers of Henry's
grandchildren. It was Bennett's thugs who brutally beat Walter Reuther
and other union organizers during the infamous Battle of the Overpass
in 1937. It was Bennett who installed cronies and spies throughout the
company, rising to a seat on the board of directors and turning an erratic
autocracy into a money-hemorrhaging thugocracy.

Henry II took his time getting a grasp on the company's colossal dys-
function and then, as the peacetime economy picked up, he began cleaning
house. He got rid of Bennett and a thousand of his minions and replaced
them with qualified managers. His most inspired hire was Ernie Breech,
president of Bendix Aviation and a former protégé of Alfred Sloan at
General Motors, who made an inspired hire of his own when he lured

another former GM executive, Lewis Crusoe, out of semiretirement to bring order to the company's chaotic finances. They, along with a cadre of number-crunching former Army Air Corps officers known as the Whiz Kids—an elite group that included Robert McNamara—gradually turned a money-losing mess into a humming modern corporation. Put another way, Henry II turned a dysfunctional thugocracy into a profitable meritocracy.

As the company came back from the grave in the fifties, it became apparent to Henry II and both of his younger brothers (and their sister) that there was room for only one Ford at Ford Motor Company. This was a lesson their father had learned the harshest way imaginable. The corporate culture had changed since the War, symbolized by the sleek new twelve-story headquarters building known as the Glass House, where the casual camaraderie of the old Administration Building was supplanted by a rigid hierarchy of status and perks. It was a chilly place, increasingly dominated by McNamara and his numbers people. At the top of the ladder was the occupant of the spacious twelfth-floor office suite, Henry II, the increasingly autocratic lord who could survey his domain through large plate-glass windows. Much lower on the ladder were his two brothers. After a series of mid-level posts, Benson was made head of the Dealer Policy Board, a eunuch's job; and after the Continental fiasco, Bill's Siberia was the Design Center. More than a few observers remarked that Henry Ford's grandchildren were not merely prisoners of the family's history—they were doomed to relive it. Henry II, at the center of the show, was becoming their power-drunk grandfather, while Bill, relegated to the sidelines, was becoming their talented, stylish but ineffectual father. Both younger brothers started drinking, with Benson heading toward an early grave and Bill embarking on his long lost weekend.

The stark differences between the eldest and youngest brothers would be revealed in their handling of their chosen challenges. To revive the company, Henry II absorbed the gospel of his archrival Alfred Sloan, who never turned a wrench or learned to drive a car but nonetheless transformed

General Motors into an industrial behemoth through his philosophy of decentralized operations with coordinated control. This expressed itself in a system of five autonomous divisions, from entry-level Chevrolet up to Pontiac, Oldsmobile, Buick, and finally top-of-the-line Cadillac. Sloan's genius was to elevate qualified people and then get out of the way and let them do their jobs—while keeping a sharp eye on their performance. He expressed the virtue of decentralization in his typically dry way: "Any plan that involved too great a concentration of power upon a limited number of executives would limit initiative . . . and would reduce efficiency and development. Further it would mean an autocracy, which is just as dangerous in a great industrial organization as in a government."

Or, he might have added, in a professional sports franchise.

This was a lesson Bill Ford would never learn. To revive the Lions and return them to glory, he went in the opposite direction preached by Sloan and followed by Henry II. Like many rich owners of sports teams, Bill Ford viewed the Lions as his personal toy to play with as he pleased. It was also his lifeline, the ideal salve for the beating he had taken over the Continental Mark II—and for the painful realization that there was no room for him in the rigid hierarchy of the family business. Since the Lions had no shareholders to answer to, Bill was free, as he'd put it, to conduct board meetings in a phone booth. He could hire and fire at will. And because of the privileges he'd always lived with, he was free to judge people not on their merits but on their loyalty and, perhaps worse, on their *likability*. In the ensuing years, Bill Ford would surround himself not with people who were qualified to do their jobs but with people who were loyal and who made him feel comfortable. The Detroit Lions were on their way to becoming something that would reduce efficiency and development even more drastically than an autocracy. As the job offer to Dick Morris, the removal of George Wilson, and the hiring and firing of Harry Gilmer had revealed, Detroit's football team was already a one-man plutocracy. Which is to say it was engineered to fail.

BLANK SLATES

Bill Ford was not going to make the same mistake twice. The Harry Gilmer fiasco—hiring a head coach who had played college and pro ball and served as an assistant NFL coach for eight years—convinced Ford that experience was overrated. You learn by doing, you seek out and reward loyalty and, above all, you follow your instincts. It was why he'd put Gene Bordinat in charge of Ford's styling studios. It was why he'd made loyal Russ Thomas the Lions' director of player personnel. It was why he'd offered the general manager's job to his drinking buddy Dick Morris, and it was why he'd greeted Morris's misgivings about the job offer with such a casual dismissal: "Oh, you can handle it with your left hand."

That dismissal captured Bill Ford's linked beliefs that experience was overrated and that brains and class and a little effort could overcome any challenge. This was a telling insight into the thinking of the very rich, into the way privilege can distort calculations of effort and reward. It was also an uncanny echo of an earlier episode that has become a revelatory, if overlooked, footnote to American history.

In the summer of 1960 Henry Ford II had picked Robert McNamara to succeed him as president of Ford Motor Company. Henry II would remain as chairman. It was the first time someone outside the Ford family had held the presidency, a break with tradition that surely stung the bypassed brothers, Benson and Bill.

Seven weeks after McNamara's coronation, he received a summons to Washington. President-elect John F. Kennedy wanted to talk to him about a possible Cabinet post. McNamara's drive and swagger, his faith that any challenge could be overcome if it was understood, fit nicely with the can-do ethos of Kennedy's New Frontier.

McNamara's nearly religious worship of numbers did not turn him into a cloistered monk. Though he didn't drink and though he lived near the University of Michigan campus in Ann Arbor instead of in one of the posh Detroit suburbs favored by auto executives, McNamara occasionally put in an appearance at company social functions. While the men gathered on one side of the room talking sports and cars at one such cocktail party, Dick Morris noticed that all the women were on the other side of the room—clustered around Bob McNamara like moths drawn to a bright light. Curious, Morris drifted over and listened in as McNamara regaled the ladies with his adventures from a recent mountain-climbing trip in the Southwest. *Mountain climbing!* McNamara was surely the only auto executive in Detroit who spent his vacations climbing mountains. He also drove himself to work instead of riding in a chauffeured company car, and he traveled economy class instead of using one of the company planes. The guy didn't even play golf. But he was an engaging storyteller who radiated intelligence and a spirit of adventure, and Morris could see that the women surrounding him at the cocktail party were enthralled. It was so refreshing to hear a man talk about something other than Thunderbirds and home runs and the Lions' latest quarterback conundrum!

When McNamara arrived in Washington, Kennedy offered him his choice of two of the most powerful cabinet posts, treasury or defense. McNamara, like Dick Morris three years later at the Plaza Hotel, demurred, saying he didn't know anything about either of the jobs he was being offered. Kennedy, a son of inherited wealth, waved away McNamara's objection just as Bill Ford would wave away Dick Morris's objection.

"I don't know how to be president, either," Kennedy told McNamara. "We can learn our jobs together."

This was a blithe admission that wealth and privilege and clout—that is, the machinations of the family's ruthlessly ambitious patriarch, Joseph P. Kennedy—had landed young Jack Kennedy in a job for which he was unprepared and unqualified. Such trifles may have given pause to self-made men like Bob McNamara and Dick Morris, but they never stopped sons of wealth like Jack Kennedy and Bill Ford. One Kennedy biographer neatly summed up this blend of presumption and impatience: "He did not wait his turn."

The appointment of Robert McNamara as secretary of defense led directly to the disaster of the Vietnam War. It also illuminated the parallels between the Kennedy and Ford families, and especially between Jack Kennedy and Bill Ford. Both families were descended from Irish immigrants and had recently come into major money. Both of the current generations had grown up surrounded by opulence, told from an early age that they were destined for great things, told this so often that they came to believe it was virtually inevitable. Both families, in other words, equated inherited wealth—class—with destiny. For Jack Kennedy and his brothers, the destiny was politics, the realm of pure power that is attained not always by merit and not infrequently by convincing (or paying) enough people to give it to you; for Bill Ford and his brothers, the destiny was the family business, which proved to be such a perilous place that Bill Ford set out to create his own alternate destiny by paying a small fortune for an NFL franchise.

Both Jack Kennedy and Bill Ford offered jobs to men who were blank slates because they themselves were blanks slates, men with limited qualifications but deep faith in the power of their native intelligence and inherited wealth. *Oh, you can handle it with your left hand* was another way of saying *I don't know how to be president, either.* Kennedy might have added, *But that's never stopped me before.* To complete the parallel, both Jack Kennedy and Bill Ford grew up in the shadows of domineering older brothers, which spurred both men to want to make their mark. Neither enjoyed much success. Jack Kennedy may have been a world-class womanizer, but as a congressman, senator, and president he has come to be regarded as a mediocrity at best; Bill Ford was a washout as an auto executive, and as a football team owner he was a car wreck that was destined to keep repeating itself for the next half century.

So much for destiny.

◆

Bill Ford did not make the same mistake twice. He decided to hire blank slates like himself, men with no track records, men who would sink or swim based on talent, brains, and effort rather than on their past performances. As always, Ford would surround himself with men who were loyal, men he liked, men who made him feel comfortable.

First, Ford promoted Russ Thomas from director of player personnel to vice president and general manager. Then Ford elevated the popular assistant coach and former star linebacker Joe Schmidt to head coach and gave him a five-year contract. Schmidt, in turn, brought in his fellow former linebacker Carl Brettschneider as director of player personnel. None of these blank slates had any experience in the jobs they'd been given.

This was not lost on Joe Falls of the *Free Press*, who wrote: "It looks as if the Lions have become so desperate to put their house in order that they've cast aside their business sense and are being guided by emotions." He could have substituted "Bill Ford's instincts" for "emotions." Falls added that the Lions were "a team whose middle name was trouble."

Yet the hiring of Schmidt made some sense. He was worshipped by the fans and respected by the players—two luxuries Harry Gilmer never enjoyed. When Schmidt stated that the team was in rebuild mode and that trades and smart draft picks were needed immediately, people listened. Even so, there was something vague about the powers he would wield.

"Ford said Schmidt would have more freedom than Gilmer, although it would be hard to define just how," the *Free Press* reported. "Schmidt said he would have a free hand in trades, although he wouldn't go off half-cocked without consulting Russ Thomas, his coaches, and Ford if needed." *If needed?* Make that *without fail.* Schmidt, like Harry Gilmer, was about to learn that all draft picks and trades were subject to the approval of Thomas and Ford, and every coaching decision was subject to second-guessing by Thomas and Ford. Hands-on micromanagement was to become a corner-stone of the team's culture. On the positive side, even cantankerous Alex Karras respected Schmidt, and Ford had reason to hope that if Karras fell into line, the rest of a team whose middle name was trouble might follow his lead.

The promotion of Thomas, on the other hand, was a mystery. Yes, Ford approved of the way Thomas had handled the Harry Gilmer contract nego-tiation and, yes, Thomas understood the game of football and he'd proven his loyalty. But Ford's undying loyalty to Thomas had to go deeper than that. I've heard speculation from several sources, plausible but impossible to prove, that Thomas had covered for Bill Ford's drinking mishaps more than once and that he'd had a hand in guiding Ford into rehab. If true, it was a debt that would be impossible to repay, and it helps explain why Bill Ford remained loyal to Thomas for more than two decades as the general manager took the team on a rollercoaster ride that carried them relentlessly, dizzyingly downhill.

In time, the players would come to believe that the team's chronic problems stemmed from the sway general managers held over the owner. And they tended to blame the managers and give the owner a pass. "Russ Thomas and Edwin Anderson were two of the biggest assholes who ever walked the Earth," Sam Williams, a member of the Lions' "Fearsome Four-some" defensive line, said years after he'd retired. "They had Bill Ford so hoodwinked it was pathetic. Bill Ford never figured it out. God bless his soul, he's such a sweetheart—you couldn't find a better man in the whole world than Billy Ford Sr. I just love the man. I've been out drinking with him and having a good time, and he's just one of the boys. I've talked to him on the telephone for two hours when I was having contract troubles, and he will not go either way. He stands right there in the center and says, 'It's not my business. I hired these guys to do that. That's their job.' He will not say yes or no to *anything*."

This was decades before Ford hired the worst general manager in the history of the NFL.

◆

The NFL and rival AFL had taken a step toward their planned merger by staging the first showdown between the champions of the two leagues after the 1966 season. The powerhouse Green Bay Packers of the NFL dispatched the surprisingly stubborn Kansas City Chiefs of the AFL by a score of 35–10 at the Los Angeles Coliseum in a game now known as Super Bowl I.

When the two leagues held their first joint draft before the 1967 season, the Lions struck gold. With the seventh overall pick in the first round, they nabbed a slick running back from UCLA, Mel Farr, a player with seemingly unlimited potential. It was a smart but not particularly audacious choice. Farr was a highly publicized star at a college power-house, an obvious plum.

It was in the second round that the Lions showed their ingenuity. The team had brought in one of the NFL's first Black scouts, a Detroiter named Will Robinson who coached the local Pershing High School basketball team and had a sharp eye for basketball and football talent. At a time when Black colleges got little attention from pro football scouts, Robinson traveled the back roads seeking overlooked gems. He'd found one in 1960 at Maryland State College on the remote Eastern Shore, Roger Brown, a mammoth lineman destined for fame as an anchor of the Fearsome

Foursome. In 1967, the year Mel Farr was drafted, Robinson found another gem at Jackson State College in Mississippi: a lightning-quick cornerback named Lem Barney. The team drafted him with the thirty-fourth overall pick. To complete the trifecta, the Lions used their third-round pick to draft an All-American linebacker out of Tennessee, Paul Naumoff, who would prove to be a durable workhorse in the mold of Joe Schmidt.

The 1967 draft, conducted at the height of the civil rights movement, did not stamp the Lions as pioneers in the racial integration of pro football. That distinction belongs to the Cleveland Browns and Los Angeles Rams, who, in 1946, a year before Jackie Robinson smashed professional baseball's color barrier, each signed two Black players to a sport that was then all-white, thanks to a "gentleman's agreement" put into place by the racist owner of the Washington Redskins, George Preston Marshall. Two years later, a pair of barriers fell in Detroit: the Lions signed their first Black players, and Bill Matney of the *Michigan Chronicle* became the first Black sportswriter admitted to the Briggs Stadium press box. Matney's breakthrough was noteworthy because the stadium was named for the owner of the Detroit Tigers, the industrialist Walter O. Briggs, an unapologetic racist who hotly resisted the integration of his ball club. The scabrous expression around town was "No jigs with Briggs." It wasn't until 1958, six years after Briggs's death, that the Tigers signed their first non-white player, the Dominican-born infielder Ozzie Virgil. Of the sixteen teams in the major leagues, only the Boston Red Sox were slower to integrate.

The Lions' record was better, but not by much. During their 1957 championship season, their roster included just one Black player, the bruising fullback John Henry Johnson. When Bill Ford bought the team, he inherited a handful of outstanding Black players, including Roger Brown and the feared cornerback Dick "Night Train" Lane. After Lane retired as a player in 1965, Ford had made him the first Black member of the team's front office—"a sort of good-will man-about-town for the club," as one reporter put it. The Lions may not have been pioneers, but the hiring of Lane along with the drafting of Farr and Barney did announce that Bill Ford was, at least compared to Walter O. Briggs, a relative progressive on racial issues.

Scouting was an imprecise science in those precomputer years. The Lions were members of the BLESTO (Bears-Lions-Eagles-Steelers Talent Organization) scouting combine, and they also had their own scouts. The team sent hundreds of highly unscientific questionnaires to college seniors every year. A typical question: "Please name the five best players you have played against during the past season." Since few of those questionnaires went to players at historically Black colleges and universities, and since all of the Lions' scouts were white before the arrival of Will Robinson, it's hardly surprising that the team drafted few Black players in the pre-Ford years. Joe Schmidt, for one, did not believe this was driven by racism. "I don't think the coaches had anything against signing Black players," he said. "I think it was more of a case of scouting not being very sophisticated in those days. Hell, they were still drafting some guys out of magazines. Nobody was paying much attention to those small Black colleges." With the hiring of Will Robinson, that began to change.

But before Mel Farr and Lem Barney played their first game for the Lions, while they and the rest of their teammates were sweating through training camp in the July heat, the city of Detroit exploded.

THE MOTOR CITY
IS BURNING

It may have been the Summer of Love in San Francisco and other American cities. Not in Detroit.

In the steamy early-morning hours of Sunday, July 23, 1967, Black revelers were packed into an illegal after-hours club on Detroit's West Side, known locally as a blind pig, celebrating the safe return of two neighborhood men from tours of duty in Robert McNamara's worsening nightmare in Vietnam. Well past midnight, a squad from the largely white Detroit police force smashed its way into the club and broke up the party. A crowd gathered at the corner of 12th Street and Clairmount Avenue to watch the familiar spectacle of white cops herding dozens of Black celebrants into paddy wagons. The atmosphere, festive at first, quickly turned brittle. There was some vigorous taunting of the cops. Someone threw a bottle. Then someone smashed a window. And then, like a whirlwind, five days of looting and shooting and burning swept the streets of Detroit, leaving forty-three people dead and reducing vast swaths of the city to smoldering rubble.

Many people at the time saw this as a senseless, self-defeating spasm of violence, and they called it a riot or, more pointedly, a race riot. In fact, it was the logical, possibly inevitable response to a decades-old pattern of racism in the way Detroit policed, housed, educated, and employed its Black citizens. No less an authority than Philip Levine, a blue-collar Detroiter who went on to win a Pulitzer Prize and become America's poet laureate, acknowledged this distinction. Levine, whose poetic apprenticeship had taken place in the unlikely cauldrons of Chevy Gear & Axle and other Detroit factories, rightly called the events of that summer "the great rebellion of 1967." It was, he added dryly, "labeled 'riots' by the newspapers."

That Sunday afternoon, as the fires spread and ribbons of acrid black smoke spiraled up from the West Side, the Detroit Tigers played a doubleheader against the New York Yankees three miles away in Tiger Stadium. After the second game, the Tigers' popular homegrown slugger Willie Horton, the team's first Black star, ignored instructions to go straight home and instead drove to the heart of the fray. These were the familiar streets where Horton had delivered the *Michigan Chronicle* as a boy, and he was shocked by the chaos—the fires, the sirens, the shattered storefronts and overturned cars, the brazen looting, the crackle of gunfire, cops everywhere. Horton claims in his memoir that he climbed onto the roof of his car and started shouting at the crowd to stop what they were doing. There is no documentation of such an impromptu plea, and some people dispute the veracity of Horton's story. But there's no doubt that Willie Horton was powerless to stop the city's fury. After he drove away, the rebellion, as it is now widely known among Detroiters, raged on.

Detroit has always been a musical town—before the flowering of Motown and rock 'n' roll there were vibrant blues and jazz scenes—so it's not surprising that the conflagration of 1967 haunted and inspired its musicians. Among them were the Temptations and Marvin Gaye, Motown stars who would now begin moving away from boy-meets-girl ballads toward rougher, more socially conscious material. Another was the raw thwanking bluesman John Lee Hooker, a foot soldier in the Great Migration who had come up to Detroit from his native Mississippi during the Second World War to toil in a Ford factory before his musical career took off. Hooker's song, "The Motor City Is Burning," later covered by the proto-punk Detroit rockers the MC5, cleverly linked the war being fought on the streets of

Detroit to the war being fought halfway around the world in the jungles and rice paddies of Vietnam. After all, the former war was sparked by the return of two soldiers from the latter war. Hooker's electric guitar has the sting of a cattle prod, his voice is mystified and anguished. He admits he's powerless to stop the violence, doesn't really understand what it's all about. All he knows is that his hometown's burning down to the ground—and it's "worster than Vietnam."

Bad, worse, worst, *worster*. Standard English cannot capture the extremes that have always existed side by side in the ethnic crazy quilt of Detroit—boom and bust, artistry and drudgery, mansions and slums, Arctic cold and hellish heat, neighborliness and racism and waves of adversity that never stop coming but always run up against the city's unkillable spirit. Detroiters are, in Philip Levine's words, people who've "survived everything America can dish out." Since its founding as a French trading post in the early eighteenth century, the place has always been about hard work, making things, taking risks, and either getting rich or barely getting by. It came to be known as "an eight-finger town," thanks to the treacherous machinery inside its thundering factories. Not a place for the delicate or the faint of heart.

Yet it was a city with undeniable beauty, even grandeur. Leveled by fire in 1805, it was rebuilt on a plan devised by Augustus Woodward, chief judge of the Michigan territory, who was inspired by Charles L'Enfant's recent layout of the young nation's new capital at Washington, DC. The Detroit plan called for spokes radiating from a central hub located downtown by the river, "the Grand Circus." Streets grids were laid over the spokes and the result is a vast platter encompassing 139 square miles, stretching from the Detroit River on the south to Eight Mile Road on the north, from Grosse Pointe on the east to Henry Ford's Dearborn empire on the west. It's big enough to contain the entire cities of Boston and San Francisco, plus the island of Manhattan. In keeping with its origins, many of the city's streets bear Anglicized French names—Livernois (LIVER-noy), Gratiot

(GRASH-it), Dequindre (de-KWIN-der), and many more. The city's name itself is an Anglicized French word, *D'étroit*, "by the straits," a reference to its riverfront location, pronounced DEE-troyt by many natives. By the time Bill Ford was born, the city was essentially in place: a cluster of high-rise stalagmites rising from the riverbank downtown, most of them built in the golden early decades of the twentieth century, surrounded by miles and miles of single-family homes packed side by side, punctuated by factory smokestacks, machine shops, steel mills, church steeples and, of course, the beckoning signs of car dealerships. The deal in Detroit was straightforward: get a job and you can own a house and a car (or two), maybe a boat, and you'll be a member of the middle class. In the fiery summer of 1967, one resident offered this vivid snapshot: "A city of streets. Freeways. Overpasses, railroad tracks, razed buildings and weedy vacant lots and billboards and houses, houses, blocks and acres and galaxies of houses, stretching out forever."

Bill Ford understood his hometown's extremes because he'd spent his life locked inside one of them—the uppermost reaches of the upper class. A month before the streets exploded, he had overseen a rite of passage emblematic of his class: the lavish coming-out party of his first-born, Muffy, who'd just completed her freshman year at Vassar. Bill Ford's mansion on Lake Shore Road was lit up like Christmas on the big night, thronged with family and friends. The Fords were Motor City royalty, and these events were treated as major news. According to the society pages of the *New York Times*, the debutante wore a long pink-and-white Staron of Bayadere dress at dinner, and for the after-dinner dance, which featured the Meyer Davis Orchestra and a rock band called the Young Rascals, she changed into "a fragile, full-length gown of white silk organza in the princess style, sleeveless and with a high neckline. It was embroidered with roses of the same material. . . . Each rose petal had been cut out, shaped, and appliquéd individually. Slim pendant beads of iridescent crystal hung in tiny clusters to the hem."

A month after that high-society soirée, with the fires creeping peril-
ously close to the Lions offices across the street from Tiger Stadium, Bill
Ford wasn't thinking about Staron of Bayadere dresses, the Meyer Davis
Orchestra, or the Young Rascals. He was worrying that hundreds of thousands of freshly printed tickets for the 1967 season would get incinerated
or, worse, looted. He called Ford Motor Company and asked for vans and
drivers, but an executive turned him down, said no driver was willing to
risk going into the war zone. Ford then recruited a Black janitor and his
good-will man-about-town Dick Lane to help with the mission. This only-
in-Detroit trio—the janitor, the former football star, and the debutante's
multimillionaire father—wove through the burning streets and retrieved
the precious tickets.

◆

A week after the last fires were extinguished, the Joe Schmidt era began
with a dubious distinction: the Lions lost to the Denver Broncos in their
preseason opener, marking the first time a team from the supposedly inferior AFL had beaten a team from the established NFL.

The Lions opened the regular season in Green Bay, hoping to make
another run at the defending champions. The first time a ball was thrown
his way, Lem Barney made an acrobatic interception, somersaulted, then
bounced to his feet and sprinted into the end zone. It was an auspicious
beginning to his career and the team's season, but the game ended in a tie
after the Lions squandered a seventeen-point lead. They left town feeling
it was a game they should have won.

They followed the disappointing tie with a convincing win at home
over a solid Cleveland Browns team, playing to a packed house. For Joe
Schmidt, it was a flashback to that glorious championship game in 1957.
Then the rollercoaster started downhill, gaining speed as it went. The team
lost three games in a row, six of the next ten, managing just two wins and

two ties. Schmidt seemed out of his depth at times, but the Lions closed the season with back-to-back wins, finishing with a 5–7–2 record, in third place in the newly configured four-team Central Division. There were positives. Schmidt was learning on the job, getting better, and Mel Farr and Lem Barney were named, respectively, offensive and defensive rookies of the year. The players and management—and owner—allowed themselves to feel optimistic about the future.

The 1968 draft revealed the team's ingrained discord. Schmidt wanted a premiere defender. Will Robinson was promoting a Black tight end named Charlie Sanders. Brettschneider believed the Alabama quarterback Ken Stabler would cure the team's most chronic problem. And Russ Thomas was fixated on a quarterback prospect of his own, Greg Landry from the University of Massachusetts.

"I wanted to draft quarterback Ken Stabler, who had been recommended by the BLESTO scouting services," Brettschneider recalled in a radio interview nearly fifty years later, still seething over the events of that long-ago day. "But Russ Thomas came up with his usual lies. He claimed that he spoke with Bobby Layne and that Layne had recommended Greg Landry, saying he was the best quarterback in the country. So of course Bill Ford listened to Russ Thomas." In another interview, Brettschneider offered a peculiar reason why the team shunned Stabler: "Bill Ford said he can't play. He's left-handed."

Of course Bill Ford listened to Russ Thomas before the draft. Bill Ford would spend the next twenty years listening to Russ Thomas. Meanwhile, word was out that the front office had turned into a snake pit.

"The head coach did not trust the general manager," wrote Jerry Green of the *Detroit News*, who covered that year's draft. "The general manager did not trust the head coach. It was not a secret that they were enmeshed into an office feud. The entire town knew of the bickering between Joe Schmidt and Russ Thomas."

When the team, on Ford's orders, picked Landry in the first round, Schmidt didn't even stick around to feed the usual platitudes to the sportswriters gathered in the team's offices. He bolted out the back door and roared off to his home in Bloomfield Hills, boiling with anger. Halfway out the Lodge Freeway he had cooled off enough to turn his car around and return to the scene of the crime.

Things actually improved after that. With another first-round pick the Lions drafted Earl McCullouch, a speedy wide receiver from Southern Cal, and in the third round they heeded Robinson's advice and nabbed Charlie Sanders. McCullouch would be named Rookie of the Year, and though no one knew it at the time, Sanders was destined for stardom.

This time, before Greg Landry, Earl McCullouch, and Charlie Sanders played their first game for the Lions, the entire nation exploded

BALL OF CONFUSION

It would not be a stretch to say the United States suffered a nervous breakdown in 1968. It began in late January, when North Vietnamese and Viet Cong troops launched the tightly choreographed Tet offensive, attacking scores of South Vietnamese cities, towns, and military installations, even breaching the walls of the US Embassy compound in Saigon. Though the Tet offensive failed to achieve its military goals—the collapse of the South Vietnamese regime and the departure of its American puppeteers—it was a major propaganda victory. For the first time, Americans saw proof on their TV screens that their government had been feeding them rosy lies about the war's progress. Robert McNamara had recently announced his resignation as secretary of defense, and he would leave the job shortly after the Tet offensive, content to let others mop up his mess. The job would require seven more years of senseless bloodshed.

In March the NFL owners held their annual meeting in Hawaii, and Bill and Martha Ford decided to make it a family vacation. The liberal Minnesota senator and antiwar candidate Eugene McCarthy had nearly bested President Lyndon Johnson in the recent Democratic primary in New Hampshire, a clear indication of the nation's growing disaffection with the war. Ford's eldest child, Muffy, the debutante who'd nudged him into rehab, had already volunteered to work on the McCarthy campaign, and in Hawaii she and her father had long talks about the war. Though Robert F. Kennedy had just entered the race as another antiwar candidate, Muffy

expected to have a hard time selling her father on the evils of America's
war effort and the appeal of a long shot liberal like McCarthy. He surprised
her. "Well, anybody who's against this war can't be all bad," he told his
daughter. "Maybe I'll go to work for him, too, when we get back home."

On the day the family returned to Grosse Pointe, President Johnson
stunned the nation with the announcement that he would not run for
reelection that fall, the clearest sign yet of the war's cascading political
toll. Bill Ford, true to his word, called McCarthy's local headquarters and,
after overcoming some initial skepticism among campaign volunteers that
a member of Detroit royalty was in favor of the iconoclastic McCarthy,
Ford enthusiastically hosted fundraising events and became chairman of
Michigan Businessmen for Eugene McCarthy. "I had a wonderful time,"
Ford recalled. "It was one thing for Henry to pal around with Johnson. His
politics were business politics. But I was doing this thing *voluntarily*. That's
what made it fun. My mother particularly thought I was off my rocker."
His nearly boyish enthusiasm for this unlikely crusade has a hint of the
euphoria common to the newly sober. Bill Ford was free of his demons at
last, and he didn't care if his family and every Republican in Grosse Pointe
thought he was off his rocker. In fact, he liked the way it made him feel.

◆

Four days after Johnson's shocker, on the evening of April 4, a drifter,
feckless career criminal, and recent escapee from a Missouri prison entered
the communal bathroom in a shabby rooming house in downtown Mem-
phis, Tennessee. He locked the door behind him, then stepped into the
bathtub and removed a bulky object wrapped in a green blanket. It was a
high-powered Remington .30-06 rifle. He rested the rifle's barrel on the
windowsill above the bathtub and peered through the Redfield scope at
the motel across the street. And all of a sudden there he was, bigger than
life in the scope's crosshairs: the elegantly dressed, freshly shaved Black

man who'd been causing so much trouble. The man was leaning on the motel's second-story balcony railing, chatting with some men lounging around a Cadillac in the courtyard below.

The single shot entered the right side of the Black man's face just below his mouth, shattering his jaw and spinal cord and throwing him against the door of Room 306 of the Lorraine Motel. As aides rushed to him, the man sprawled on the floor of the balcony in a spreading pool of blood, drawing his last ragged breaths.

James Earl Ray's assassination of the civil rights icon Martin Luther King Jr. ignited rioting in more than one hundred American cities, from Washington, DC, to Chicago to San Francisco. Yet Detroit, still reeling from the previous summer, remained almost eerily quiet. Shortly before midnight, police dispersed an amped-up crowd from 12th Street, and there were half a dozen reports of shots fired, some of them aimed at police. A few storefronts were smashed, a few cars were pelted with rocks and bottles. The following day, Black students walked out of several city schools, and Black autoworkers walked off the assembly line at a Chrysler plant. Taking no chances on a repeat of 1967, Gov. George Romney sent National Guard troops into Detroit. When the fever passed, one person was dead.

It may not have been a repeat of the bloody summer of 1967, but for Detroit, as for the rest of America, it was a season of raw nerves. The city's population, declining since 1950, now began to plunge. The increasingly Black city and its largely white suburbs crackled with rumors and the emotions they breed—suspicion, loathing, fear. Much of it was racially motivated, to be sure—a white teenager in a novel set in Detroit at that time is terrified that Black people are out to *scalp* him. A young writer named Joyce Carol Oates was teaching at the University of Detroit that year and living in the mostly white Green Acres neighborhood, and she wrote to a friend that Detroit "does not seem very healthy." Yet Oates was enthralled by the place—"the quintessential American city," she called it—and she worked up this vivid sketch: "Hazy skylines. Chemical-red sunsets. A yeasty gritty taste to the air—how easy to become addicted!" This addict understood that the trouble lived right next door. "Perfectly nice people," she said, "often turn unbelievably nasty over the question of integrated neighborhoods." The result was white flight, which the Temptations, in their soon-to-be-released hit "Ball of Confusion," depicted as people moving out and others moving in for one simple reason: "the color of their skin."

Oates and her husband, Raymond Smith, joined the exodus that year when they accepted teaching jobs at the University of Windsor. It was there, at a writing table facing north across the river toward Detroit, that Oates completed her novel *them*, the unflinching story of a poor white family scuffling in the slums of Detroit until they're swept up into the fires of 1967. The title is lowercased, a signal that these people are outsiders, insignificant, invisible to *Us*. The novel won the National Book Award and launched Oates on the road to literary stardom.

While she was writing it, James Earl Ray, object of the most intense manhunt in FBI history, passed undetected through Detroit and Windsor on his way to Toronto, where he boarded a flight to London. In Europe the fugitive managed to elude his pursuers for two months before he was arrested at the London airport and extradited to the US to face trial.

◆

The breakdown worsened two months later. After winning the California Democratic primary, a jubilant Robert F. Kennedy was walking through the kitchen of the Ambassador Hotel in Los Angeles in the early hours of June 5 when a Jordanian immigrant named Sirhan Sirhan approached from behind and shot him three times at point-blank range in the head, neck and back. After undergoing hours of surgery, Kennedy died the next day.

The nation was reeling. Martin and now Bobby dead, cities torched, Johnson on the way out, nonviolent civil rights protests giving way to shouts of "Black Power," college campuses and city streets convulsed with antiwar protests, Nixon on the rise promising "law and order." In Chicago that summer, Mayor Richard Daley's cops brutalized antiwar protesters at the Democratic National Convention, and at the summer Olympics in Mexico City the black American sprinters Tommie Smith and John Carlos stepped onto the stand to receive their medals shoeless, their black-gloved fists raised in a Black Power salute during the playing of the national anthem. The gesture infuriated millions of Americans and inspired millions more.

In such divisive, nerve-jangling times, it's natural for people to seek escape from the daily onslaught, and in Detroit the old staples of music and sports proved reliable tools for forgetting. Motown acts were drawing exuberant crowds to the Flame Show Bar, the 20 Grand and other clubs, and fans packed the Fox Theatre downtown for that year's Motortown Revue, starring the Temptations, Stevie Wonder, and Gladys Knight & the Pips. A Detroit disc jockey named Russ Gibb had reincarnated an old big-band dancehall on the West Side as the Grande (rhymes with "candy") Ballroom, which was now a mecca for homegrown rock bands, including the MC 5 and the Stooges, the local bluesman John Lee Hooker, as well as the Byrds, Jimi Hendrix, the Velvet Underground, Blue Cheer, Cream, and many others. The place was a typhoon of grinding and soaring electric guitars, pounding drums, a decibel level equal to any Detroit factory. To top it off, the crowds were a sweaty, thrashing, unleashed beast. Bands loved to play the Grande.

That summer Detroiters found another welcome distraction in the performance of the Tigers, who seemed determined to make amends for having lost the pennant on the last day of the '67 season. The '68 team had a knack for dramatic late-inning comebacks, and as the summer progressed and the wins piled up, larger and larger crowds were drawn to the snug confines of Tiger Stadium, a hermetically sealed world that could make the cares of the larger world magically vanish for a few hours. Those crowds were a mix of Black and White, working class and wealthy, city and suburb. The balm of baseball seemed to soothe the city's nerves, and the rising enthusiasm turned into citywide euphoria when the Tigers walked away with the American League pennant and got ready to take on the heavily favored St. Louis Cardinals in the World Series. The Detroit players and fans relished the role of underdog. It fit them and their city like a bespoke suit.

Meanwhile, after another fruitful draft and several inspired trades, anticipation was running high for the Lions' second season under Joe Schmidt. Russ Thomas had dealt the unloved quarterback Milt Plum to the Los Angeles Rams for the veteran Bill Munson, a move that was universally regarded in Detroit as an upgrade. The quarterback question was no longer "Plum or Morrall?" Now it was "Landry or Munson?" The answer may not have been any more apparent than it had been in years past, yet even quarterback-loathing Alex Karras liked what he saw. "This is the best quarterback situation since I've been here," he said before the season. "I feel like I was traded."

The NFL, like the rest of the nation, was becoming richer, more sophisticated, and more contentious by the day. TV revenues and ticket sales were turning even small-market teams into blue-ribbon cash cows. Computers were turning scouting from a guessing game into something resembling a science—and leading to the drafting of a new generation of gifted Black players. And the NFL Players Association, first formed in 1956, was awakening from a twelve-year slumber and demanding a bigger share of the owners' growing pile of money. The association declared itself an independent union and presented the owners with a twenty-five-page list of demands. This new assertiveness was part of the rising nationwide chorus demanding civil rights, women's rights, gay rights, an end to the Vietnam War, and equal pay for equal work. The cordial, nearly paternalistic relations between NFL owners and players that had existed for thirty years were beginning to change. Bill Ford, whose father had urged cooperation with organized labor in Ford factories (against old Henry's wishes), now tried to reason with his fellow NFL owners. Bill Ford once sat across the bargaining table from Walter Reuther of the United Auto Workers, and he developed great respect for the man and his dedication to his cause. Cooperation, Ford told his fellow owners, was better than confrontation. Change was inevitable, and not necessarily bad. His message was not warmly received. These rich men were not accustomed to having their employees tell them how to run their businesses.

The president of the players' union was the Lions' veteran offensive lineman John Gordy, who'd been a rookie on the 1957 championship team and was one of the players fined by Pete Rozelle for gambling on the 1962 NFL championship game. Dan Shulman, a sharp-elbowed lawyer for the players, was unhappy with the way Vince Lombardi, a member of the management negotiating team, was condescending to the players at the bargaining table, pushing them around. Shulman pulled the players aside and urged them to shake the owners up, use some salty language, tell them to go fuck themselves. Back at the table, Gordy stumbled in his mission to get tough. "We've got to, we've got to get these . . ." Then Gordy found his legs. "We've got to get these negotiations . . . these . . . these *fucking* negotiations off center!"

Lombardi exploded at the use of such language, according to his biographer, David Maraniss, and Shulman responded by leaning across the table and shouting, "FUCK! FUCK! FUCK! FUCK! Vince, the word is FUCK!" The coach and the lawyer sprang at each other, but order was restored before any punches were landed.

It got uglier. With the talks stalled in early July the players voted to strike, and the owners responded by announcing a lockout. Some owners wanted to bring in scab players, but they abandoned the idea when Lombardi refused to go along. Finally, on July 14, the bitter opponents reached a deal. The owners agreed to make a sizable contribution to the pension fund, raise minimum salaries to $9,000 for rookies and $12,000 for veterans, and pay players $50 for every appearance in an exhibition game, which in years past brought no money but ample opportunity for career-ending injury. It might seem like a modest victory by today's standards, but it was the beginning of a new era when power would tip from the owners to the players. The agreement announced that players were no longer willing to be treated as the perpetual personal property of rich white men. Plantation days, with a captive labor force, were coming to an end in the NFL.

THIS LOVE AFFAIR

Alex Karras's optimism going into the 1968 season may have been understandable, but it couldn't paper over the Lions' ruinous flaw: the festering animosity between the offensive and defensive units. Begun by that last-minute loss to Green Bay in 1962, it had now hardened into a permanent state of internecine warfare. Tex Maule of *Sports Illustrated* described those lingering "old wounds" in his preview of the 1968 season. "In years past," he wrote, "the beleaguered and overworked defenders have barely spoken to an offensive unit, which was apt to appear only long enough to run three plays and punt, leaving the brunt of the game to the defense." No savvy draft choice or trade could wipe away such history. And it was becoming apparent that no one in the front office or on the coaching staff knew how to heal the old wounds on a team whose middle name was trouble. Dissension and finger-pointing were becoming embedded in the team's DNA.

After a lopsided loss to the Dallas Cowboys in the season opener, the Lions delivered solid back-to-back wins over division rivals Chicago and Green Bay. Then everyone took a breather as Hollywood paid an overnight visit on Detroit. The movie version of George Plimpton's bestseller, *Paper Lion*, had its world premiere at the Adams Theatre in downtown Detroit on October 3. Spotlights stroked the night sky and a one-hundred-piece high school marching band blasted away as the theater filled with a giddy crowd, fueled by the sense that Detroit was on a roll. The Lions were off to a respectable start, and earlier that day the Tigers had whipped the

Cardinals in St. Louis to even the World Series at one game apiece. After a twenty-three-year absence, the World Series was coming back to town that weekend. And now, to top it off, Hollywood had come calling.

Several Lions played themselves in the movie, including Schmidt, Barney, Gordy, and Alex Karras, who showed up for the premiere sporting a double-breasted blazer and puffing a fat cigar, his wife Joan on his arm swaddled in a mink stole. The veteran linebacker Wayne Walker was decked out in a powder-blue Nehru jacket with a medallion dangling from a chain around his neck. *So* groovy. No one ever mistook Detroit's Woodward Avenue for Hollywood Boulevard, but the city and its football team were not going to pass up this chance to dress up and play Tinseltown for one night.

Alan Alda stars as hapless George Plimpton, but it's Alex Karras who steals the show—and takes his first step toward a second career as a successful actor in movies and TV shows. During a "talent show" put on by the Lions players during training camp, the emcee announces that the next performer is Joe Schmidt. Onto the stage strolls Karras, dressed as a World War II German soldier, carrying a bullwhip and leading a German shepherd on a leash. "I vant discipline!" Karras/Schmidt says, cracking the whip. "Bill Ford vants discipline! My assistants vant discipline! And ve are going to get discipline!" The whip cracks to raucous laughter.

What *is* this? This is Nazi humor—another symptom of America's collective nervous breakdown. People who are dismayed and confused by everything will laugh at anything, including something that would have been unthinkably tasteless just a few years earlier. A desperate need to laugh—that is, a desperate need to forget—could make anything mainstream. Even Nazi humor.

Lost in the opening-night hoopla were memories of Joe Schmidt's grousing during the six-week movie shoot earlier that year in Florida. Lions players were paid between $350 and $1,500 a week to play themselves—some serious coin at a time when pro football players had to work offseason jobs to make ends meet—but Schmidt had bigger things on his mind. "It was kind of fun to do it, but it was also a pain in the ass, to tell you the truth," he recalled. "I was worried about preparing game plans for the next season, and I'm thinking, 'What the hell is the season going to bring when we're jacking around in Florida?' It took a long time to get the players' minds off the damn movie and concentrate on football. Everyone thought they would be movie stars."

Film critic Roger Ebert was a bit more forgiving: "I don't know what to make of *Paper Lion* as a movie—it will not be immortal, I guess—but as wish fulfillment, it's crackerjack." He added that Alex Karras "emerges as an engaging actor," the first evidence of a gift that would lead to a lucrative second career after his retirement from football. Ebert gave the movie three of a possible four stars.

It may not have been immortal, but it was a hit in Detroit, especially among Lions fans, and it revealed the essence of the team's appeal. Now, as in years past, the team was full of colorful personalities who combined to give the team a collective personality that matched the blue-collar fabric of the city. The Lions didn't always win, but they always showed up, and they weren't afraid of the dirty work and when you played them you knew you'd been in a fight. In the past it was Dutch Clark, Doak Walker, Les Bingaman, Bobby Layne, Tobin Rote, and "Night Train" Lane administering the pain; now the team's roster mirrored the city's demographics. There were Black players up from the South (Barney, Sanders, defensive lineman John Baker). There was an assortment of reliable lug wrenches from the industrial Midwest (Schmidt, Karras, wide receiver Bill Malinchak, running back Tom Nowatzke, defensive back Dick LeBeau). By way of sprinkling a little glitter on the grit, there was a handful of glamor boys from the West Coast (Munson, McCullouch, Farr), but no high-watt showboats like Broadway Joe Namath of the New York Jets. Detroit had no use for showboats. The result was an iron bond between the team and its lunch-pail fans, a bond so strong that nothing could break it, not even some of the sorriest seasons in the history of the sport.

A week after the *Paper Lion* premiere, the Tigers stunned the base-ball world by beating the Cardinals in game 7 in St. Louis to win the World Series. Detroit exploded again—this time with joy. There was interracial dancing in the streets, a mad gabble of car horns, blizzards of confetti, delirium not seen since the Lions' last championship in 1957. The euphoria didn't make the city's mounting problems go away, of course, but Detroiters had learned long ago to let the good times roll when they come your way—because it's a given they're not going to last.

◆

The Lions' home game against the Packers on October 20 was a microcosm of their season: a fast start followed by a disappointing finish. The Lions jumped to a 14–0 lead on a couple of slick Earl McCullouch touchdown catches, then took their foot off the gas pedal and allowed the Packers to tie the score in the fourth quarter. When the Lions recovered a Green Bay fumble to snuff a possible game-winning drive in the final minute, Schmidt, still haunted by that last-minute interception and loss to Green Bay in 1962, elected to play it safe and run out the clock. The tie put the Lions in first place in their division, but the starved Detroit fans wanted wins, not ties. For the first time during his tenure as head coach, Schmidt heard boos raining down from the stands, an unsettling echo of the music that had sent Harry Gilmer offstage after his final loss. This time, merci-fully, there was no barrage of snowballs.

After climbing into first place with that tie, coach and team seemed to lose something—their nerve, their footing, their *mojo*. In Detroit-speak, their wheels came off. They lost their next four games and six of their last eight, sprinkling in just one win and one tie.

They hit bottom on Thanksgiving Day against the winless Philadelphia Eagles. A day and a half of incessant rain had pounded Detroit before the game and turned the field into a swamp, which inspired this burst of poetry from a visiting *Philadelphia Inquirer* sportswriter: "Tiger Stadium's turf made the average pig's quarters appear to be wall-to-wall carpeted by comparison." The only way to distinguish the mud-slathered players was by the color of their helmets. Neither team scored a touchdown, but the Eagles, after illegally substituting dry footballs, kicked four field goals for a 12–0 win that knocked the Lions out of playoff contention. A season that had begun with such high hopes was now a mud-caked wreck.

Free Press columnist Joe Falls bumped into a disconsolate Bill Ford in the Lions' locker room after the game. This was Ford's fifth season as owner, and he was now on his third coach of a team headed for its fourth straight losing season. It was becoming apparent to Detroit fans that something was fundamentally wrong, that Bill Ford had no clue how to return the Lions to glory. In the next morning's paper, Falls produced a revealing sketch of Ford: "The image he has with most of the people in our town is that of spoiled rich man who treats the Lions as his private play toy. He has been depicted from time to time as a meddler, a second guesser, a guy who lets Van Patrick tell him what to do. In short, not a very sound football man."

Now Falls shifts gears.

"But if you could see this man after one of these ball games—such as the Lions played on Thanksgiving Day—you might have just a little different opinion of him. He stands there in the dressing room trying mightily to hold his head high, when deep down, where it counts, you know he is dying a thousand deaths. More than anything else in life, he wants to have a winning football team in Detroit. Maybe he doesn't know how to go about it. Maybe it would be better if he just stepped back from the whole thing and never went near the front office, the dressing room, or the field."

After floating that suggestion, Falls takes a step back.

"What is most impressive about Bill Ford—even beyond this love affair he has with his football team—is his utter and complete honesty. I have never known him to back off a question or give you the old double dribble. It almost gets scary interviewing him after the games because you know he is going to say something and it's usually something that will make a headline. But it is going to be what he thinks—exactly what he thinks—and he'll never back off after reading it in print."

Then Ford tells Falls exactly what he thinks about losing: "Sure, it's killing me. This thing is eating me up."

"And that," Falls concludes, "is what this poor little rich boy thinks of the Lions. Criticize him, ridicule him, complain about him . . . but don't tell me he doesn't care . . . Some of the players would do well to care as much about winning as does the man who signs their checks."

To the frustrated fans, Joe Schmidt's second season was a replay of Harry Gilmer's second season—a step backward, a 4–8–2 record and a last-place finish in the Central Division. But a closer look suggests that the team was making progress. The personnel was coming together. Schmidt was gaining confidence, and the players still believed in him. Other than the thrashing administered by the Cowboys in the season opener, the losses were close, with an average margin of defeat of just ten points. They were games that could have been won—without that dropped pass or that missed field goal, without that stupid holding penalty, with a few good breaks here and there.

After the 1967 season, the popular placekicker Garo Yepremian had enlisted in the US Army Reserve, and when he came back to Detroit after his discharge hoping to get his old job back, Joe Schmidt was against offering him a contract. "I think soccer-style kicking is a fad," Schmidt said. It was a small but telling illustration of another trait that would come to define this team: the tendency to keep the wrong people and let the right people get away. Garo Yepremian would soon join former Lions assistant coach Don Shula and former Lions quarterback Earl Morrall on the Miami Dolphins. Together they were headed for football immortality. The Detroit Lions were not.

A LUCKY MAN

Dick Morris's attempt to steer Bill Ford into rehab had failed, but Morris had been wrong to believe that taking his concerns to Henry II was his death sentence at Ford. As it turned out, Morris had a second act at the company. He managed to walk out of Bill Ford's shadow—not an easy thing to do—by engineering a transfer to the public relations staff at Ford Division, the pumping heart of the company, which was then run by a high-octane salesman and self-promoter named Lee Iacocca. When Morris reported for work, Iacocca offered a terse welcome: "You realize you've joined the infantry, don't you?" And compared to the leisurely pace of the styling division—where Morris had been the executive assistant of a man who didn't execute much of anything—Morris found that he had indeed landed on the front lines. Ford was then locked in mortal combat to outsell Chevrolet, and the pace was brutal. "If ever there was a fast track in American industry, that was it," Morris recalled. "We came to work with our track shoes on in the morning and never took them off."

Morris's duties included promoting the company's racing program, and he was present when Fords won the 24-hour of Le Mans four years in a row in the late 1960s, a feat immortalized in the popular movie *Ford v Ferrari*. Beating one of Europe's storied car brands was a major ego-boost for Henry II, who had embarked on his midlife phase of self-discovery and self-indulgence. His appetites had become Falstaffian. His face was now puffy and pink from the heavy drinking, and his weight, thanks to the rich food and sauces and booze, had ballooned to 250 pounds. He could be moody and boorish, as coarse as a cheese grater, especially when drunk. He bedded women at will. In the executive dining room at the Glass House, a Swiss-Italian chef would prepare whatever the executives fancied, from oysters Rockefeller to Dover sole or roasted pheasant. But Henry II, the unreconstructed Irish peasant, preferred to have the chef send an inch-thick New York strip steak through a meat grinder and serve up a nice juicy burger. Henry II liked his served with a side order of peas.

Eventually, inevitably, Henry II shed his first wife, the old-school Eastern socialite Anne McDonnell, and took up with a divorced Italian jet-setter named Cristina Vettore Austin, a sometime model who was everything Grosse Pointe wives were not. She was worldly, willowy, brazenly sexy. The Ford children were outraged. It was a scandal in Grosse Pointe. It was also the most predictable—and predictably expensive—move in the middle-aged American male's repertoire. It led to an ugly and costly divorce that stood in sharp contrast to the newfound stability and sobriety of Bill Ford's life. Anne McDonnell had married Henry II at least partly because of his money, while Martha Firestone, heiress to a fortune of her own and no fan of dynastic couplings, married Bill *in spite of* his money. Henry II would cycle through three wives, each divorce further depleting him financially and spiritually, while Bill and Martha stayed together until the day he died. They had arrived at an understanding that marriage and family were forever, and they were devoted to their four kids, who, unlike many of their cousins, appeared headed for productive lives. Henry's jet-set crowds in St. Moritz and the Côte d'Azur were not Bill's "cup of tea," as he put it. He was content to stay home with his family and run his football team into the ground. With good reason, he saw himself as a lucky man.

As general managers came and went at the Ford Division—much as coaches would come and go from the Detroit Lions—Dick Morris fell out of favor and wound up getting shuttled into a dead-end job running the company's publications. He'd had enough. In the summer of 1969, while an acid-zonked throng wallowed in the mud at Woodstock and a man walked on the moon, Morris agreed to take a PR job at Carrier, the air-conditioning manufacturer headquartered in Syracuse, New York. For my two younger sisters and me, the move was like getting shipped from Moscow to Siberia, where we didn't know a soul and where the gulag winters were, impossible to believe, even colder, snowier and bleaker than Detroit's.

As Morris was cleaning out his office in the Glass House, a question arose about his bonus since he was leaving in the middle of the year. In boom-or-bust Detroit, the executive bonus is the grease that keeps the wheels spinning. In a good sales year, it could equal, or surpass, a man's salary; in an off year, it might fail to materialize. This tool of reward and punishment was about to teach Morris a lesson about the cost of disloyalty to a man like Bill Ford.

The final bonus due to Morris was, he guessed, about $20,000. When it was denied on a technicality—the timing of his departure rather than the quality of his work—Morris decided to turn to an old friend. He called Bill Ford and told him that if he would simply sign off on the bonus, the personnel people assured him, it would sail through. Ford never responded. After seventeen years of service to the company, Morris left town feeling wounded, wondering how to read Ford's silence. Was it payback for Morris's perceived disloyalty—for turning down the Lions' GM job, for telling Henry II about his brother's drinking problem, for walking away to the job at Ford Division after a decade as a loyal bag carrier? Could it be an even deeper anger that Morris was betraying the company by taking the job at Carrier? Or was it something less sinister, merely Bill Ford's lack of interest in boring clerical details? Morris thought back to Gene Bordinat's remark about Bill Ford's failure to pick up a single check at the Dearborn Inn: *"When it came to big stuff, man, he was generous. And that little piddling stuff, you know, 'I'm paying these guys enough. Let them pick it up.'"* The bonus was big stuff to Morris, but maybe it was little piddling stuff to Bill Ford. Morris never figured it out.

The episode taught him that Harry Bennett may have been long gone, but the spirit of Machiavelli lived on in the offices of Ford Motor Company and, by extension, in the front office of the Detroit Lions. And powerful men like Bill Ford could conjure that spirit any time they chose to, by an act as simple as declining to sign a piece of paper. In the end, Morris probably should not have been surprised. For men who demanded and delivered loyalty as fervently as Bill Ford did, any hint of disloyalty was seen as a betrayal. Final and fatal. Impossible to redeem.

◆

From his first game as a Lion, Charlie Sanders was on a mission to revolutionize the position he played. Before Sanders, with a few notable exceptions—John Mackey in Baltimore and Mike Ditka in Chicago among them—the tight end was a workhorse offensive lineman who protected the quarterback and cleared openings for the running backs and caught an occasional short pass. Sanders, at 6'4" and 225 pounds, was big enough to work the trenches, but he was also surprisingly agile, an excellent basketball player who had what are known as "soft" hands, pillows that seemed to swallow up any ball thrown in his vicinity. Not only was he athletic enough to get open on the football field and catch passes, he could then turn and gobble up valuable yardage while eluding or flattening tacklers. He transformed the tight end from a utilitarian foot soldier into a potent offensive weapon, and his style played well on the rising medium of television, which was helping to transform the game from trench warfare into balletic aerial combat. Best of all, the innovation of instant replay allowed television viewers to witness Sanders's acrobatics from numerous angles. He was made for TV, and vice versa.

In his rookie season Sanders caught forty passes for 533 yards and was named to the Pro Bowl. In his second season he actually improved, catching forty-two passes for 656 yards and again getting named to the Pro Bowl. He was under a three-year contract that paid him $16,000 the first year, $17,000 the second and $18,000 the third. Having established his worth after his first two seasons, Sanders approached Russ Thomas before the 1970 season and asked for a raise.

Thomas turned him down flat. "We don't renegotiate contracts," he told Sanders. Translation: *You made your bed, now sleep in it.* Or, more to the point: *We don't reward excellence around here.*

After being named to his third straight Pro Bowl that season, Sanders demanded his pound of flesh: a new contract starting at $40,000 a year. Thomas turned him down again, pointing out that Sanders was asking the team to more than double his pay. Sanders, fully aware of the math, stood firm. When Thomas refused to come around, Sanders was a no-show at training camp. As the season opener with Green Bay approached, the adversaries reached a compromise. "When I did sign, it was for a little less than $40,000," Sanders wrote in his memoir, "so I never got what I wanted." What he wanted went beyond money; he wanted acknowledgment of his contributions to the team. And he never got it.

The arc of those contract negotiations with Sanders—stellar performance on the field, a request for a reward, rejection of the request, a holdout and, finally, an unsatisfactory compromise—became the template for contract negotiations with Russ Thomas. The GM's tightfistedness at the bargaining table was a major contributor to the team's perennial mediocrity on the field, which in turn would lead numerous frustrated Lions, including their biggest star, to walk away from the game in the prime of their careers.

Dick Morris's question from the Plaza Hotel in 1963 had become newly relevant: *What are the chances for success in an organization that's run like that?*

The Lions began to jell in 1969, though the season was a reversal of form: a slow start followed by a fast finish. They dropped their opener against the underwhelming Pittsburgh Steelers—the only game the Steelers would win all season—and it proved a costly loss. With Lombardi's retirement as head coach, the Packers had come back down to Earth but now it was the Vikings who were the immovable object in the Lions' path. They lost both games to Minnesota, including a deflating shutout at home in a howling snowstorm on the traditional Thanksgiving Day game. Detroit finished 9–4–1, their first winning record since 1964. But again they missed the playoffs—for the twelfth season in a row.

◆

As his duet partner Tammi Terrell fought a losing battle with brain cancer, the Motown star Marvin Gaye had slid into a creative funk. He stopped performing and recording, spent his time getting high and arguing with his wife Anna (one of Berry Gordy's sisters), arguing with his strict Pentecostal father, arguing with the world. Eventually it came to him that sports might be a way out of his rut. A gifted athlete, Gaye for years had dreamed of playing professional football, and now he approached his two buddies on the Lions, Mel Farr and Lem Barney, about the possibility of getting a tryout with the team. Farr and Barney didn't discourage Marvin's dream. After all, the team let that pencil-necked Ivy Leaguer George Plimpton try out at quarterback, right? To get ready, Marvin lifted weights and bulked up from 160 to 207 pounds, a physical transformation so extreme that he had to buy an entire new wardrobe. But after letting Gaye work out briefly with the team, Joe Schmidt, possibly remembering the distractions of the *Paper Lion* movie shoot and premiere, suggested that Marvin should stick with his singing.

Though devastated by the team's rejection and Terrell's death in the spring of 1970, Gaye pulled himself together and returned to the Hitsville studio. Motown staff writer Al Cleveland and Obie Benson of the Four Tops had written a song expressly for Marvin. It would be a major departure for him and for Motown—a darker, deeper kind of song, in keeping

with the mood of the singer and the mood of the nation. It was destined
to revive Marvin's career and revolutionize American pop music.

◆

In 1970, Joe Schmidt finally succeeded in turning the Lions around. They
opened the season with convincing wins against the Packers, Bengals, and
Bears, and suddenly, after missing the playoffs for a dozen years, they were
being touted as potential championship material. In early October the *New
York Times* wrote: "The unbeaten Detroit Lions, on a track toward the Super
Bowl, are proof that a chaotic pro football operation can be turned around
and it doesn't take forever."

In this case, it took four years.

"Four years ago," the article continued, "the Detroit fans, who can be
almost as mean as Philadelphia's, were throwing snowballs and invective
at Harry Gilmer, the coach. The players were rebellious and the president,
Bill Ford, indecisive."

The reporter attributed the team's turnaround to Schmidt's growth as a
coach, the hiring of capable assistants, savvy trades, and smart draft choices.
Even the general manager came in for praise: "[Russ] Thomas, who had
once been the object of derision within the N.F.L. circles, gains the credit
for the improved drafting." There was no mention of any contribution from
the team's owner.

After building a 5–2 record, the team fell victim to an implausible stroke
of bad voodoo in the eighth week of the season. In New Orleans to play the
woeful Saints, winners of just one game all season, the heavily favored Lions
didn't bother to show up. They led just 7–6 after a lackluster first half, then
found themselves trailing late in the fourth quarter. After regaining the lead
at 17–16 when Errol Mann kicked a field with fourteen seconds left, the Lions
were able to exhale and get ready to slink out of town after snatching victory
from the jaws of what would have been an embarrassing defeat. The Saints

returned the ensuing kickoff, then completed one pass. With two seconds left on the clock, the home team got ready to attempt a desperation field goal from its own thirty-seven-yard line—which would require a kick that broke the existing NFL record by seven yards. Onto the field lumbered the Saints' 264-pound placekicker, Tom Dempsey, who was born without fingers on his right hand or toes on his right foot. He wore a specially fashioned shoe with a flat front that turned his kicking foot into a powerful club. With the Lions getting ready to celebrate, Dempsey lined up for the kick. The snap was crisp. The Lions defenders, fearing a fake attempt and viewing the game as won, mounted a listless rush. Dempsey's flat shoe smacked the ball and it rose and rose and rose, spinning end over end, then beginning its lazy descent. All the air was sucked out of Tulane Stadium as the ball came down out of the sky.

"I don't believe this," the CBS announcer Don Criqui gasped as the ball neared the goal posts. Pause. *"Ohhhh, it's good! I don't believe it! The field goal is good from sixty-three yards away! It's incredible! Tulane Stadium has gone wild . . ."*

Jack Saylor of the *Free Press* went wild, too. His recap of the game's unforgettable finish opened with this unforgettable line: "They say football is a game of inches but today the Lions were beaten by half a foot." The editors back in Detroit shared a laugh over Saylor's wit before good taste dictated that they rewrite his lede.

There was no laughter in the Lions' locker room. A furious Joe Schmidt smashed a blackboard while most of the players sat at their lockers, staring into space, too stunned to speak. The freak loss proved, at the very least, that the Lions were snake-bit. But more than a few people in Detroit saw it as further proof that the Curse of Bobby Layne lived on.

◆

Again the Lions picked up momentum, but even victories didn't always satisfy the hungry Detroit fans. In a home game against the St. Louis

Cardinals on Dec. 10, for instance, the Lions took a 9–3 lead in the third quarter on three short field goals by Errol Mann. The team's most prolific scorer was booed every time he stepped onto the field—not because he was unpopular but because the fans wanted the team to go for touchdowns instead of playing it safe, which had become a Joe Schmidt trademark. He believed you should never come away empty-handed when you drive deep into enemy territory; half a loaf is better than none at all. Mel Farr scored the game's only touchdown late in the fourth quarter to seal the win, vindicating Schmidt's strategy. But the booing was a reminder just what a tough town Detroit could be, and as he left the field Schmidt raised a gnarled middle finger to the boo birds. The love fest between coach and fans was beginning to lose its luster.

After beating the Rams in Los Angeles on *Monday Night Football* for their fourth straight win, the Lions needed to beat Green Bay in the season finale to make the playoffs. With a blizzard raking the Midwest, most of the players decided to wait out the storm on the West Coast after the Monday night win. They locked the barroom doors at the team hotel and threw themselves a party. As the liquor flowed, Schmidt sang and banged on the piano. At the end of the night, a woozy Alex Karras scribbled Russ Thomas's name on the check. Bill Ford, a man who never picked up a check, picked up that check.

"It was," said linebacker Mike Lucci, "one of the great times."

Mel Farr missed the party. He'd dislocated his shoulder during the game—one of numerous injuries that would soon cut his career short—and he flew back to Detroit with Ford on a private plane so he could get immediate medical attention. He said later that the hours alone with Ford changed his life.

"That plane flight did wonders for me," Farr said. "It made me dream, dream of owning my own plane." In more down-to-earth moments, Farr, who worked at Ford Motor Company during off-seasons, also dreamed of owning a Ford dealership. In time, both dreams would come true, and Farr would never forget his debt to the owner of the Lions. "He was very real and genuine, and he really *really* wanted to do the very best thing for the players," Farr said of Ford. "But unfortunately he chose some poor, poor, poor managers . . . and some of the people that he'd stick with were not very good. No one can say anything bad about Mr. Ford other than the fact that he's too loyal."

The Lions, playing without Farr, shut out the Packers in the season finale. In the week after the game, Ford passed out $100 bills in the locker room so the players would have some pocket money for Christmas and for their upcoming trip to Dallas. "That may not sound like much now," said an appreciative Charlie Sanders, "but that was a lot of money back then."

The Green Bay win was not quite enough to catch the Minnesota Vikings, but under the new wild card format, each conference's three divisional champs would be joined by the second-place team with the best record in a four-way playoff to determine who went to the Super Bowl. The 10–4 Lions were slotted to play the Cowboys at the Cotton Bowl in Dallas on the day after Christmas.

It was a game Scrooge would have loved.

The Lions' defense kept Dallas out of the end zone all day, including a stout goal line stand in the fourth quarter. But Dallas scored on a first-quarter field goal and then sacked Greg Landry in the end zone in the fourth quarter to take a 5–0 lead. When Bill Munson replaced Landry at quarterback, the Lions sprang to life, mounting a desperation drive that looked like it might produce the winning touchdown—until a pass skipped off Earl McCullouch's fingertips into the waiting hands of the Dallas defensive back Mel Renfro. Game over. The Lions gained just 92 yards passing and 38 yards rushing—and no defense could compensate for that. It was the lowest scoring playoff game in NFL history and the first without a touchdown in twenty years, an abiding embarrassment.

Scrooge was all smiles.

Four weeks after that dispiriting loss in Dallas, Marvin Gaye, the would-be Lion, released the single of "What's Going On." It opens with the sounds of a boisterous party. Mel Farr's and Lem Barney's voices cut through the hubbub, a couple of brothers lighting up at the sight of one another.

"Hey, what's happenin', brother? . . . How ya doin'? . . . This is a groovy party, man . . . I can dig it . . . Solid!" Then a silky sax riff gives way to a very different Marvin Gaye, tormented, aching, carrying the woes of a broken nation.

Berry Gordy had balked at releasing the record because it was such a radical departure from Gaye's suave style. Instead of singing about how sweet it is to be loved by you, Gaye was now delving into such weighty matters as the Vietnam War and urban unrest. This time Gordy's infallible instincts were off. The record captured the zeitgeist and became an instant hit, spending five weeks atop *Billboard*'s soul charts, selling two million copies, and serving as the foundation for the forthcoming album of the same title, a record that addressed the war, environmental degradation, police brutality, and much more. It announced a new era at Motown and arguably stands as the label's single greatest achievement. And it included the voices of two of Detroit's biggest sports stars. Not only had the Lions made it back to the playoffs; suddenly they were hip.

DODGING THE ZIGGY

Coaches of professional sports teams in America understand that they're hired to be fired. Joe Schmidt even coined a term for the inevitable moment when the ax falls. He called it "the ziggy."

For now, Schmidt appeared to be ziggy-proof. He still had a year left on his contract, but as a reward for returning the team to respectability, if not quite Super Bowl–quality, Ford gave him a new three-year contract starting at $60,000, a show of largesse few Lions players would ever experience. Other changes were on the way.

Most notably, the Lions released thirty-six-year-old Alex Karras before the start of the 1971 season. The official reason for the surprise move was that the team was embarking on a youth movement, though Karras speculated, loudly, that he was guilty of expressing his strong opinions about Pete Rozelle and a lot of other things, including the quality of the ownership and management of the Detroit Lions. Russ Thomas said the decision to let Karras go was the head coach's. Schmidt called it "the roughest I ever had to make."

Going back to his college days at Iowa, Karras had never been shy about letting the world know how he felt. During the 1965 season, Harry Gilmer's first, the Lions won three of their first four games and were primed for a showdown when the undefeated Packers came to Detroit. A win would move the Lions into a tie for first place, and they raced to a 21–3 lead at halftime. As the teams were moving toward their locker rooms, Karras spotted Lombardi and barked at him: "Whadaya think of that, ya big fat wop?"

Poking the bear proved unwise. The Packers woke up, scoring four unanswered touchdowns in the second half and winning the game going away. That, essentially, was the season for both teams. The Packers went on to win the NFL championship while the Lions tumbled to a sixth-place finish. Karras's big mouth, as it turned out, was not always a big asset.

Schmidt's decision to let him go was driven by other factors as well. "Alex's attitude had changed," Schmidt said recently from his retirement home in Florida. "He wasn't playing up to his standards." Karras was, for instance, conspicuously missing in action during the playoff loss to Dallas. "He'd been in the movies and that affected him," Schmidt went on, "and I had to look at how that influenced the whole team. The decision to let him go was a combination of his playing, his attitude, and the distractions." And so, after twelve tempestuous seasons with the Lions, Alex Karras was gone.

Even without him, the team got off to a fast start in 1971, winning four of its first five games and once again appearing headed for the playoffs. If the previous year's loss to New Orleans on a fluke last-second field goal had been the stuff of farce, now the Lions experienced genuine tragedy.

In the sixth game of the season they hosted the Chicago Bears at sold-out Tiger Stadium. It was a back-and-forth brawl, and after several lead changes the Bears scored a touchdown late in the fourth quarter to go back on top, 28–23. With 1:40 left in the game, Greg Landry began marching the Lions up the field from their own twenty-yard line. The fans were standing, roaring, trying to will the team to the clinching touchdown. A key play in the drive was a thirty-two-yard pass reception by the little-used wide receiver Chuck Hughes. It was his first catch of the season—and his last. The next play was a pass over the middle to Charlie Sanders. It appeared to be catchable, but just as the ball met Sanders's soft hands, Chicago linebacker Dick Butkus flattened him with a neck-snapping tackle, breaking up the play. The whole stadium groaned as Sanders struggled to his feet.

Sixty-two seconds on the clock. As the Lions were jogging back to their huddle, Chuck Hughes suddenly clutched his chest, then fell face-down on the turf as though he'd been poleaxed. Several Chicago players thought Hughes was faking an injury to buy time, but Butkus was waving to the sidelines for help. Team doctors and trainers hurried onto the field to find that Hughes had stopped breathing. They pounded his chest, gave him mouth-to-mouth resuscitation. Nothing. The stadium was now quiet as a church. In the radio broadcast booth, Van Patrick, the Voice, kept saying, "This doesn't look good. This doesn't look good at all . . ." A stretcher was wheeled out and Hughes was carried off to a waiting ambulance. The eerie wail of the siren racing to Henry Ford Hospital was audible inside the stadium as the game resumed.

After the Detroit Lions failed to score, the Bears ran out the clock. At 4:41 P.M., doctors at Ford Hospital pronounced Chuck Hughes dead. An autopsy would reveal that he had undiagnosed hardening of the main artery that supplies blood to the heart, and a clot had formed in the artery, shutting off the flow of blood and causing a massive heart attack. Hughes was probably dead before he hit the Tiger Stadium turf.

A twenty-eight-year-old player dying during a game. It qualified as one of those "things that happened to us," as Bill Ford would put it when he mused about the fateful timing of his purchase of the Lions on the day John F. Kennedy was assassinated. The shocking death of a player was, in Ford's eyes, additional proof that a "stigma" was attached to anything that took place on that "awful day" of Nov. 22, 1963—including the marriage of the Ford family and the Detroit Lions. Maybe the team really was cursed.

After flying to San Antonio, Texas, to bury Hughes, the Lions tied the Packers the following Monday night, but their hearts were no longer in it. They dropped four of their last six games, fading to a distant second-place finish behind Minnesota and once again missing the playoffs. The players didn't see it as the end of the world. Veteran linebacker Wayne Walker put it in perspective: "After that day, the only thing that really mattered to me was going back to the locker room with the same number of guys I'd gone out there with. Screw that 'winning is everything' nonsense."

◆

Over the course of that tragedy-marred season, Mondays turned into torture for Schmidt, especially after a loss. He and his assistant coaches started the day by reviewing the previous day's game film, then Schmidt was summoned into a closed-door postmortem with Russ Thomas and Bill Ford that often lasted into the night. For hours the trio dissected the game film, and the owner and GM demanded an explanation for every miscue, every penalty, every dropped pass and missed block.

"Being subjected to Bill Ford and Russ Thomas got to be a nuisance and a very difficult situation when you lost," Schmidt said. "It was like a death march. Losing is one thing, but being criticized and having to answer all these questions the next day was nerve-racking. I had to worry about those two guys and I had to worry about what was going on with the team. From a coaching standpoint, I had to carry a double load."

But the problems, as the 1968 draft had revealed, went deeper. Schmidt and Thomas did not play well with each other. Schmidt still speaks enviously of Green Bay's Vince Lombardi, who, during his run of five championships in the 1960s, had total control of his team. As both head coach and general manager, Lombardi not only ran the team on the field, he also made draft picks, negotiated player contracts, and set the tone down to the minutest detail. He attended league meetings with a team lawyer and did most of the talking. In negotiating player contracts, Lombardi was surgical where Russ Thomas was ham-fisted. When Bob Skoronski, an anchor of the Packers' offensive line, asked for a raise, Lombardi pulled a piece of paper from a desk drawer and reminded Skoronski that he'd missed a crucial block on a third down with one yard to go in the Rams game. Skoronski, like many other Packers, wilted under Lombardi's microscope.

"He could even tell his players what color of socks to wear!" Schmidt said, which was not much of an exaggeration. After taking over from laissez-faire Scooter McLean in 1959—who in his single season at the helm had compiled a horrific 1–10–1 record—Lombardi laid down the law. You showed up early for team meetings. Training camp was boot camp and practices were warfare. No more sweatshirts or T-shirts on the road; players were the face of the organization on and off the field, and when the team traveled the players wore team sport coats and neckties. No exceptions. Lombardi even dictated the bars where players were allowed to drink and which ones were off-limits.

The Packers were unusual in other ways. The team was a publicly owned nonprofit corporation, and the shareholders were the fans, who'd first bought shares in 1923 to rescue the team from financial collapse. The corporation was run by a board of directors—"a contentious group of forty-five know-it-alls," in the words of Lombardi biographer David Maraniss. The directors subjected McLean to torture similar to what Schmidt would endure years later. "With every loss," Maraniss wrote, "the board interfered a bit more openly with Scooter's decision-making, demanding that he appear before them every Monday to explain what had gone wrong on the field the day before and outline his plans to correct the team's glaring mistakes." But after those know-it-alls got rid of McLean and brought in Lombardi, they had the good sense to get out of the new coach's way and let him do his job—much like Alfred Sloan at General Motors. It helped that Lombardi was supremely qualified, a genius in the minds of more than a few football people.

The situation in Detroit was very different. Schmidt was able to pick his assistant coaches, but Thomas had the final say on draft picks, contract negotiations, and many other facets of the operation. Thomas also had Bill Ford's ear, and Ford, as sole owner, answered to no one but himself. Why was Thomas so notoriously stingy? There was no salary cap in those days, so why didn't Bill Ford, one of the richest men on the planet, hand Thomas

a stack of blank checks and tell him to go shopping for the very best football talent money could buy? Schmidt has a theory: "I think Thomas was
trying to show Mr. Ford that he could put together a good football team
and still make some money. Thomas was always worried about the money.
I didn't give a shit about the money—I just wanted good football players.
In a situation like that, you're bound to get pissed off."

Here's another theory: Bill Ford was driven by a powerful sense of
noblesse oblige, a belief, inculcated by his parents, that the privileges he had
enjoyed all his life demanded that he always play fair. To go on a shopping
spree for football players would have done two undesirable things: it would
have made him a pariah in the one-for-all-and-all-for one fraternity of NFL
owners, all of whom were rich but none of whom had pockets as deep as
Bill Ford's; and far worse in his eyes, it would have been a galling abuse of
his abundant privileges, a breach of an iron code. Buying a championship
would have been unspeakably vulgar. Ungentlemanly. Cheap. And Bill
Ford could not abide that kind of cheap.

Unfortunately, for reasons that remain a mystery, he did not stop listening to Russ Thomas. If Schmidt and his assistants said the team needed
a linebacker but Thomas had his eye on a running back, the running back
invariably got drafted. And the team invariably paid the price.

"The general manager has to know what's best for the team," Schmidt
said. "Why draft a running back when I've already got two good running
backs? But Bill Ford had faith in his general manager, and he listened to
him. If the general manager, the owner and the coaches agree, you can
succeed. When they don't agree, it's a very sticky circumstance. But you
have to accept the owner's ideas. If they're bad, you try to ride them as
best you can."

But as Joe Schmidt and others would learn, you can ride them only
so long.

◆

The following summer, while the Lions were in training camp, the city of Detroit suffered a psychic gut punch. Berry Gordy had been spending more and more time in Los Angeles and Las Vegas, gambling, playing golf, enjoying the sunshine, and, above all, scheming how to break into the movies. Now he packed up the last remnants of Motown Records and officially moved the company to Los Angeles. Though the axis had been tilting westward for several years, many Detroiters, including numerous Motown employees, were blindsided by the departure. When Martha Reeves, one of the label's first and biggest stars, phoned the company on a business matter, it was the operator on the other end of the line who broke the news to her that Motown had moved to California.

That year the Lions' performance was seesaw, inspired one week, insipid the next. Maybe they were still hung over from Chuck Hughes's death. Late-season losses to division rivals Minnesota and Green Bay all but killed hopes of a return to the playoffs. Those losses also revealed a troubling trend. The "youth movement" that had led to the release of Alex Karras was not producing much youthful talent. Though no one knew it yet, a long decline had begun. Years after his retirement, Charlie Sanders was able to see the source of the decline in retrospect. Without naming names, he pinned the blame on the man in charge of acquiring players through drafts and trades. Sanders said, "The downfall of the Lions in the 1970s, I believe, was because they never, over a reasonable period of time, replaced those older guys with good, young players. The transition wasn't gradual, but sudden, and that's why the rest of the decade saw the Lions struggle most of the time."

As the final game of another lost season approached in December 1972, Bill Ford started venting his displeasure in public. As usual, his potshots were aimed at the wrong targets. Under the *Free Press* headline FORD VOWS SHAKEUP: LIONS' ASSISTANTS 'HEADS WILL ROLL,' Ford managed to sound both jocular and savage. "Our game plan runs like the state lottery," he quipped. "You wonder what number comes out of the tube next. Yes,

I guess this probably has to be critical of the staff, but I blame everyone, including myself. It was dumb of me to let it get this far out of hand. I mentioned it earlier in the season, but when it got down to the crucial test, I flunked. You're inclined to dismiss some of the things that happened, but when it happens game after game—I mean the ones that mean something—when they fold up and take a dive, you've got to blame everyone." Everyone, it seems, except the general manager.

Ford made it clear that Schmidt's job was safe and that his assistant coaches' heads were the ones on the chopping block. Schmidt, deeply loyal to his staff, was incensed. "When that negative stuff gets in the papers," he said, "it affects the team." Instead of folding, his team responded by thumping the Rams, 34–17, in the season finale, which gave them an 8–5–1 record, an improvement but not quite good enough to make the playoffs.

After the Lions flew home, the undefeated Miami Dolphins arrived in Los Angeles to take on the Washington Redskins in Super Bowl VII. Joe Falls of the *Free Press* was in town to cover the game, and he sought out the soccer-style kicker Garo Yepremian, now a valued member of the Dolphins, for his thoughts about his former team.

"I do not understand that team," Yepremian said of the Lions. "They have very good personnel . . . but they do not win. It seems they are always bickering among themselves. The offense blames the defense; the defense blames the offense. The kickers blame the specialty teams; the specialty teams blame the kickers. What kind of way is that to play football?" He neglected to mention that the owner blamed the assistant coaches, and the head coach blamed the general manager and the owner, and more than a few of the players blamed the general manager.

The Lions, in short, had developed a culture of finger-pointing, and, like all organizational cultures, this one emanated from the top. Ford's finger-pointing in the papers the week before the game against the Rams was a deft illustration of how to build a dysfunctional culture. It was also the last straw for Joe Schmidt. This was shaping up to be a replay of Ford's first major miscue in 1964, when he'd ordered George Wilson to fire his assistant coaches and then watched Wilson walk out the door. With the Detroit Lions, history didn't merely repeat itself; it repeated itself again and again and again. It was like watching endless replays of the same instant replay.

Days after returning from the West Coast, Schmidt told Ford and Thomas he wanted out. Working under trying circumstances, he had compiled a commendable 43–34–7 record over six seasons and had returned the team to the playoffs, but he was cooked. Two days later, the trio held a press conference to announce Schmidt's resignation.

With Ford sitting to his right and Thomas to his left, Schmidt told the gathered reporters: "I really don't enjoy coaching anymore. It got to be a burden more than a fun-loving game. I promised my family and myself when I started coaching that I would get out when it stopped being fun. Unfortunately, it's reached that point."

For Schmidt, walking away from the team after twenty years was a bittersweet moment. "The Fords were very kind to me and very good to me," he said recently, "but I felt like I was being released from prison."

On the day he resigned, Schmidt joined George Wilson in a very exclusive club. In six decades of Ford family ownership, the Detroit Lions employed twenty head coaches before the current coach, Dan Campbell, was hired. One of those coaches died of a heart attack while under contract—another "one of those things that happened to us"—and all but two of the rest got fired. Schmidt and Wilson are the only ones who walked away before the ax fell.

They alone dodged the ziggy.

AN OVERKILL OF MEDIOCRITY

(1973-1989)

TWIST THIS!

For years Bill Ford had dreamed of watching his team play in a stadium designed expressly for football. After the long baseball season and months of football practices and games, the turf at Tiger Stadium was always a lumpy, tattered mess by year's end. The rest of the old iceberg wasn't in much better shape. As one wag wrote, "It is John Barrymore with a three-day beard and mustard on his tie." Also, the stands were separated from the football field by vast swards of outfield grass, erasing an advantage to the home team when the fans are right on top of the action, an audible physical presence, almost like having a twelfth player on the field. The brutal Michigan weather added fuel to Ford's dream. His meteorological misgivings had come to a head during that notorious Mud Bowl game against the Philadelphia Eagles on Thanksgiving Day in 1968.

So Bill Ford wanted a new football stadium, but where to put it? There had been talk about building one on the riverfront in downtown Detroit, or at the State Fairgrounds at Eight Mile and Woodward, or even out in the suburbs of Troy or Walled Lake. But the talk never turned into shovels in the ground.

That began to change in the 1960s thanks to a University of Detroit architecture and urban planning professor named Don Davidson, a native of Pontiac, Michigan, a fading GM factory town thirty miles north of Detroit. Davidson bought into the popular myth that a key to salvation for his hometown was to build new stadiums—specifically, new stadiums for the Lions and Tigers on the spot that was virtually at the center of the state's population, vacant land on the east side of Pontiac where I-75 and highway M-59 intersect. Plans were drawn up for side-by-side stadiums that could be covered by a sliding roof.

By the late 1960s, Bill Ford had joined southeastern Michigan civic and business leaders on the Metropolitan Stadium Committee, which began considering half a dozen possible sites for new stadiums for the Lions and Tigers in and around Detroit. A separate committee was exploring sites within the Detroit city limits, and Mayor Jerome Cavanagh warned that moving the Lions out of town would be "an extremely devastating blow" to the city. Other committees were exploring other possible sites. "At present," Pete Waldmeir wrote in the *News*, "there are almost as many stadium committees in Detroit as there are Frank Sinatra fans."

Meanwhile, big brother Henry II was about to get involved in a construction project of his own. Shaken awake by the fiery summer of 1967 and the Kerner Commission's conclusion that America was becoming two societies, "one white, one black—separate and unequal," Henry II realized he was in a unique position to address that inequality. He had all of the company's outside parts suppliers surveyed, and the company began pressuring white-owned suppliers to hire more minorities, and it pumped up contracts to black-owned businesses. Henry II also launched a minorities hiring program, an ambitious effort to turn unemployed city dwellers into productive Ford workers. It may not have revolutionized the city's economy like his grandfather's $5 day, but recruitment centers were set up near 12th Street, the required written tests were waived, and applicants' police records were overlooked. The company even set up special bus service to ferry workers from the inner city to the Rouge plant, then back home after their shifts. Some 1,500 Detroiters lined up outside the recruitment centers before dawn on the first day they opened, hungry for a chance. Though the program was a mixed success, it showed that Henry Ford II was serious about attacking his hometown's festering ills. But he wanted more.

William Clay Ford Sr. and his pet project, the elegant Continental Mark II in 1955. "There was more attention paid to detail in that car than anything I've ever been exposed to before or since," he said. When the car was taken out of production after just two years, Ford bought into the syndicate that owned the Detroit Lions. In 1963 he paid $6 million to become sole owner of the team. *Courtesy of Ford Motor Company.*

The Fords at a Detroit Tigers baseball game in 1937 (left to right) Edsel Ford; his father, Henry Ford; Edsel's twelve-year-old son, William Clay Ford; Edsel's daughter, Josephine Ford; and his wife, Eleanor Ford. *Courtesy of the Detroit Lions.*

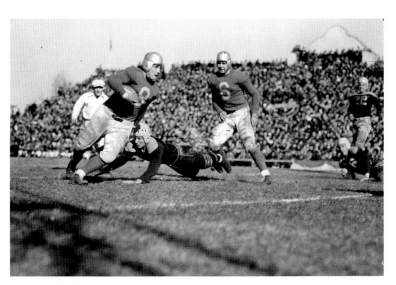

Detroit Lion Bill Shepherd carries the ball against the Green Bay Packers in a 1937 game at Dinan Field at the University of Detroit. It was the first of the Lions' four homes—and the place where young William Clay Ford fell in love with the team. *Courtesy of Walter P. Reuther Library, Archives of Labor and Urban Affairs, Wayne State University.*

A 1951 photograph shows company founder Henry Ford (top right); his only son, Edsel (top left); and Edsel's three sons, (left to right) Henry II, Benson, and William Clay. *Courtesy of Walter P. Reuther Library, Archives of Labor and Urban Affairs, Wayne State University.*

Backup quarterback Tobin Rote blasts into the end zone for another
touchdown as the Lions overwhelm the Cleveland Browns to win the
1957 NFL Championship, the last in franchise history. *Courtesy of
Walter P. Reuther Library, Archives of Labor and Urban Affairs, Wayne
State University.*

ABOVE: Legendary Lions quarterback Bobby Layne (left), on crutches with a broken ankle, hugs his backup, Tobin Rote, after the Lions beat the 49ers to win the Western Division title in 1957. A week later they battered the Cleveland Browns, 59-14, in Detroit. It was the last time the Lions won the NFL Championship. *Courtesy of AP Photos.* BELOW: On Thanksgiving Day 1962, the Lions mauled quarterback Bart Starr and the rest of the Green Bay Packers, handing them their only loss of the season. The Lions finished second while the Packers went on to beat the New York Giants and win the NFL Championship. *Courtesy of the Detroit Lions.*

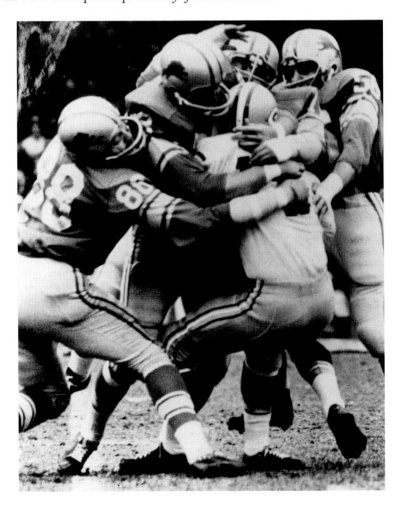

Bill Ford (bottom left) in a rare calm moment in the Tiger Stadium press box during a Lions game in 1964, shortly after he became sole owner of the team. *Courtesy of the Detroit Lions.*

Berry Gordy Jr., the founder of Motown Records, outside the Hitsville U.S.A. studios in December 1964. Among the Motown acts topping the Billboard charts that year were Mary Wells, the Supremes, Martha and the Vandellas, the Four Tops, and the Temptations. *Courtesy of The Tony Spina Collection, Walter P. Reuther Library, Archives of Labor and Urban Affairs, Wayne State University.*

ABOVE: Martha Parke Ford (center) with her parents on the night of her debut in Grosse Pointe in June 1967. A month later, the inner city of Detroit exploded in a week of arson and looting that left forty-three people dead. *Courtesy of Walter P. Reuther Library, Archives of Labor and Urban Affairs, Wayne State University.* BELOW: Detroit erupted, this time with joy, after the Tigers won the American League pennant in 1968. The Tigers went on to beat the heavily favored St. Louis Cardinals in the World Series. *Courtesy of The Tony Spina Collection, Walter P. Reuther Library, Archives of Labor and Urban Affairs, Wayne State University.*

On August 23, 1975, more than 62,000 fans, then the largest crowd in franchise history, showed up to watch the Lions inaugurate the Pontiac Silverdome in a preseason game against the Kansas City Chiefs. *Courtesy of The Tony Spina Collection, Walter P. Reuther Library, Archives of Labor and Urban Affairs, Wayne State University.*

After twenty-two years on the job, general manager Russ Thomas (left) was forced to retire after the 1989 season, and Bill Ford replaced him with Chuck Schmidt (right), an accountant. The new man's first task was to sign the No. 1 draft pick, running back Barry Sanders. The contract negotiations turned into a dog fight. *Courtesy of the Detroit Lions.*

After signing his first contract, a wide-eyed Barry Sanders gets a tour of the Silverdome from head coach Wayne Fontes, a man of many memorable sweaters. *Courtesy of the Detroit Lions.*

Matt Millen (far left) succeeded Chuck Schmidt and turned out to be one of the worst executives in the history of American professional sports. His Waterloo was the draft room, where he consistently made disastrous picks. His explanation: "I gave more credit to guys who've been in the business longer. I should have stuck with my gut. I should have trusted myself, and I didn't. Like an idiot." Here he's pictured in the draft room with Lions vice chairman William Clay Ford Jr. (holding paper), sitting beside his father, William Clay Ford Sr. No one looks terribly confident about the looming pick. *Courtesy of the Detroit Lions.*

Author George Plimpton (left) with Alex Karras and Bill Ford at the 40th reunion of the *Paper Lion* team at Ford Field on September 21, 2003. Four days after the reunion, Plimpton died of a heart attack at 76. *Courtesy of the Detroit Lions.*

After William Clay Ford's death in 2014, his widow, Martha Firestone Ford (in dark glasses), became principal owner of the Lions. She handed the reins to her daughter, Sheila Ford Hamp (standing to her right), in 2020. Sheila promptly traded star quarterback Matthew Stafford (#9 at right) and began to rebuild the team. *Courtesy of the Detroit Lions.*

When Lions general manager Brad Holmes (center) pounced to draft him with the team's first pick in 2021, offensive lineman Penei Sewell (left) said of Holmes, "If he asked me to go swim 200 miles, I'd swim 200 miles. I'd go as far as he wants me to go." *Courtesy of the Detroit Lions.*

Dan Campbell, the head coach who vowed to bite off kneecaps, working his magic. *Courtesy of the Detroit Lions.*

He wanted something that would serve as a symbol of the city's undying belief in itself, something that would show the world that the Motor City was worthy of its motto: *Speramus Meliora; Resurget Cineribus—We Hope for Better Things; It Shall Rise from the Ashes.*

And so the idea of the Renaissance Center was born. Henry II brought in the architect John Portman, whose mammoth Peachtree Center was being touted as the savior of musty downtown Atlanta even though it contained many design flourishes that walled out the surrounding city. It was less "a city within a city" than "a suburb within a city," a cluster of towers linked by sky bridges that removed pedestrians from the streets, a hermetically sealed world of shops, galleries, offices, meeting spaces, and hotels that wanted no part of the city it was supposedly saving. Many of these design flourishes were destined for Detroit. "Babylonian ziggurat hotels," Tom Wolfe called Portman's confections, "with thirty-story atriums and hanging gardens and crystal elevators."

To pay for such an insular fantasy—"as remote as a cloud-ringed Disneyland castle," in the opinion of the *New York Times*—Henry II put together a consortium of fifty-one investors, including Ford Motor Company, General Motors, and Chrysler, plus an armada of banks, advertising agencies, parts suppliers, and other businesses that relied on the Big Three for their livelihoods. Henry II then proceeded to twist arms mercilessly until he'd raised the $257 million needed to break ground. The owners of those arms did not always enjoy the experience. "The logo of the Renaissance Center should have been a twisted arm," one investor griped. Another said, "It was little more than a sophisticated protection racket . . . I got the distinct impression, although nobody ever said it in words, that if we didn't kick in X number of dollars, our contracts with Ford and G.M. might be reevaluated and we might not end up with as much business as we have now. What does that sound like to you?"

Henry II had morphed into a cross between Captain Ahab and Vito Corleone, and the RenCen, as it is known among Detroiters, had become his white whale. He was pouring all of his energy—and a considerable amount of Ford Motor Company's treasure—into making his obsession a reality. He could not be stopped. When inflation and rising prices pushed constructions costs up by another $100 million just as a major recession began to clobber American automakers, Henry II's white whale began to look like a white elephant. There was talk of abandoning the project. Rather than cut his losses and bail out, though, Captain Ahab doubled down, traveling to Los Angeles, Chicago, New York, and London to shake old money trees and find new ones. He dispatched a Ford vice president to knock on doors at U.S. Steel, Firestone, and dozens of other companies with ties to the auto industry. Investors grumbled about throwing good money after bad, but they ponied up. Construction moved forward.

The result was the largest private development on the planet, a seventy-nine-story glass cylinder ringed by four shorter towers and two outlying buildings that originally had the feel of a walled fort. There was even a massive concrete berm on Jefferson Avenue to keep the city at a safe distance. "The message is clear," said the urbanist William H. Whyte. "Afraid of Detroit? Come in and be safe."

Indeed, the city's crime rate was very much on Portman's mind as he designed the complex. When he visited Detroit, the staff at his hotel advised him never to walk on the downtown streets—always take a taxi to restaurants and take a taxi back to the hotel. "To understand the Renaissance Center, you have to understand the basic situation of Detroit when we started," Portman said later. "Cities, and certainly Detroit, have at least the image of being unsafe places. To reverse that, we have to give people city environments where they feel safe."

After a major renovation in the 1990s, the berm is gone and the complex has a welcoming entrance on Jefferson Avenue. It now houses General Motors' headquarters, ironically, after the giant automaker bought the complex at the fire-sale price of just $72 million. Though much improved, it's still a confusing, monstrous maze. On a recent visit I had to ask directions how to get out of the place.

Given the tenacity of his commitment to the RenCen project, Henry II surely tried to persuade his brother to heed the mayor's admonition and keep his football team in the city. To have his own brother pull the beloved team from their hometown would be another psychological blow for Detroit, right up there with the departure of Motown—not to mention a humiliating loss of face for Henry II. But Bill was growing impatient with all the competing presentations, feasibility studies, public hearings, and other mind-fogging machinations involved in choosing a stadium site. In 1970 he signed a tentative agreement to move the Lions to Pontiac—with an escape clause if Detroit came up with a viable stadium plan within six months. The agreement effectively tossed the political hot potato back to the city group. If they couldn't come up with an acceptable plan and the Lions left town, it would be their fault, not Bill Ford's. "Imposing a deadline ensures action," Ford said after signing the agreement.

Except it didn't. In early 1971, his deadline long past, a fed up Bill Ford sent a letter to the head of the Pontiac Stadium Building Authority, giving the group the green light to proceed with the construction and lease of a stadium for the Detroit Lions. Harold Cousins, chairman of the stadium authority, was ecstatic. "This," he crowed, "is one of the most momentous days in the city's history!" The remark proved one of two things: either Cousins, like Don Davidson, believed in the magical healing powers of stadiums; or Pontiac's history suffered from an acute shortage of momentous days. Maybe both. In making his announcement, Bill Ford anticipated the backlash from his brother and the other boosters who wanted to keep the Lions in Detroit.

"I think I ought to say something before the downtown group gets all whomped up and spends a lot of money on more studies," Ford told reporters. "It's getting to the stage where it's unfair to withhold my opinion." And his opinion, quite frankly, was that the backers of the riverfront site were nothing but a bunch of "drumbeaters, promoters and buglers, sounding the charge without any cavalry to back them up." He did not name names. He didn't need to. Everyone knew that Henry II was a prominent member of the bugle corps.

Bill Ford claimed that he preferred the Pontiac site because the land was cheap, vacant, centrally located and ready for construction to begin, while the downtown Detroit site was comparatively expensive and inaccessible, it lacked adequate parking space and would require major infrastructure work and the rerouting of traffic patterns. In addition, though he didn't say so publicly, it was not politically astute to push for a multimillion-dollar playpen for white people in the heart of a dying Black city that had far more pressing needs. (The team's fan base, then as now, was largely white and largely from outside the city.) Ford neglected to mention one other consideration, and it may have been the biggest of all: a stadium at the downtown site would literally sit in the shadow of its soaring next-door neighbor, big brother's RenCen.

Bill Ford sounded like a man trying to justify his decision to himself. "This isn't an anti-Detroit move," he insisted. "I love the city. I was born here. I don't feel that I'm stabbing anybody in the back by moving out of town. I'm going to an area where the greatest concentration of population is."

With the Lions willing to move to Pontiac and the Tigers content to remain at Tiger Stadium, Don Davidson and a team of architects drew up plans for a football stadium with 80,638 seats, an inflatable roof, artificial turf and 102 luxury suites, the must-have amenity in the new generation of stadiums that were popping up across the country like mushrooms after a downpour. The $55.7 million cost would be covered by general obligation notes, revenue bonds, and state subsidies, and it would be owned by the City of Pontiac Stadium Building Authority. Which is to say that, profit-maker or money-loser, it would be the responsibility of city and state taxpayers. The Lions would continue to rent, not own, their workplace.

In the calculus of fraternal rivalries, payback might be hell for the receiver, but it can be sweet bliss for the deliverer. And after the long-ago killing of his Continental Mark II, after the years of coming to terms with his second-fiddle status in the family and the family business, the Kid finally had the chance to deliver a little payback to Lard Ass. Henry II may have been able to bully others, threaten them, twist their arms—"kick ass," as one friend put it—to make his outlandish dream come true, but he had no leverage on his kid brother when he urged him—begged him—to keep his football team in Detroit. Bill Ford was free to do as he pleased, and there's no doubt he derived more than a little pleasure from having the upper hand for once. "Bill's ass," as the historian Robert Lacey put it, "evidently, was not for kicking."

Put another way, after watching his brother twist dozens of arms, Bill Ford could smile at him and say, in so many words: *Twist this!* Then he was free to pick up his football team and walk away to Pontiac.

MAYOR MOTHERFUCKER

What happened on the field in the Lions' final two seasons playing in Tiger Stadium was largely forgettable. Bill Ford had overlooked prior experience when he'd hired Joe Schmidt as head coach, and now he reversed course and went after a proven winner. Two weeks after Schmidt's resignation, Ford hired former Baltimore Colts head coach Don McCafferty, a speedy succession that suggests Ford had been quietly working the levers long before Schmidt quit. McCafferty, known to his players as "Easy Rider" for his laid-back manner, had coached the Colts to their second Super Bowl win after the 1970 season and he'd led them to the AFC Championship game the following season. But after the team got off to a sluggish start in 1972 and McCafferty refused to bench the veteran quarterback Johnny Unitas, the Colts fired him. Three months later, Bill Ford scooped up the unemployed McCafferty, hoping to import some of his Super Bowl magic to Detroit.

That fall, while the enclosed stadium was under construction in Pontiac and the glass silos of the Renaissance Center were rising on the riverbank in downtown Detroit, Egypt and Syria launched a surprise attack on Israel that triggered the Yom Kippur War. The fighting lasted less than three weeks, but its repercussions rippled for years. When the Organization of Petroleum Exporting Countries, angered by the United States' support for Israel, announced a 5 percent reduction in oil production, President Richard Nixon, not willing to be pushed around by a gang of rich Arabs, responded by shipping $2.2 billion in arms and supplies to Israel, though the Israelis had asked for just $850,000 in matériel. It was, US Secretary of State Henry Kissinger admitted later, a "mistake." It was a colossal mistake. OPEC, not willing to be pushed around by a smarmy Western pol, responded by curbing oil production and ending all shipments to the US and other countries that were supporting Israel in the war. The price of oil quadrupled in the next six months, plunging the global economy into a recession. For years Detroit automakers had been drunk on cheap gas and the big, profitable cars it allowed—encouraged—them to produce. Suddenly car buyers were abandoning their gas guzzlers and flocking to economical Japanese and European imports. Detroit was caught flat-footed.

A month after the beginning of the Arab oil embargo, Detroiters elected Coleman Young the city's first Black mayor. Born in Alabama, Young had grown up hustling on the streets of Black Bottom, a lively, largely black neighborhood on the East Side of Detroit that was erased to make way for the Chrysler Freeway, which wiped out 10,000 businesses, displaced 40,000 residents, and greased the exodus to the suburbs. City planners called it "urban renewal," while residents of Black Bottom called it "urban removal." (The neighborhood's name came not from its racial makeup but from the rich riverside soil that made ideal farmland in the city's pre-industrial years.) Young trained with the Tuskegee Airmen (though he never saw combat), worked in Ford's River Rouge plant, became a fiery union organizer and then a state senator before running for mayor. In his first inaugural address as mayor, on Jan. 2, 1974, Young, famous for his salty tongue, inadvertently set the tone for a reign that would run for the next twenty years. "To all dope pushers, to all rip-off artists, to all muggers . . . it's time to leave Detroit. Hit Eight Mile Road," Young said, referring to the street that separates the city from its northern suburbs. "I don't give a damn if they're Black or white, or if they wear Super Fly suits or blue uniforms with silver badges. Hit the road."

Such talk sent a spasm of panic through the city's largely white suburbs, where Young's remarks were misread not as a vow to clean up Detroit but as a threat to drive the city's sizeable criminal element into pristine suburbia. Detroit was now the nation's most racially segregated metropolitan area, and with Young in the mayor's office and the chasm between city and suburbs widening—and with population and jobs evaporating as the Big Three built factories in the business-friendly, nonunion Sun Belt—Detroit became the largest majority black city in the nation. It also became shorthand for the ills that were ravaging many American cities, especially in the Rust Belt: unemployment, drugs, crime, shrinking population, and rotting infrastructure. In the second year of Young's tenure, Detroit would record the nation's highest murder rate. The Motor City was now known as Murder City. It had lost so much—jobs, population, its world-famous record company, its belief in a future of boundless prosperity—and now it was even losing its football team.

As Young tried vainly to reverse the city's decline, he came to be seen as the avenging angel by Black Detroiters and as the devil incarnate by many white suburbanites. He relished both roles, which made him an unlikely precursor to another divisive politician of a very different stripe. As unalike as Coleman Young and Donald Trump were, they shared a vital essence: their supporters did not take them literally but did take them seriously, while their detractors took them literally but did not take them seriously. The sharply divided reactions to Young's inaugural address were the first of many illustrations of this fact. In his autobiography, *Hard Stuff*, Young's explanation for his election as mayor was characteristically blunt: "I was taking over the administration of Detroit because the white people didn't want the damn thing anymore. They were getting the hell out, more than happy to turn over their troubles to some Black sucker like me." Young kept a plaque on his desk that read M.F.I.C—Motherfucker in Charge. The book's ghostwriter, the late Lonnie Wheeler, told me that Young wanted to title the book *Mayor Motherfucker*, but the publisher didn't think that was such a good idea.

◆

Don McCafferty failed to import his Super Bowl magic from Baltimore to Detroit. The Lions continued to stumble, finishing 6–7–1, once again in second place, once again out of the playoffs.

The following summer, on July 28, 1974, with veteran players in the midst of a six-week strike that had shut down all training camps, McCafferty decided to spend that Sunday afternoon mowing his lawn. After finishing the job, he experienced chest pains then collapsed inside his home. A doctor who lived in the neighborhood rushed over to administer heart massage, but McCafferty was pronounced dead on arrival at a Pontiac hospital. The cause was a heart attack. He was fifty-three.

First President Kennedy. Then Chuck Hughes. Now Don McCafferty. It was beginning to appear to more than a few people that this team truly was cursed.

The next day, Bill Ford reversed course yet again and elevated the Lions' offensive backfield coach, Rick Forzano, to interim head coach. A middling college coach with no experience as an NFL head coach, Forzano was the opposite of Easy Rider—a workaholic martinet who let it be known that "permissiveness kind of drives me up a wall." Forzano was the sort of boss who showed up at the office on Mother's Day, a Sunday, two months before training camp opened—and expected his assistant coaches to show up, too. After NFL players agreed to go back to work without a contract, Forzano put the Lions through two-a-day sessions at training camp, which the players loathed, along with his "rah-rah Joe College" style.

The team was coming apart, and then a national scandal hit. Days after McCafferty's death and Forzano's promotion, the Watergate agony finally came to an end when Richard Nixon resigned the presidency and rose off the White House lawn in a helicopter, headed for exile in his own private St. Helena on the California coast. Bad news followed good. In the

Lions' final preseason game, quarterback Greg Landry suffered a fractured shoulder and was knocked out of action for at least two months.

The Lions responded to all this adversity by posting a 7–7 record that year. In their final game at Tiger Stadium, on Thanksgiving Day, they lost to Denver, 31–27, despite a valiant fourth-quarter rally led by a newly healthy Greg Landry. It was the team's seventh straight second-place finish. Home games were no longer sold out, as fans lost interest in this perennial mediocrity and realized it was almost worse to be repeatedly tantalized and disappointed than to have a truly wretched team you could boo with abandon.

What took place on the Tiger Stadium field during those last two seasons may have been forgettable, but something happened inside the Lions' locker room that left a lasting impression on many of the players. Bill Ford, nearing fifty and obviously thinking about the future, regularly showed up before games with his teenage son, Bill Ford Jr., to deliver a little pep talk to the team. Fifty years later, Jim Thrower, Lem Barney's backup, still had vivid memories of those locker room visits.

"The coach would introduce him," Thrower recalled, "and Mr. Ford would say, 'Let's go out and win this game.' He ended it by saying: 'Give me the best that you have and that's all I can ask of you.'"

Ford's speech may not have had the inspirational juice of Knute Rockne's "Win just one for the Gipper," but Thrower and the other players in that locker room realized they were getting more than a pep talk; they were witnessing preparations for a royal succession. "Mr. Ford would always bring his son in the locker room with him," Thrower said. "I later realized he was getting his son ready for the future, and I was really impressed by that."

The message was clear: win or lose, the Detroit Lions and the Ford family were destined to stay married long after Bill Ford Sr. was gone.

THE BIG MUFFIN

Pontiac Metropolitan Stadium—originally known as PonMet, soon to be rechristened the Silverdome—opened for business on Aug. 23, 1975, with a preseason game between the Lions and the Kansas City Chiefs. The stadium was finished on time and on its $55.7 million budget, which, backers proudly noted, was exactly one-third the cost of the newly opened Superdome in New Orleans. A crowd of 62,094 showed up for the debut of the cavernous stadium, the largest crowd up to that time to witness a Detroit Lions home game. The house was not close to being full and it was not quite ready for prime time. Parking lots were unfinished, some toilets failed to flush, and several Teflon-coated fiberglass panels were missing from the ten-acre roof, which allowed rain to soak parts of the field and forced crews to hurriedly patch the holes and bring in blowers to inflate the roof. The balky ventilation system left a pall of cigarette smoke hanging over the field and stands. For good measure, traffic was horrendous. Unfazed, the fans roared when the Lions scored three touchdowns in the fourth quarter for a 27–24 win. Everyone went home happy.

Six weeks later, the stadium had its formal coming-out party in a nationally televised *Monday Night Football* game between the Lions and the Dallas Cowboys. Now in its fifth season, *Monday Night Football* had become a national institution, welcomed by millions of football junkies desperate for a fix after their weekend of binge-watching games. It was their tapering-off drug—a perennial top twenty–rated TV show and a weekly warm-up for that year's Super Bowl, which would pit the Dallas Cowboys against the Pittsburgh Steelers in a game that was beamed all the way to Bali and became the single most-watched TV sporting event up to that time. Yes, TV and football were now joined at the hip, a fusion that had begun shortly after Bill Ford bought the Lions and had been gaining momentum—and generating bigger dollars—ever since. In Pontiac, the local and national media gushed about the new stadium, calling it everything from the Football Palace to the Taj Mahal. One wit, inspired by the vast puffy roof, dubbed it the Big Muffin. The sportscaster Howard Cosell, no stranger to bombast, proclaimed it "the most magnificent football structure of its kind." But it wasn't destined to save the Lions or the city of Pontiac. In a sign of things to come, a big crowd showed up on opening night to watch the Lions hang around for a while, then give up three fourth-quarter touchdown passes to the Cowboys in a lopsided 36–10 loss.

It would soon become evident that the Detroit Lions organization was no better at negotiating business deals than it was at assembling football teams. While the team's thirty-year stadium lease exacted the highest annual rent in the league—the Lions now paid $700,000, nearly double what they'd paid at Tiger Stadium—the team collected nothing from parking, concessions, or the lucrative luxury suites. They also had to charge a fee of $1.50 per ticket to cover the stadium debt, and season ticket holders were hit with a surprise $27 surcharge for parking, which did nothing for the team's bottom line but led to loud grumbling. Stadium deals—not market size—had become the wellspring of value for NFL franchises, and the Lions were saddled with one of the worst deals in the league. This income squeeze contributed to management's reputation for miserliness, which in turn contributed to a mediocre product on the field. If the Lions were the big losers in the PonMet Stadium deal, the big winner was the company that controlled concessions and catering, Elias Brothers, owners of the Big Boy hamburger chain famous for its ubiquitous pitchman, a beaming pompadoured cherub in red-and-white checked bib overalls, holding aloft a sizzling double-decker cheeseburger. While the stadium hemorrhaged money from day one, Elias Brothers, home of the Big Boy, used its sweetheart contract to rake in a tidy profit of $1 million a year.

The stadium distinguished itself in other ways. By the fourth quarter, fans unwilling to wait in line at the overtaxed bathrooms simply climbed into the vacant nosebleed sections and off-loaded a day's worth of beer. Fragrant golden rivers came trickling down the stairs. For this and other booziferous behaviors, the place soon came to be known as the Drunk Bowl. When the entertainment value on the field waned, well-lubricated customers picked up the slack by engaging in rolling fistfights in the stands and concourses. One *Free Press* reporter was sent out to the Big Muffin with orders to ignore the game and just cover the fights. More often than not, they were the better show.

By now Bill Ford had rewarded Rick Forzano's mediocre first season as interim coach with a promotion to head coach and a new three-year contract. The Lions' starting center that season was none other than Jon Morris, Dick Morris's nephew, the player Bill Ford had offered to draft sight unseen back in 1963. After eleven mostly losing seasons in Boston, Morris wanted a change of venue, and his wish came true when the Patriots shipped him to Detroit—or rather, to Pontiac. Be careful what you wish for.

The veteran Morris, now thirty-three years old and hardly a candidate for a youth movement, was brought in to replace Ed Flanagan, the Lions' reliable center for the past decade who'd played out his option and signed as a free agent with San Diego, which would allow him to live near his in-laws and play in a balmy climate—far from Detroit. Flanagan claimed he left town under "happy circumstances."

His replacement arrived in Detroit under less than happy circumstances. Jon Morris found himself playing in a dazzling, state-of-the-art stadium on a team that was in a demoralizing state of disarray. Grabbing the biggest headlines that summer was the contract dispute of Ron Jessie, the team's leading receiver, a budding star. Acquired as a rookie in 1971 in a trade with Dallas, Jessie had been locked into a three-year contract that now paid him $16,000 a year and, based on his stellar performance, made him one of the more shamefully underpaid players in the league. When he approached Russ Thomas to renegotiate his contract, Jessie got the same answer Charlie Sanders, Mel Farr, Lem Barney, and other members of this not-very-exclusive club had gotten: "If I do it for you, I'll have to do it for everybody." Translation: "No. Fucking. Way."

After playing out his option in the 1974 season, Jessie became a free agent in 1975 and demanded a hefty pay raise through his lawyer and close friend, Bob Fenton. Now Russ Thomas showed his true colors. He suggested to Jessie that the two of them sit down alone, without Fenton, and try to work out an agreement, man to man. Though he had flatly refused to renegotiate Jessie's nearly criminal contract, Thomas now tried to convince Jessie that he really and truly had his best interests at heart. It proved a tough sell.

"He treated me like a dumb slave, like I didn't know what was happening," Jessie said. "He was running a con game on me. I'm from the streets, man. I know when somebody's running a con game on me."

Rather than play Thomas's con game, Jessie signed a contract with the Los Angeles Rams, who had been molded into a consistent winner by former Lions assistant coach Chuck Knox. Under the so-called Rozelle Rule, the Rams and Lions were required to work out mutually satisfactory compensation for the loss of Jessie. When they couldn't come to an agreement, Commissioner Pete Rozelle stepped in and awarded the Lions the services of Cullen Bryant, a promising but unproven third-year running back. The Lions were amenable to the deal, but there was a small hitch. Bryant refused to leave a winner in sunny California and go to work for a perennial also-ran in the frigid Midwest. He filed a lawsuit, and a federal judge issued a restraining order allowing him to stay with the Rams until the case could be heard in court. The judge also opined that the Rozelle Rule was a violation of the Sherman Antitrust Act—welcome news to the NFL Players Association, which had filed a lawsuit of its own to overturn the rule. Rick Forzano announced that he didn't care how the courts ruled—he would not accept Cullen Bryant on his team under any circumstances.

Now the dispute turned into a bare-knuckle brawl. After Rozelle awarded the Lions the Rams' number one pick in the 1976 draft in place of Bryant—and held out the possibility of additional compensation if Jessie had a stellar season with the Rams—Bill Ford fired off a scorching letter to Rams owner Carroll Rosenbloom, calling him a "hypocrite," claiming he had made a mockery of the compensation rule, and stating that Rosenbloom had "done more to harm pro football than anyone in the history of the NFL"—a reference to Rosenbloom's signing of the first free agent back in 1961, which had led to the creation of the Rozelle Rule as a way to prevent bidding wars for top talent. Ford also intimated that Rosenbloom had promised Bryant a starting role if he stayed with the Rams, then Ford sent copies of his letter to the other twenty-four team owners and the commissioner's office. Rosenbloom claimed he had made no such promise to Bryant, and he dismissed Ford's other charges as "ludicrous, irresponsible, and untrue."

The story made headlines because it was a stunning breach of the code of NFL owners, an all-boys millionaires' club where it was tacitly understood that disputes were to be aired behind closed doors, away from reporters and the public. The appearance of amity and unanimity was paramount. Owners must never do anything that would tarnish the meticulously polished NFL brand, that fecund goose that kept laying bigger and bigger golden eggs.

In keeping with that ethos, the smooth operator in the commissioner's office issued a typically anodyne non-statement. "This is a private matter between the clubs," Rozelle said, "and if there's any need for me to act on it, I will discuss it privately with the clubs."

Case closed. But the bad blood between Carroll Rosenbloom and Bill Ford would continue to flow. And it would reveal the personalities of two very different breeds of multimillionaire—an immigrant's son who had clawed his way to a fortune through hustle, street smarts, and brazen self-interest versus a tycoon's grandson who rarely had to fight, or work, for a thing in his life. An alley fight between these two very different, very rich adversaries was looming.

◆

The Lions' woes didn't stop with the Ron Jessie fiasco. Bill Munson, unhappy with his backup role, let it be known he wanted to be traded. Several disgruntled players walked out of training camp, while others grumbled about the coach and the churn on the roster. Soon they were also grumbling about aching joints, rug burns, and a painful condition called turf toe, all caused by the Silverdome's unforgiving AstroTurf. Some rug burns got infected and led to blood poisoning. The field never got muddy, but the inflatable roof sprang so many leaks that some fans showed up for games toting umbrellas, and there are pictures of Charlie Sanders literally making a splash after catching a pass and landing in one of the ponds that dotted the playing surface. Crowds were bigger than they'd been at Tiger Stadium, but the PonMet was rarely sold out. The fans who showed up found that they'd arrived in a no man's land surrounded by a whole lot of nothing—no nearby bars or restaurants, just a postindustrial wasteland where two highways crossed. When the Lions tried to persuade Jimmy Butsicaris to open a new Lindell AC near the stadium, Butsicaris did the math. There were maybe ten football games at the PonMet every season, plus assorted concerts and events, and Butsicaris asked himself: who would venture to that moonscape the other 300-plus days a year? He decided against opening a Lindell outpost in Pontiac.

More importantly, the players tuned out Forzano and his schoolmarm style. This was revealed in the little things. Morris rarely lifted weights and typically smoked three or four cigarettes during halftimes, a common practice in those days, captured most memorably by a photo of Kansas City Chiefs quarterback Len Dawson during halftime of Super Bowl I, puffing a meditative cigarette, a half-drunk bottle of Fresca resting by his feet. When a Lions assistant coach approached Morris and suggested that smoking cigarettes might not be the best thing for his health, Morris, at 6'4" and 245 pounds, looked down at the guy and said, "If I was worried about my health, you think I'd be playing this fucking game?" The assistant coach had the good sense to laugh and walk away, but the message was clear: *Get out of my face.*

No number of smokes in the locker room could obscure what was happening on the field. "It was constant turmoil," Morris recalled recently. "A merry-go-round. Players coming and going all the time. You can't expect to win under those conditions."

He placed the blame on one man: "When you think of the word idiot, Russ Thomas comes to mind. He wasn't with the program, and the results speak to that. If you've got the right guy on the sideline and the right guy in the GM's office, it's not that complicated." But the Lions rarely had the right guy in either place, and as long as Russ Thomas occupied the GM's office they never had the right guys in both places. The blame for that belongs to one man: the owner. Yet Morris, like so many Lions before and since—Sam Williams, Joe Schmidt, Mel Farr, Jim Thrower, and Charlie Sanders, to name a few—gave Bill Ford a pass. "William Clay Ford was around quite often," Morris said. "He was in the locker room after games. He was a good guy—the Fords treated us right."

At least Ford's Lions were consistent. They inaugurated their new stadium with yet another 7–7 season, yet another second-place finish, yet another no-show in the playoffs. But a curious thing happened in the locker room after a season-ending loss to the playoff-bound St. Louis Cardinals. Instead of hanging their heads over a disappointing repeat of seasons past, everyone was in a surprisingly upbeat mood. Like battle-hardened soldiers, the players had pulled together in the face of incessant adversity—most notably the loss of both quarterbacks, Landry and Munson, to season-ending knee injuries in a Week 6 loss in Houston.

After those devastating injuries, third-string quarterback Joe Reed had gamely led the Lions to three straight wins and a 4–4 record the rest of the way—nothing spectacular, but no worse than they had been with their two top quarterbacks. Given all the adversity and distractions—Ron Jessie's contract dispute, the walkouts, the dissension, the cascading injuries—there was reason to feel good about the 1975 season and optimistic about 1976, when the Lions would have two first-round draft picks, thanks to the Rozelle Rule.

Even Bill Ford got in the spirit when he pried open his wallet and announced that he was giving Rick Forzano a fatter raise than his contract called for. "The coaching staff did a fantastic job," Ford said in the boisterous locker room after the St. Louis game, adding, "I think I enjoyed this season almost more than any since I owned the club. The last few years it seemed I had to get sore and tell off the team publicly for playing a bad game. Not this year. The spirit is there."

Only in Detroit—underpaid star players can't get a raise while a coach with a so-so record gets a pay bump without even having to ask.

Jon Morris had planned to retire at the end of the season, but now he was singing a different tune. "This is a great bunch of guys," he said as he cleaned out his locker. "I hope I'm coming back next year. This team is going to be okay—I think we can win a championship."

YOOPERMAN AND YOOPERWOMAN

There was no way to know if this team would soon—or ever—win another championship, but one thing was beyond doubt: the people of Michigan, from the Upper Peninsula to the Detroit suburbs to the Ohio state line, still loved their Pontiac-based Lions. The team may have been locked forever in second place, and it may have been locked for the next three decades into a nightmare stadium lease, but it drew 513,383 paying customers during the PonMet's inaugural season, second by a whisker only to the Buffalo Bills. The novelty of a new stadium may partly explain that staggering attendance statistic, but something deeper had to be at work when more than half a million people were willing to pay to see a team that hadn't won a playoff game in almost two decades and still wasn't even close. After so much losing, why did fans continue to pour by the hundreds of thousands through the turnstiles of the Big Muffin?

For starters, Michigan is a state where people tend to stay put—only Louisiana has more native-born residents—and it's a place where traditions get passed down through the generations, including the tradition of rooting for the state's long-established college and pro sports teams. It's not uncommon for season tickets to be passed from father to son and then from son to grandson, and the Lions are not the only beneficiaries of the resulting ingrained loyalty. While the Lions were drawing an impressive average of 73,000 fans to their home games in 1975, the nearby University

of Michigan's Orange Bowl–bound football team drew more fans than any
other college team in the nation—an average of 97,000 per home game.
It didn't hurt that Detroit teams' rosters over the years have glittered with
some of the most luminous stars in the American sports firmament. There
were the aforementioned Lions and, more recently, Barry Sanders, Calvin
Johnson, and Matthew Stafford; the Tigers fielded Ty Cobb, Hank Green-
berg, Al Kaline, and Willie Horton; Gordie Howe, Ted Lindsay, and Steve
Yzerman skated for the Red Wings of the NHL; Isiah Thomas and the Bad
Boys of the Pistons won back-to-back NBA titles; and perhaps the greatest
of them all was another son of Alabama who grew up in Detroit's Black
Bottom, the Brown Bomber of the boxing ring, Joe Louis.

Of course Detroit fans, like fans everywhere, crave championship and
hate losing. But in Detroit, as in few other towns, there is a nearly unkillable
sense of loyalty that has managed to trump this craving, and by the time the
Silverdome opened in 1975, that loyalty had held steady through forty seasons. This is remarkable because the diehard sports fan faces guaranteed risks
and uncertain rewards. Championships come rarely, even for the best teams.
Dynasties come and go. So being a die-hard fan requires not only learning
to live with disappointment but learning to embrace it. For the hardened
Detroit Lions fan, heartbreak is not a deal-breaker, it's merely a test, the price
of admission, and if it chases you away then you weren't a true fan in the first
place. It could even be argued that history has acquainted Detroit with more
heartbreak than any other city in America, and that Detroiters—people who
"survived everything America can dish out," in the words of the poet Philip
Levine—have learned to handle adversity with an iron brand of fatalism,
with no hint of chest-thumping or complaint. This is true of all Detroiters,
but it's especially true of the long-suffering Detroit Lions fan.

In the end, this devotion to the city's sports teams can be seen in
one of two ways: as a lowly form of escapism or as an exalted form of
caring—caring about something that means little in the larger world but
has deep resonance among the initiated, the dedicated, the tribe. This caring

delivers a nearly mystical reward: a sense of belonging to something larger than yourself, which in turn bestows the sense of being truly alive, even if just for a few hours on a Sunday afternoon. This payoff was expressed sublimely by Frederick Exley in his classic "fictional memoir" from 1968, *A Fan's Notes*, the story of an unstable alcoholic schoolteacher in upstate New York who has a passion for the great New York Giants teams of the 1960s, most especially their star running back Frank Gifford. Anxiously standing before a barroom TV set while awaiting the Giants' opening kickoff one Sunday, this fan asks *the* question:

> "Why did football bring me so to life? I can't say precisely. Part of it was my feeling that football was an island of directness in a world of circumspection. In football a man was asked to do a difficult and brutal job, and he either did it or got out. There was nothing rhetorical or vague about it . . . It had that kind of power over me, drawing me back with the force of something known, scarcely remembered, elusive as integrity—perhaps it was no more than the force of a forgotten childhood. Whatever it was, I gave myself up to the Giants utterly. The recompense I gained was the feeling of being alive."

The late Roger Angell, one of the most decorated American sportswriters, was not ashamed to admit that he was a fan first and a journalist second. "It is foolish and childish, on the face of it, to affiliate ourselves with anything so insignificant and patently contrived and commercially exploitative as a professional sports team," Angell wrote in his 1977 baseball book, *Five Seasons*. "What is left out of this calculation, it seems to me, is the business of caring—caring deeply and passionately, really *caring*—which is a capacity or an emotion that has almost gone out of our lives."

It never went out of Donnie Stefanski's life. He was born and raised in the hamlet of Goetzville (pop. 419), on the remote eastern end of

Michigan's Upper Peninsula, or U.P., where natives called themselves Yoopers. Stefanski owned Yooperman's Bar and Grille in Goetzville, which he turned into a shrine of Lions memorabilia, and after a friend gave him Lions season tickets in 1994, he never missed a home game—for the next twenty-five years. He and his daughter Megan would leave home at two o'clock on Sunday mornings and drive the 350 miles, give or take, to the Silverdome in Pontiac and, later, to Ford Field in downtown Detroit, where they were always welcomed as members of an extended family of tailgating fans. The team honored Donnie on the field at his one hundredth consecutive game. Then again at his two hundredth. After he died of a heart attack before the start of the 2019 season, his daughter carried on the family tradition. She still shows up for every home game, sitting in her dad's old seat just above the tunnel: Section 100, Row 18, Seat 14. "That's my seat now," Megan recently told the *Free Press*. "I could've upgraded over the years . . . but I don't care to. I like our seats. I like the people around us. It's a family, and those were his seats, so it'll always be my seat."

Which brings us to the greatest paradox of all. The undying devotion of fans such as Donnie and Megan Stefanski, Frederick Exley, and Roger Angell doesn't automatically translate into championships. On the contrary, it gives inept team owners like Bill Ford a license to put an inferior product on the field, year after year after year. Such owners—and Ford is by no means the only example—may yearn to produce a winner, but they know that the quality of the product doesn't matter all that much because the customers will always come back. Diehard fans, in a sense, are enablers of these owners' worst tendencies.

Bill Ford was lucky. During his lifetime, most Detroit Lions fans never lost their capacity for caring deeply about the team. If subsequent history and recent events are any measure, it seems unlikely they ever will.

◆

In the closing days of 1975, a federal judge in Minneapolis declared that the Rozelle Rule was an unfair restraint of trade because it restricted players' freedom of movement, decreased their bargaining power, and kept their salaries lower than if competitive bidding were allowed. Rozelle said the NFL was "disappointed" by the decision; John Mackey, a retired Baltimore Colt and one of the plaintiffs in the suit, called it "a victory for every man in America." One thing beyond dispute was that the owners' years of controlling their players' destinies were coming to an end. The owners howled that they would be bankrupted by bidding wars for the best players, but it was a hollow cry. Everyone—the players and, especially, the owners—was about to get a whole lot richer.

After that high courtroom drama, a bit of political theater—the comedic variety, opera buffa—visited the Lions during the offseason. Having failed to win the Democratic presidential nomination in 1968 and 1972, Eugene McCarthy announced that he was running for president as an independent in 1976. He'd brought a lawsuit challenging campaign-finance laws that resulted in the US Supreme Court striking down limits on the amount of money a political candidate could spend on his or her own campaign. This way lies plutocracy. Americans are still paying for that Supreme Court decision and similar ones that followed. The result is that today the country enjoys the best democracy money can buy.

Less than a week after the ruling, McCarthy announced that his running mate would be his unlikely supporter from 1968, William Clay Ford. There were widespread sniggers that the cash-strapped McCarthy campaign was less attracted by Ford's political cheek than by his prodigious checkbook.

McCarthy's motive didn't matter. With the Vietnam War over and no galvanizing issue to buoy his campaign, McCarthy failed to resonate with voters. Possibly sensing that he had signed up with a sure loser, Bill Ford withdrew from the campaign six days after signing on, citing a legal technicality in some states that required stand-in vice presidential candidates to be a resident of those states. McCarthy, who would name some three dozen vice-presidential candidates in the course of the campaign, said he "regretted" the necessity of Ford's decision. In the November election, McCarthy got slightly less than 1 percent of the popular vote while Bill Ford got a new line on his résumé: "Vice Presidential Candidate for Slightly Less Than One Week."

ON THE COUCH

The good vibes in the Lions' locker room at the end of the 1975 season did not survive the winter. During training camp leading up to the 1976 season, Herb Orvis, a normally mild-mannered mastodon who played defensive tackle, exploded into a shouting match with Rick Forzano in front of his teammates. After he was suspended for "challenging the authority of the coach," Orvis demanded to be traded. Bill Munson finally got his wish when he was gifted to the expansion Seattle Seahawks for less than a song—a fifth-round draft choice, which showed just how highly the Lions prized the one big name their trade-averse general manager had brought in from another team. Altie Taylor, the Lions' all-time leading rusher, ached so badly to get out of town that when trade talks hit a snag he wound up in Ford Hospital undergoing psychiatric treatment for "mental fatigue." Running back Steve Owens, a Heisman Trophy winner, announced he was retiring after seven injury-marred seasons—though there was open speculation that the real reason behind Owens's early exit was that he refused to work for the current coach. He was not alone. Four assistant coaches decamped for other jobs, one of them with the lowly Cleveland Browns. The sentiment was nearly unanimous: anything was better than working for Rick Forzano.

It was an open mutiny. One headline read: REVOLT RIPS LIONS—FORZANO IS TARGET. And an unnamed veteran player—was it Jon Morris?—offered an unscientific estimate of players' attitudes toward their head coach: "I'd say 95 percent of the guys don't respect him."

While the Lions were suffering through their summer of discontent, the rest of the nation was shaking off its hangover from Vietnam and Watergate and trying to get into the spirit of America's rolling, coast-to-coast two hundredth birthday party. That bicentennial summer the Detroit Tigers were once again the talk of the baseball world, thanks to a gangly, curly-haired rookie pitcher named Mark Fidrych. Nicknamed the Bird after the *Sesame Street* character Big Bird, Fidrych augmented his superb pitching skills with a repertoire of eccentricities that endeared him to Detroit fans—and would soon turn him into a national sensation. Before stepping up on the pitcher's mound, the Bird got down on his knees and smoothed the dirt with his hands. When an infielder made a nice play, the Bird hopped across the diamond to congratulate him. And the Bird talked, talked, talked to the baseball, urging it to behave and avoid that big piece of lumber in the batter's hands. If he gave up a hit, he would return the baseball to the umpire in the hope it would mingle with its mates in the ball bag and mend its ways. "Maybe it'll learn some sense," Fidrych explained, "and come out as a pop-up next time."

Fidrych's local fame went national in late June on a *Monday Night Baseball* broadcast on ABC. For the first time, millions of Americans witnessed the Bird's antics—and also saw him mow down a powerful Yankees lineup in a 5–1 Tigers win. Overnight, Detroit had a superstar. He would go on to start in the All-Star Game and win rookie of the year.

The city of Detroit needed such a feel-good story now even more than it had in the troubled summers of 1967 and 1968. A shrinking tax base and ballooning budget deficits had forced Mayor Coleman Young to slash city services, including the temporary layoff of nearly 1,000 police officers. On the night of Aug. 15, the Average White Band and Kool & the Gang played a concert at Cobo Hall, a few hundred feet from the RenCen construction site. Because of the police layoffs, security was light. The night turned into a horror when hundreds of members of two rival gangs from the East Side, the Black Killers and the Errol Flynns, swept through the arena, robbing and beating concertgoers. The violence spilled outside and led to more fighting and robberies, window smashing, and a brazen gang rape.

The Average White Band was a group of young Scots enthralled by American jazz, Motown, and funk. The day after the riot at Cobo, Alan Gorrie, bassist and guitarist with the AWB, noted that gang fights used to be common at concerts in their native Glasgow, especially in hard times. The Scottish gangs called themselves the Fleet and the Tones instead of the Black Killers and the Errol Flynns, but the script was much the same. "It happens everywhere," Gorrie told the *Ann Arbor Sun*. "If unemployment goes up in Scotland, so does the fighting. Just violence. The two things always seem to go hand in hand. It was a great disappointment for us because we'd been looking forward to playing Detroit for weeks." And he insisted that the violence at Cobo was an aberration. "I'm sure it wouldn't happen again here," he said. "It was just one occasion."

Detroiters, Black and white, were not reassured. And white suburbanites had one more reason to stay away from the inner city.

◆

After witnessing a punch-less exhibition season and a 10–3 loss to the Chicago Bears in the season opener, Bill Ford once again started airing his displeasure in the papers. These public tutorials in the Bill Ford School of Business Mismanagement did little to improve the product but succeeded magnificently at alienating the coaching staff and demoralizing the players. This session had a new wrinkle. This time Ford threatened not only the head coach but also the previously untouchable general manager.

"I jumped on Rick and Russ after the game in Chicago," Ford told Jerry Green of the *News*. "I told them their necks were on the line. Frankly, I didn't want a debate or a rebuttal. I said one goes, you both go. I told them

I wouldn't pay to see this team. If I didn't own it and it was a nice day, I wouldn't go. I'd go play golf or go out on a boat."

Then Bill Ford, the colorful quote machine, delivered an ultimatum for the upcoming game against Atlanta. "I figured if we lost this game and were 0–2 with the Minnesota Vikings coming up next week, I just would have to do something drastic." He left no doubt that if the Lions lost to Atlanta, he would give Forzano and Thomas the ziggy. "I would not tie the can to one without tying it to the other," Ford vowed.

It was management by threat of execution, not a proven technique for building self-confidence or nurturing success. Forzano coached the Atlanta game while staring into the basket of a guillotine, waiting for the blade to drop. Despite his desperate situation, he was unable to coax a score out of his players for the first forty-five minutes, and the Lions limped into the fourth quarter trailing 10–0. Starting quarterback Joe Reed was so mercilessly booed that Forzano benched him and inserted Landry. Then, with the blades poised to separate Forzano and Thomas from their heads, a minor miracle happened. The Lions, led by Landry, erupted in the fourth quarter and breezed to a 24–10 win.

Forzano lived to coach another day. Make that another fifteen days. After a 10–9 loss to Minnesota and a 24–14 loss to winless Green Bay, both division rivals, a distraught Forzano submitted his letter of resignation—obviously under pressure from Ford. While Forzano was composing his letter, the can somehow came untied from Russ Thomas, who would cling to his job for another dozen seasons. So it went in the dark and mysterious hallways of the Bill Ford School of Business Mismanagement.

Joe Falls of the *Free Press*, for one, was not fooled by Ford's one-goes-you-both-go vow. "Those who know Ford and his relationship with Thomas knew that such a statement didn't mean much," Falls wrote. "William Clay Ford was no closer to firing Russ Thomas as his general manager than he was to hiring me as his first-string quarterback." But the question hangs in the air: *Why?* Why was Thomas so ziggy-proof?

Jerry Green of the *News*, a perceptive chronicler of the team and its owner, offered this postmortem after Forzano resigned: "Billy Ford has two months to think about revising his system as another football season wastes away for the Lions. He has employed five coaches in eleven years of ownership of the Lions. The coaches lacked authority. They served under the power of a general manager whose faulty advice was too often accepted by the owner. The Detroit method has been an abysmal failure. Ford knows it . . . So now he has to consider changing the mode of the Lions' operation or watch the treadmill process continue through another succession of coaches."

Green cited teams that were successful because the coach was given total control—Vince Lombardi in Green Bay, obviously, and more recently George Allen in Washington, Don Shula in Miami, Chuck Fairbanks in New England, and Chuck Noll in Pittsburgh. Green suggested that Ford "ought to hire a strong coach and give him total authority." The alternative was to let Russ Thomas continue to deliver more of the same: "an overkill of mediocrity."

◆

Later that day Ford proved he had not lost his gift for hiring the wrong head coach. This time he tapped Tommy Hudspeth, the team's coordinator of personnel and scouting, who, like Forzano, had enjoyed limited success as a college coach and had zero head coaching experience in the pros. You would think a smart guy like Bill Ford would learn from his past mistakes. But you would be wrong.

Hudspeth kept the team's overkill of mediocrity humming right along, winning half of the games he coached and losing the other half as the Lions finished with a 6–8 record. It was respectable, considering the season's dreadful start under Forzano, but once again the team was far out of the playoffs.

Sports-mad Detroit in those days was the kind of town where columnists doubled as armchair psychiatrists, and one of the city's most prominent amateur head-shrinkers put Ford on his couch immediately after that disappointing season. Joe Falls of the *Free Press* opened his psychoanalysis session with an exploration of motive: "Ford likes to run his team. It is the one thing which makes him so viable. It is his one contact with the public—and make no mistake about it, this is a man who likes to be in the public eye, whether or not he will ever admit it."

A secret love of the spotlight.

Then Falls explored Ford's fatal flaw: "I am not too sure he would ever accept a secondary role even if it were good for the team. I don't think his vanity would ever permit it. But as long as Ford remains around and exerts so much influence on the operation of the team, the Lions are going to be in the same situation they're in now—going around in circles, promising much and producing little."

Overblown self-regard.

And the cure? "The big change has to be in Ford's philosophy," Falls concluded. "Does he have the stuff to step back from his operation and let others—the professionals—run it for him? I don't think so. The Lions are the thing he loves most in his life and he is not about to give them up. The problem is that Ford is like so many NFL owners. He is a fan and he reacts like a fan. He has surrounded himself with people who are loyal to him and tell him what he wants to hear. His loyalty to Russ Thomas must even be embarrassing to Thomas."

Misplaced loyalty.

The therapy session had revealed the sources of the team's ongoing futility—and a possible way to break out of it. When he got up off the couch, though, an angry Ford blistered Falls and his fellow psychiatrists in the local press. Ford noted that he traveled all over the country, and in his opinion the Detroit sportswriters were "the worst hatchet men in the business."

The therapy, in short, did not take.

OUT-OWNERED

The Lions, as noted, had developed a knack for keeping the wrong people and letting the right people get away, and Ford now openly admitted that one of the latter was Chuck Knox, an assistant Lions coach Ford had declined to elevate to head coach after Joe Schmidt resigned in 1973. Knox promptly accepted the top job with the Los Angeles Rams, who were owned by Ford's sworn enemy Carroll Rosenbloom, a shrewd operator who had swapped his Baltimore Colts in 1972 for the Rams in a no-cash transaction that saved him $4.4 million in capital gains taxes. Knox had blossomed as head coach in L.A., leading the Rams to four consecutive division titles—but so far no trips to the Super Bowl.

Ford, for some reason, was convinced he could convince Knox to walk away from all that California sunshine and all that winning and come back to iron-gray Detroit to step onto the coaching treadmill of a proven loser, where, as an added bonus, the local sportswriters were the worst hatchet men in the business. All it would take, in Ford's mind, was a little money. Ford, who'd scoffed at the "ridiculous" $20,000 contract the Kansas City Chiefs had offered the rookie quarterback Pete Beathard back in 1964, was now willing to pay Knox $2.5 million for a five-year contract to coach the Lions, including a home in Detroit and an insurance policy. In letting this record-shattering offer get into the papers, Ford had broken the poker player's first commandment: Thou shalt never let your opponent know what you want or how badly you want it.

Sitting across the poker table, Carroll Rosenbloom must have been licking his chops. Raised in Baltimore—H. L. Mencken lived in the neighborhood for a time—Rosenbloom went to work in the family textile business during the Depression, did well for himself and eventually added an eclectic web of other businesses to his portfolio, ranging from a film and theater production company to the American Totalisator Co., which leased tote machines to racetracks, to a very tall pile of Warner Bros. stock. Silver-haired, square-jawed, perpetually tan, Rosenbloom played golf with Joe Kennedy and hung out with Frank Sinatra. He owned a home on the Jersey Shore and was a late-night prowler in Atlantic City's casinos, a high roller, well connected, a fierce competitor at everything he did. A worthy adversary, in other words, and nobody's idea of a choirboy. Press reports usually included the adjectives "ego-centric," "spiteful," and "vindictive." One veteran sportswriter offered a summation of Rosenbloom's character: "This was a man who either won or lost but rarely—if ever—compromised."

And this uncompromising man was unhappy when reports began to circulate that the Lions were talking to Chuck Knox through a secret back-channel liaison, possibly Joe Schmidt, and that Knox was reportedly open to the idea of returning to Detroit. The reason for Knox's openness was pretty simple: "I have a chance to make more money than you could ever believe."

Rosenbloom, unlike Ford, kept his cards close to his vest. "They have not sought permission to talk to my coach," Rosenbloom said, citing a tenet of the NFL constitution that forbids tampering with coaches or players who are under contract. "They must have that first. If they want to talk to him, that's fine. But first we must negotiate on a price and determine how much they are willing to pay me to take my coach." Sounding like a riverboat gambler holding a royal flush, he added: "We'll see just how much Mr. William Clay Ford wants my coach after we sit down and talk."

So Bill Ford boarded a plane to Los Angeles with his checkbook in his pocket and Russ Thomas at this side. Also in Ford's pocket was a list of the players he was willing to sacrifice to persuade Rosenbloom to part with his coach, mostly aging veterans such as Greg Landry, Charlie Sanders, and Lem Barney.

Ford and Rosenbloom and their general managers huddled for four hours in a Bel Air hotel but failed to come to terms. While Ford was offering used goods, Rosenbloom made it clear he wanted "young bodies" to compensate for the loss of his highly successful and highly respected coach. When Ford returned to Detroit the next day he predicted the deal would be finalized "in a few days."

Rosenbloom, meanwhile, was spinning a different narrative, scoffing at the players his visitors from Detroit had offered. "They think if a guy can walk, he can play football," said Rosenbloom, who was holding all the cards and knew it. "It's up to Mr. Ford to satisfy me; I don't have to satisfy him. I don't blame them for wanting Knox—Chuck Knox is the best coach in football. But I'm not stupid. I'm not going to give him up unless I'm fully compensated."

For three days after Ford and Thomas returned from Los Angeles, the Detroit papers were peppered with speculation about the negotiations. One reporter called the drama a "cloak-and-dagger thriller." Then Knox abruptly killed the suspense by announcing that he was staying with the Rams. The worst hatchet men in the business showed Ford no mercy.

ROSENBLOOM BEATS FORD AGAIN, read one headline. Joe Falls tarred Ford and Thomas with the same brush: "They never should have gotten themselves in the position where Rosenbloom could dictate to them."

Over the past twenty seasons there had been countless headlines about the Lions getting outplayed, out-hustled, out-maneuvered, and out-coached, but now the newsroom wordsmiths took it to the next level. One headline said it all: THE LIONS WERE OUT-OWNERED.

Red-faced and empty-handed, Ford did the thing he had done so many times before: he rewarded Tommy Hudspeth's middling performance as interim coach with a three-year contract. The thought of three more years of plodding football under Hudspeth led one sportswriter to suggest that the Elias Brothers should stock the Silverdome concession stands with ample supplies of NoDoz. Hudspeth did his part by delivering a déjà vu 6–8 record and third-place finish in the NFC Central Division in 1977, once again far out of the playoffs.

So far, in fact, that a state legislator named Thomas Holcomb introduced a resolution in the state's house of representatives that November, calling for the ouster of Russ Thomas because the team he managed had become an embarrassment to the entire state of Michigan.

At first the news reports played the story for laughs, but Holcomb, a Democrat from Lansing, made it clear he wasn't joking. "The state of Michigan, through its $800,000 subsidy of the Silverdome, has a financial interest in the performance of the Lions," Holcomb said by way of explaining his push for Thomas's ouster. "We looked at his record, his performance, the coaching manipulations, the decisions he's made, the operation and management of the team—and we think they are questionable and inferior. I think the government has a legitimate gripe when we're asked to finance these [stadiums]."

Most fans agreed. In a newspaper reader poll, fans supported Holcomb's resolution by a healthy 3-to-1 margin. Meanwhile, a group in Grand Rapids calling itself Save the Lions began soliciting $2 donations to pay for newspaper ads directed against the team's poor ownership and management, promising to include a list of all contributors by name. "This is no joke," the solicitation said. "We are serious and angry fans who want to see a winner. Hit Ford in the pocketbook!"

That pocketbook happened to be bulging. Once again the team drew more than half a million fans despite its losing record, which again was second best in the league, this time surpassed only by the New York Giants. Despite that dreadful stadium contract, the take at the gate and TV revenue added up to an income of $7.8 million, and in the coming season the team's TV revenue was scheduled to more than double. No matter how badly Bill Ford got out-ownered, he just kept getting richer.

◆

After another season-ending loss to another playoff-bound team, this time division rival Minnesota, the upbeat mood was gone from the Lions' locker room. Players talked openly about a collapse of team spirit, inadequate effort, a tendency to point fingers, and, yes, questionable coaching decisions. Bill Ford was absent, as he'd been for most of the season, a sure sign that he was dissatisfied with the team, especially its anemic offense.

"The Lions' offense is a joke, but nobody's laughing," Mike O'Hara wrote in the *News*. "It has made them outcasts in their own stadium, where they are greeted by bitter boos." He then offered a succinct analysis of how a team's culture works: "Winning is a quality that runs through an entire organization—from the owner to the last man on the roster." The Lions were proof that the same could be said of losing.

Jon Morris, who kept putting off his retirement plans, had just been chosen most valuable offensive player by his teammates. In that subdued locker room he summed up the prevailing sense of dismay that the well-liked Hudspeth was headed for the ziggy. "Tommy's a helluva nice guy," Morris said. "He deserves better."

By season's end, in response to the growing unrest from Lansing to Grand Rapids to Pontiac, the rumor mill in the team's front office began grinding yet again. This time the speculation centered on possible new candidates for head coach, not general manager. Nothing, it seemed, could threaten Russ Thomas's job security.

One name conspicuously absent from the list of coaching candidates was Chuck Knox. Ford had no appetite for reopening that can of worms. Knox had led the Rams to yet another division title in 1977, his fifth in five seasons, but again the Rams failed to reach the Super Bowl when they lost to the Vikings on a sloppy field in Los Angeles. After fighting so hard to keep him, Carroll Rosenbloom, bored by Knox's groundhog offense and dissatisfied with his postseason record, let his once-coveted coach shuffle off to the Buffalo Bills. The mercurial Rosenbloom wanted Super Bowl rings, and nothing less would do. For his part, Knox was glad to get out from under the thumb of the domineering owner.

What a difference a year makes. And what a vivid portrait of the differences between Carroll Rosenbloom and Bill Ford. When he owned the Baltimore Colts, Rosenbloom claimed wealth couldn't touch the thrill of winning football games. After his team won back-to-back championships in the late '50s, the owner said, "I don't want any yachts, and I don't want any castles. I would just like to have about thirty more championships, and then I'd be all set." He was an astute judge of talent, unlike Bill Ford. Rosenbloom saw the potential of the assistant coach Don Shula, architect of the Lions' league-leading defense, and after the 1962 season he wooed him away from Detroit with an offer to be head coach of the Colts. That was the birth of the feud between Rosenbloom and Ford, but Ford had no one to blame but himself for letting Shula slip away. Ford may have cared deeply about the Lions and he may have died a thousand deaths every time they lost, but, unlike Rosenbloom, his will to win was not accompanied by an ability to make the requisite tough, smart decisions—such as hanging on to promising assistant coaches and cutting loose his albatross of a general manager. A longtime writer on the Lions beat pinpointed this shortcoming: "Bill Ford was funny, had a quick wit. He had a flaw, though. He cared about the team, but he sort of took things as they came. He didn't have a burning desire to win." Rosenbloom's desire to win burned white-hot and led him to hire Shula and Knox away from the Lions, and it's a safe bet that he would not have tolerated Russ Thomas for two seasons, let alone twenty-two.

Despite these differences, Rosenbloom and Ford did have one thing besides their wealth in common: a shared loathing of Pete Rozelle. For both men, it originated with the gambling investigation way back in the early 1960s. At the time Ford had made no secret of his displeasure with Rozelle's actions, while Rosenbloom's displeasure went even deeper. He had helped broker the deal that ended the logjam among the owners in 1960 and resulted in Rozelle's election as commissioner—partly because, as Rosenbloom said years later, he thought young Rozelle was "just another harmless ass-kisser." But Rosenbloom soon came to regret his diplomatic handiwork. His reputation as a high-stakes gambler came to the attention of Rozelle's investigators, and a story hit the papers alleging that Rosenbloom had once bet more than $50,000 *against* his own Baltimore Colts. The charges were eventually proved groundless, but Rosenbloom felt that Rozelle, in his quest for sensational headlines, had paid insufficient attention to the news of Rosenbloom's exoneration. It appeared in most newspapers, as *Sports Illustrated* dryly noted, "in small print next to the dog and cat ads."

Vindictive by nature, Rosenbloom never forgot Rozelle's slight. For years he plotted his revenge, telling his fellow owners that the commissioner had become an emperor in his capacious Park Avenue palace, master of a small army of minions who were loyal to Rozelle instead of to the people who signed their paychecks, the owners. Hell, Bert Bell used to run the league from his kitchen table in Philly. By the time the owners gathered for their annual powwow in San Diego in March 1976, Rosenbloom was ready to pounce.

His first salvo was a proposal to create a committee that would govern the league, severely undercutting the commissioner's power. There was tepid support from Oakland but stone silence from the other teams, including Detroit. The next day Rosenbloom uncorked a rambling anti-Rozelle speech, and the hotter he got the more alarmed and enraged his fellow owners became. To defuse the situation, a lunch break was called. After the break, venerable George Halas, owner of the Chicago Bears and one of the founders of the NFL, spoke passionately on Rozelle's behalf. Lamar Hunt, an oil tycoon who had helped launch the AFL and now owned the Kansas City Chiefs, then gave a pro-Rozelle speech of his own. Every man in the room gave the two owners a standing ovation.

Rosenbloom had left the building during the lunch break so he missed the speeches and the applause, but he continued to hammer away at Rozelle. When the owners reconvened in New York that fall, Rosenbloom showed up with the Rams' lawyer, who read a long list of grievances against the commissioner. When the charges were met with more silence, another lunch break was called. Furious at the failure of his coup attempt, Rosenbloom marched out of the room with his lawyer, barking over his shoulder at Rozelle, "If I can't get you in here, I'll get you out there!" The IRS was soon combing through the NFL's books, almost certainly at the instigation of the well-connected owner of the Los Angeles Rams.

Rosenbloom's angry exit from that second meeting was a replay of Bill Ford's angry exit from Ford Motor Company's executive committee meeting two decades earlier, after his Continental Mark II was sent to an early grave. Now it was Carroll Rosenbloom whose fury was pathetic, the yelp of a beaten man. Down but not out, Rosenbloom would continue his campaign until April 2, 1979, the day he drowned while swimming alone in the surf off Golden Beach, Florida. Rosenbloom never swam alone, according to his family, and there was speculation that his drowning was not an accident, that his past as a high-stakes gambler with shady connections had caught up with him. The evidence was thin, however, and no charges were ever filed.

More than 900 people attended Rosenbloom's memorial service at his Beverly Hills home, including Howard Cosell, the movie stars Cary Grant, Jimmy Stewart, Kirk Douglas, and Warren Beatty, as well as fifteen NFL owners. Bill Ford was not among the mourners.

DETROIT CHAINSAW MASSACRE

After returning to Detroit from his vacation home at Smoke Tree Ranch near Palm Springs in early January 1978, Bill Ford was tanned, rested, and ready to fire up the chainsaw. He promptly announced the wholesale firing of Tommy Hudspeth and all eight of his assistant coaches. Once again Ford let the wrong guy get away—this time it was the man in charge of special teams and select offensive duties, Bill Belichick, who, like Don Shula and Chuck Knox, was destined for spectacular success elsewhere as a head coach.

Two days after the mass firing, Ford introduced Hudspeth's imposing successor, 6'6" 265-pound Monte Clark, a former offensive tackle with Cleveland and one of Don Shula's offensive assistants in Miami when the Dolphins were amassing their unblemished 17–0 season and two Super Bowl titles. More recently, Clark had been head coach of the San Francisco 49ers for one season, turning a perennial loser into an instant winner—until the team was sold and a new general manager told Clark he would have to relinquish his coveted control over drafting and trades. Rather than accept a diminished role at increased pay, Clark quit, which won him glowing press for being a man of principle. He spent the 1977 season away from the game and was hungry to get back in.

In Detroit he was given the titles of head coach and, far more significantly, director of football operations. Bill Ford had undergone a radical change in his philosophy, along the lines Joe Falls had advocated during that futile 1976 head-shrinking session. "[Clark] will run the draft, scouting, waivers, and trades," Ford announced, "although the trades will be subject to my approval." Clark also had control over assistant coaches, trainers, even secretaries. Clark was being given the power Joe Schmidt had yearned for but never received because Bill Ford had finally decided to step back and give control of the operation to a true professional. At Clark's insistence, there would be no more dreaded Monday postmortems among the head coach, owner, and general manager. Of course all this meant that Russ Thomas's role was being sharply diminished—he was now relegated to handling contract negotiations and league business matters.

Which led Jerry Green of the *News* to offer another Nixonian allusion: "We're not going to have Russ Thomas to kick around anymore. And that's so good."

Ford gave a simple explanation for this belated transfer of power from the general manager to the head coach: "I wanted Monte to control his own destiny." Ford also admitted to making mistakes. The biggest was in 1972, when Ford had ignored Don Shula's advice to hire his offensive assistant Monte Clark away from Miami and instead pursued Baltimore's Don McCafferty. Easy Rider's untimely death, in Ford's view, was the turning point. "That's when things got out of control," he said. "We were trapped. We had to take what was available"—Rick Forzano—"and then when that didn't work out we had to turn to inside our own organization"—Tommy Hudspeth. He made no mention of the botched attempt to woo Chuck Knox. "We've been rocking along in dead center ever since."

Or maybe Ford had finally begun to listen to the chorus from the stands and the press box and the state legislature, which had been trying to tell him for years that Russ Thomas was a disaster. Whatever the reason behind this sudden change, there was a sense in Detroit that under Clark the Lions, for the first time in memory, had a chance.

◆

Clark showed no reluctance to wield his vast powers. In April he called in the veterans for strength, agility, speed, and endurance tests. Appalled by the results, he put them on tailor-made workout programs and ordered them to report for training camp in top shape. He did the same with the rookies. Then he started shuffling the deck of players as effortlessly as a Las Vegas blackjack dealer—trading, cutting, waiving, drafting. When the disgruntled veteran Herb Orvis failed to show up for the minicamp, Clark promptly dealt him to Baltimore. Message delivered: there will be no dissension on this team. The Lions deftly signed a gifted punter, Tom Skladany, who had turned down Cleveland's contract offer. Clark made some solid picks in the draft, then he declined to offer thirty-six-year-old Jon Morris a new contract, traded another veteran lineman, Rockne Freitas, and waived two others, Larry Hand and Jim Yarbrough. Then, in a shocker, Clark waived the popular but aging Lem Barney. Another aging fan favorite, Charlie Sanders, listened to his aching body and announced his retirement after ten stellar seasons. When the veterans showed up for training camp in July, their physical conditioning was much improved from the spring, delighting Clark. He had scored his first small victory. Though he had taken his own chainsaw to most of the veterans on the roster, Clark traded for Denver's center Mike Montler, an easygoing veteran who had played in that year's Super Bowl and, it was hoped, would provide some glue for the inexperienced offensive line.

The glue didn't stick. The day after his fourth game as a Lion, Montler suddenly realized he could not get in step with Clark's hard-driving style. What used to be relatively relaxed four-to-five-hour days in Denver were now seven-to-eight-hour days in Detroit. "Maybe it's the intensity of it," the thirty-four-year-old journeyman said of Clark's system. "His approach is quite foreign to me." When it came his turn to slam his body into a blocking dummy at that Monday workout, Montler had an epiphany: "I said, 'What am I doing?' I hit it and it just went through my mind that this is crazy for me. I'm not enjoying this."

What he was not enjoying was the way TV money was changing the game. The NFL and three networks were in the midst of a four-year, $576 million contract, the richest to date in television history. As the stakes climbed ever higher, the coaches became more demanding and the players started taking themselves—and their bodies—more seriously. No more offseason pickup basketball games, for fear of sprained ankles or blown-out knees. Agents, once unheard-of, were now a fixture, and the contracts they negotiated kept growing zeroes. In addition to computers, scouting for many teams included the Wonderlic aptitude test and such psychological tests as the Minnesota Multiphasic Inventory. Teams were now measuring mental alertness and that elusive quality called character. Practices, as Mike Montler had discovered, were longer and more rigorous. While old-school players like Jon Morris and Alex Karras had avoided the weight room as though it harbored infectious diseases, the new generation of players wore out the Nautilus machines, watched their diets and their drinking and, of course, rarely touched cigarettes. (Drugs, to enhance both performance and pleasure, were another matter.) The days of pro athletes mingling with fans at bars like the Lindell AC were long gone. NFL football was no longer a fun game played by accessible roughnecks. It was now a very big business watched by millions and played by increasingly remote millionaires.

For Mike Montler, like Joe Schmidt before him, the fun was long gone. So, after having his epiphany at the blocking dummy, Montler turned to the offensive line coach and said, "That's it." Then he walked off the practice field, packed up his van, and drove home to Boulder, Colorado.

Monte Clark, for one, was not sorry to see the veteran go. "The best thing that happened to us was when Mike Montler took off," Clark said, "getting rid of a guy who didn't want to work, who was distracting from what we were trying to accomplish."

After Montler drove off into the sunset, the Lions lost their next three games to fall to 1–6. Clark had said before the season that he was not a miracle worker, and now it was beginning to look like he knew what he was talking about. He also knew that the team had arrived at a crucial juncture. He still believed his system would pay dividends—*if* the players stuck with him and didn't, figuratively speaking, pack up their vans and drive home to Colorado.

With the season not yet half over but already a lost cause, Clark didn't waver. "We all believe we're right on track even though our win-loss record doesn't indicate that," he said. "I don't think we're that far off, and it might surprise us when things start going our way."

Surprisingly, things started going the Lions' way the very next Sunday. Playing before the smallest crowd ever at the Silverdome, the team exploded for thirty-one points in the first half as the new starting quarterback, Detroit native Gary Danielson, threw three touchdown passes in a 31–14 win over the shell-shocked San Diego Chargers. The Lions were getting their money's worth—Danielson's $60,000 contract, a Russ Thomas special, made him the lowest-paid starting quarterback in the league.

Bill Ford had stopped traveling with the team to away games, and he was less visible at the Silverdome again that season—he was now referred to as the "reclusive" millionaire owner—but displeasure with the team was no longer the main reason for his absence. Before the season began, there had been a major bloodletting inside the Glass House that served as a reminder that Bill Ford's heart may have been with the Lions, but his soul was forever welded to Ford Motor Company.

For years Henry II had been feuding with his No. 2 man and heir apparent, Lee Iacocca. In the spring of 1977, Henry II had shuffled the chairs in the executive suite, creating an unwieldy three-headed beast to run the company known as the Office of the Chief Executive. Henry II would continue as chairman of the board and chief executive officer, Philip Caldwell was named vice-chairman, and Iacocca remained as president.

Iacocca was furious at being distanced from the throne—especially by a cautious, plodding teetotaler like Caldwell, who one rival referred to as "plain vanilla." Not Lee Iacocca's favorite flavor.

Henry II had been hospitalized in early 1976 with a serious heart ailment, and he'd made it known that he intended to step down soon as CEO and give up the chairmanship in 1982 when he reached the mandatory retirement age of sixty-five. Shortly after his release from the hospital, Henry II offered his thoughts on the looming succession: "I think the public really wants, after I go, to see somebody called Ford right at the top of the company."

In the summer of 1978, Henry II rearranged the furniture in the executive suite yet again, turning the Office of the Chief Executive from a trio into a quartet. Bill Ford was brought in as chairman of the executive committee. Iacocca, still president but knocked down another peg, seethed at the prospect that Henry II was positioning his kid brother to take over.

One headline asked the question Iacocca and a lot of other people in Detroit were asking: Is WILLIAM CLAY FORD MOVING UP?

On the afternoon of July 13, with rumors of Iacocca's demise swirling, Henry II summoned him into his office. When Iacocca arrived he was surprised to discover that he and the boss were not alone. Sitting at the marble conference table was Bill Ford, the new fourth wheel in the Office of the Chief Executive, whose presence Iacocca could have read in one of two ways: Bill Ford was a friend and an ally, so maybe he was there to argue against Iacocca's beheading; on the other hand, Bill Ford was also the largest single shareholder in the company, so his presence could have been a signal that whatever happened in that room was final.

Iacocca recounted in his autobiography that his mind was racing: *"Bill promised he would fight for me, but I can't count on his support because he has never stood up to Henry in his life."*

And he didn't stand up to him that day. After feinting for half an hour, Henry II finally dropped the ax. Overcoming his initial shock, Iacocca angrily demanded to know why he was being fired after thirty-two years of loyal service that had earned the company billions. "Well," Henry said with a shrug of his imperial shoulders, "sometimes you just don't like somebody."

Iacocca played his last chip. "What about Bill over here," he said. "I'd like to know what he thinks."

Henry cut him off. "I've already made the decision."

Iacocca then launched into a lengthy recitation of his many achievements, real and imagined, at the company. "Your timing stinks," he told Henry II, his voice rising. "We've just made a billion eight for the second year in a row. That's three and a half billion in the past two years." He was nearly shouting now. "But mark my words, Henry, you may never see a billion eight again. And do you know why? Because you don't know how the fuck we made it in the first place!"

The storm passed. As the meeting wound down, Bill Ford took a stab at changing his brother's mind, but it was far too little and far too late. Bill Ford was in tears when he walked out of the office. "I'm sorry, Lee," he told Iacocca. "I'm sorry. He's ruthless. He didn't even give you a reason. You really laid him out—nobody in his life ever took him on like that."

Iacocca had come to the understandable, if too simplistic, conclusion that blood was thicker than gasoline. The episode carried deeper resonances that touched on class and style and ancient family history. It meant, in the end, that the cosseted WASPs of Grosse Pointe had no room in their world for this flashy, grasping son of Italian immigrants from Bethlehem, Pennsylvania. The old adage about the Irish could be applied to the clannish Ford family: The outsider is always wrong.

Two weeks after the outsider was ousted, Benson Ford suffered a fatal heart attack aboard his yacht *Onika*, the one place where he felt at home and at peace. The papers gave more prominent play to the aftermath of Iacocca's sensational firing than to the anticlimactic death of the forgotten, nearly invisible Ford brother.

◆

The drama inside the Glass House led Mike O'Hara of the *News* to jump to a misconception shared by many Detroiters, including Bill Ford. In the introduction to his mid-season interview with the Lions' owner, O'Hara wrote: "As he is being phased into a position as chairman of the board of the Ford Motor Co., Ford has been less directly involved with his football team than in previous years. Still, he keeps close contact with the team."

Asked about his impression of Clark's first half-season, Ford replied: "Probably two important things stand out. One is he's got discipline. And probably second, and maybe they go hand in hand, is that he has the respect of the ball team. He's kept them together, despite the losses. They're hanging in there together. There's no bickering, there's no backbiting. There's no dissension. There's no finger-pointing. He's got their attention. They respect him. They know he's been there. They know he's got a sound program. They believe in him."

Their belief was about to lead to a mid-season turnaround that would be replicated, with uncanny precision, forty-four seasons later by another 1–6 Lions team. Suddenly the 1978 team started clicking, stopped making stupid mistakes and reeled off six wins in its last nine games. One of the most impressive wins came when the Lions hosted the powerful Denver Broncos in their traditional Thanksgiving Day game before 71,000 fans and a national television audience. With the score tied 7–7 at halftime, the crowd came to its feet when a tall man in a three-piece suit walked onto the field with a noticeable limp, accompanied by his wife and their six children. The house shook with cheers for a recently retired Lion legend.

At the age of thirty-two, Charlie Sanders could no longer run or ride a bicycle, he had difficulty climbing stairs, and his knees frequently locked—the legacies from his ten seasons as a pro football player. As he stood out there on the field bathing in the cheers, Sanders embodied a brutal truth about the game: playing with pain, and paying for it later in life, is part of the job description of every man who has ever worn an NFL uniform. There are two reasons for this. The first, of course, is the mad-dog violence at the heart of the enterprise—and remember that Sanders retired long before the NFL acknowledged the rash of brain traumas and banned intentional helmet-to-helmet hits. The second reason is an economic imperative: players have always understood that if they allow an injury to hamper their performance or, worse, keep them off the field, they will soon be looking for another job. "You learn to keep your mouth shut, to be part of the system," as Sanders put it. "You gotta eat."

When he'd suffered a dislocated shoulder and was told he would be out for eight weeks, Sanders was back in action three days later, his shoulder wrapped in a harness. When his battered knee locked, he was wired and shot with electrical charges to relieve the pain, then heavily bandaged and sent out onto the field. His wife likened him to Dennis Rainer, a marathoner who got shot in the head during a race in Michigan but kept running on pure adrenaline, unaware that a bullet was lodged in his skull. After Sanders suffered another knee injury in 1976, a team doctor looked at an X-ray and assured him it wasn't serious, a diagnosis any player would eagerly believe. Some Lions coaches suggested that Sanders was feigning injury, goldbricking, even though his knees had to be repeatedly drained. Shortly after Monte Clark came in as head coach and started shedding aging veterans, Sanders was in the weight room trying to strengthen his battered knee, which was making popping and clicking noises. When the coach walked past, Sanders called to him with a laugh, "Hey, Monte, listen to this knee!" Clark didn't bother. "If you want sympathy," he said, "it's in the dictionary." Then he walked away. The two never spoke again.

Finally, after the knee swelled to twice its normal size, the team sent Sanders to a Toronto specialist to undergo a long-overdue arthroscopy. "The bone is completely rotted out," Dr. Robert Jackson reported. "The femur is all chewed up." Back in Detroit, a former team doctor who had repaired ligaments and cartilage in the damaged knee made it official.

"Charlie," he told Sanders, "I know how much football means to you, but your career is over."

And now, a year after receiving that devastating verdict, Sanders stood on the Silverdome field, waving to the crowd. He would admit later that being forced into early retirement by his many injuries sometimes drove him into a "depressed state." But on that day before the adoring fans and the TV cameras, Charlie Sanders was all smiles.

The Lions put the finishing touch on a seemingly perfect day by scoring a late touchdown to beat the favored Broncos. But there are few perfect days when the Detroit Lions are involved. On that day George Wilson, the genial coach who had led the Lions to their last championship in 1957, suffered an aneurysm and died hours later in a Detroit hospital. He was sixty-four, another forgotten man.

◆

The team's strong finish included that Thanksgiving Day win over playoff-bound Denver and blowouts of cellar-dwelling San Francisco and playoff-bound Minnesota, a game that featured five touchdown passes by Gary Danielson. Given their bumbling start, the Lions' final record of 7–9 was respectable—and a legitimate cause for optimism.

Clark pointed out that the team's seven wins were only one fewer than division champ Minnesota's. Maybe he was right. Maybe the Lions were getting close.

THE CHARLIE BROWN
OF DETROIT

The dreamy optimism that prevailed before the 1979 season—including a prediction by the oddsmaker Jimmy the Greek, among others, that the Lions would win the NFC Central Division title—gave way to a prolonged nightmare. That season would replicate every flaw, foible, failure, and miserable stroke of luck that had dogged this franchise since the day a jubilant Joe Schmidt was carried around the field after winning the championship in 1957.

Before the nightmare 1979 season unfolded, though, there was a dollop of good news. Meeting in Honolulu in March, the NFL owners voted unanimously to play the 1982 Super Bowl in the Pontiac Silverdome, the first time the game was awarded to a cold-climate city. The vote was seen as reward to the auto industry, especially Ford Motor Company, for being such reliable advertisers on NFL broadcasts. The local media gushed that the game would generate a $70 million cash infusion to the Detroit metro area, which was being battered by a recession and a vicious auto-industry slump. When asked about potential problems presented by Michigan's winter weather, Pete Rozelle quipped, "They say the ice-fishing is excellent." The attempt at humor would become a grim prophecy.

The Lions' nightmare of 1979 began before the season began. Greg Landry—former No. 1 draft pick, now a wobbly-kneed backup—was granted his wish when Clark traded him to Baltimore. To fill out the requisite trio of quarterbacks, Clark drafted Jeff Komlo out of Delaware in the ninth round with the 231st overall pick and signed him to a bargain-basement contract. As insurance policies go, this one would demonstrate that you get what you pay for.

In the final game of the exhibition season, Gary Danielson, the Lions' starting quarterback and centerpiece of the hoped-for turnaround, wrenched his knee. The injury was worse than originally suspected—a torn ligament—and the next morning Danielson underwent surgery and was declared out of action for four to eight weeks. Monte Clark called it a "disaster." When he went looking for a new No. 3 quarterback, he learned that quality quarterbacks were not sitting around waiting for a phone call from Detroit. Clark took what he could get—Scott Hunter, a journeyman who, after getting cut by Atlanta, and had gone back home to Mobile, Alabama, to manage an appliance store.

It got worse. In the opening game of the regular season against Tampa Bay, Danielson's understudy Joe Reed aggravated a groin injury and had to be helped off the field. This was a double disaster. Thrown into the breach, third-string Jeff Komlo promptly fumbled his first snap. Its confidence shattered, the team absorbed a 31–16 whipping.

More than a few people claimed they were hearing the whispers of Bobby Layne.

Clark, desperate for another No. 3 quarterback, scraped the nearly empty barrel and signed Jerry Golsteyn, who'd played sparingly in a three-year career with the New York Giants and Baltimore Colts.

Komlo performed adequately in his first start, but the Lions squandered a three-touchdown comeback and lost to Washington. The next Sunday they were humiliated by the winless New York Jets. Now the grumbling began. Clark called the loss to the Jets "embarrassing" and "disturbing." Jerry Green speculated in the *News* that these Lions might be destined for history—the first team to record an 0–16 season. The speculation proved to be a bit premature. Green added that the Lions were "the worst team in pro football." Bill Ford had a long powwow with Clark to assess the team's condition and direction. "It was a very amicable thing," Ford said, adding that Clark's job was secure. "I wasn't chewing him out."

The Lions finally won a game, 24–23, when an Atlanta field goal attempt sailed just wide as time expired. But the next week they lost to Minnesota, and the grumbling descended into internecine warfare. "After yesterday's game," the *Oakland Press* reported, "players and coaches turned on each other."

Now all the team's trademarks that Bill Ford thought Clark had laid to rest—bickering, backbiting, dissension, finger-pointing—came out of hiding. Gary Danielson, still recuperating from knee surgery and soon to be eligible for free agency, was growing so frustrated with Russ Thomas's unwillingness to negotiate his contract that the quarterback floated the possibility of playing in the Canadian Football League. As for Monte Clark, it was now apparent that giving him the freedom to control his destiny had come at a cost. In taking a chainsaw to the team's roster, Clark had shed too many quality veterans in favor of young players he could mold to his system, but those young players kept making rookie mistakes, which had a way of snowballing into more mistakes. As if to prove the point, two rookies were about to make the worst kind of mistake. The kind that gets into the papers.

After a surprising shutout win over Chicago on Thanksgiving Day that ended an eight-game skid and "improved" the team's record to 2–11, the internal strife finally spilled into the open. At a bar in suburban Rochester, Jeff Komlo was enjoying a few beers with one of his roommates, Keith Dorney, an offensive tackle who was the team's top draft pick that year. A dispute arose—possibly over Dorney's displeasure with Komlo's three interceptions during the Chicago game, possibly over Komlo's displeasure with the quality of pass protection he was getting from Dorney and his offensive linemates. Soon, for whatever reason, the two rookies went at each other. The 200-pound Komlo, punching well above his weight against the 265-pound Dorney, realized he needed an edge and so he picked up a beer mug and whacked his roommate in the face with it, cutting the skin and blackening his right eye. Fight over. When Dorney showed up for practice the next day wearing sunglasses, the team's PR office tried to weave a yarn that he and Komlo, who also sported facial cuts, had been in a car accident. The truth about the bar fight soon came out, along with the news that Clark had fined the roommates $1,000 apiece. So much for peace, love, and understanding. The bar fight seemed to let the last air out of the team's withered balloon. They hit bottom the next Sunday in a 44–7 loss to Philadelphia. After the game several Eagles players remarked that the Lions had given up—when you hit them, they didn't even hit back.

The only bright note was the appointment of Bill Ford Jr., who had recently graduated Princeton, to the unpaid post of team treasurer. Lions fans, ever optimistic, took this as a sign that the heir apparent had arrived, and the reign of Bill Ford Sr. now had an expiration date.

◆

Bill Ford Sr.'s dream of assuming a top role at Ford Motor Company was, like his football team, headed for trouble. His name was in the conversation as a possible successor to Henry II as chief executive officer, the guy who ran the company day to day, or as chairman of the board, the guy who ran the board meetings half a dozen times a year. Bill Ford was having second thoughts about taking on the CEO job. "At first I thought, well maybe this would work out for me," he said, "and maybe it would be a good experience. Then, the more I thought about it, I decided I really didn't want the day-to-day responsibility it would entail. I would have to give up the Lions completely, which I didn't want to do."

Henry II took care of this problem by anointing plain vanilla Phil Caldwell to succeed him as chief executive officer. Bill was secretly relieved—the thought of those stacks of briefing books that went with the CEO's job made his head swim—and he was still hoping to be named chairman of the board when Henry II relinquished that role, which would involve little heavy lifting. It would also allow him to continue devoting most of his time and energy to the Lions. The family favored such a move, and Henry II seemed inclined to go along with it.

The Lions, meanwhile, finished the season with a 2–14 record, in last place in the NFC Central—tied with San Francisco for the worst record in all the NFL—which made Jimmy the Greek look more like an idiot than a savant.

Monte Clark, without going into full Pollyanna mode, tried to stress the positives, which is what coaches of losing teams usually do. Considering the twin quarterback disasters, the bar fight, and the inevitable deflation that comes with losing, Clark pointed out that the team had remained surprisingly competitive. "Even with all the problems last season, we weren't that far off," Clark insisted. "We were ahead in ten games and couldn't hold the lead. There were eight games that we lost by eight points or less. I know we can show that we're a better team than the records indicate." After two seasons, the records indicated that he was 9–23 as head coach.

As Ford Motor Company's board of directors prepared to meet in March 1980, vice-chairman Bill Ford and many others, both inside the company and inside the Ford family, expected Henry II to anoint Bill his successor as chairman of the board. But on the day of the meeting, without any advance warning, Henry II walked into Bill's office and told him there had been a change of plan. Phil Caldwell wanted to be CEO *and* chairman, and Henry II had decided to grant his wish. Bill Ford, according to the historian Robert Lacey, exploded.

"You treat your staff like that, you treat your wives like that," Bill roared at Henry II, who was in the process of negotiating a $16 million divorce settlement with Cristina so he could make Kathy DuRoss his third wife. "You treat your children like that—and now you treat your own brother the same way!"

It was the last battle in this bitter sibling rivalry, the completion of a circle begun that day a quarter-century earlier when Henry II had blithely let Bill's Continental Mark II die. Bill must have felt like Charlie Brown after allowing Lucy to persuade him that this time she really was going to hold the football in place so he could kick it. She *really and truly* was not going to swipe it away at the last instant. And then of course she did. And Charlie Brown/Bill Ford wound up flat on his back, gazing up at the big blue sky and realizing he had no one but himself to blame for, once again, agreeing to play the sucker.

THE SAVIOR (I)

The Lions' disastrous 1979 season meant they would get the top pick in the upcoming NFL draft, which was held on April 29, 1980, at the Sheraton Hotel in New York City. It was to be a red-letter date in the history of sports television.

A fledgling, content-starved cable TV operation called Entertainment and Sports Programming Network, now known simply as ESPN, wanted to televise the NFL draft for the first time. This revolutionary idea had its skeptics, including Bill Ford and his fellow team owners, who vetoed the idea unanimously, fearing it would give even more leverage to those bloodsuckers known as agents. Also among the skeptics was Pete Rozelle, who asked, "Who the heck would want to watch the NFL draft?" Which was another way of asking, Who in his right mind would tune in to watch a bunch of middle-aged guys talking for hours into telephones in a smoky hotel ballroom? It was a reasonable question. After all, in its early days ESPN offered some programming that could be generously described as schedule fillers. These included the US National Kayaking Championships, American Legion baseball and the Great Eastern Skeet Shooting Championships. All of which inspired the comedian George Carlin to describe ESPN's early fare as "cross-country bowling and Australian rules dick-wrestling."

But ESPN persisted and Rozelle finally agreed to ignore the owners' wishes and let the network broadcast the draft free of charge. Shortly after ten o'clock on that spring morning in 1980, Rozelle stood before the ESPN cameras and announced that the Detroit Lions had used the No. 1 overall pick to select Billy Sims of Oklahoma, the sensational running back who had won the Heisman Trophy during his junior year. There was loud applause—even though it was no secret that the Lions coveted Sims and that his agent and Russ Thomas were already locked in a nasty contract dispute.

Those contracts talks were the talk of the town in Detroit, and they came on the heels of another display of Russ Thomas's negotiating skills. With a healthy Gary Danielson set to qualify for free agency on Feb. 1, Thomas had gone into turtle mode. Rather than work out a fair contract, he was content to let Danielson entertain offers from other teams, then Thomas would decide if the Lions wanted to exercise their right to match the best offer. In effect, Thomas was willing to let other teams establish the market value of his most prized player—while letting that player twist in the wind. If you want to build team morale and a winning culture, this is exactly how not to do it.

What was the source of Thomas's nearly iron-clad job security and his pathological stinginess? Jerry Green repeated a common, if vague, rumor: "For personal reasons, [Bill Ford] is indebted to Russ Thomas for life." Green speculated that there was also a financial component to their bond: "Thomas, it is said, owns some Lions stock; therefore figures in the profits." And therefore had an incentive to keep salaries low so profits could remain high. It does make sense.

After no face-to-face meetings in more than a year, the quarterback and the general manager finally sat down for a four-hour, closed-door conversation. When he emerged from Thomas's office, Danielson quipped, "No bruises, no rug burns." And no contract. Using a page from his Ron Jessie playbook, Thomas had tried to persuade Danielson that the quarterback and the general manager should work out a deal by themselves, man to man, with no agent present. Danielson was no more inclined than Ron Jessie to play Thomas's con game. He told the GM, "It's only money, Russ."

Bill Ford had come to the same conclusion. He finally put his foot down and insisted that Thomas work out a contract with a player whose value had become apparent when his knee injury led directly to the nightmare of 1979. Hours before the free agency deadline, the suddenly generous Thomas announced that he and Danielson had agreed to a $195,000 one-year contract, the richest in team history. That contract had Bill Ford's fingerprints all over it.

Sims was next into the meat grinder. His agent was Dr. Jerry Argovitz, a former dentist from Houston who favored cowboy hats, three-piece suits, and sky-high opening contract demands. Argovitz came to the table insisting that his client be paid on the level of Larry Bird, who a year before had signed a $3.25 million five-year contract with the Boston Celtics of the NBA, making him the highest-paid rookie in sports history at about $650,000 a year. Billy Sims was in Larry Bird's league, Argovitz declared, and therefore he merited a $4.5 million contract over five seasons. Russ Thomas, contending that Sims had to prove himself in the NFL before he deserved that kind of money, made a counteroffer of $700,000. The two sides were a mere $3.8 million apart.

The Lions' offer was "a joke," as far as Argovitz was concerned. "Russ Thomas is an old football man, used to dealing with old numbers," he said. "Russ Thomas ought to run for Congress because he can balance the budget."

After he was selected with the top overall pick, Sims, at Argovitz's urging, declined to pose for the traditional photo op with his new Lions jersey. Asked what it would take to get his signature on a contract, Sims said, "It would just take Mr. Russ Thomas to wake up. He hasn't woke up yet."

The *New York Times* sports columnist Dave Anderson was interviewed by ESPN on draft day, and he sensed, rightly, that what was happening in the Sheraton ballroom was part of a much larger story—the eclipse of print by the irresistible power of moving images. "I always said that the draft was the last of the great newspaper stories," Anderson said, "but that no longer holds now that ESPN is here. For years our offices would get more calls on the draft during the day of the draft than on almost any other story that goes on all year. But now, at last, it is on television. And good for you."

And bad for the *New York Times* and every other newspaper in the land.

Four decades after that red-letter day at the Sheraton Hotel, the NFL Draft has morphed into a traveling three-day media circus that includes a red carpet, concerts, autograph sessions, photo ops, and, yes, seven torturous rounds of drafting college talent. In 2023 the show drew more than 300,000 fans to Kansas City, and more than 54 million watched on television and various streaming services. This moveable feast came to Detroit in April 2024—and drew a record-shattering 750,000 fans. It is one of the events that have turned the NFL into a seamless, year-round television show, beginning with a glorified meat market called the Scouting Combine in February, at which prospects perform various physical and mental tests under the watchful eyes and stopwatches of coaches, general managers, and scouts. Then comes the draft itself, followed by minicamps, training camps and exhibition games, the regular season, the playoffs, all of it culminating in the Gaudiest Show on Earth, the Super Bowl. And then the cycle revs up all over again. The beast never sleeps, and it's always on TV.

◆

While the contract negotiations between Thomas and Argovitz dragged along, Bill Ford, now fifty-five, traveled to Houston to undergo open-heart bypass surgery. Balky hearts bedeviled all three Ford brothers. Henry II's had recently sent him to the hospital, Benson's had helped send him to an early grave, and now Bill's sent him to Texas for major surgery. The operation was a success, which was more than could be said for the contract negotiations back in Detroit. Thomas and Argovitz slugged it out until June 9, when the two exhausted adversaries reached an agreement that would pay Billy Sims $2.5 million for three years of service, with an option in the third year. The final figure was almost exactly halfway between Argovitz's pie-in-the sky opening demand and Thomas's "joke" of a counteroffer. All those months of acrimony for nothing. It was the art of the deal, Russ Thomas–style.

This, of course, was not the first time the Lions had drafted a running back out of Oklahoma who'd won the Heisman Trophy. But it soon became apparent that Billy Sims was no Steve Owens. Sims was an explosive, inventive runner, a surefire star and, just possibly, the savior of a franchise that had solid building blocks in place and was long overdue for some good breaks. Fan interest, at a low ebb six months earlier, now went through the Big Muffin's Teflon roof.

Sims did not disappoint. In his very first game, against the favored Los Angeles Rams, he ran for 153 yards, caught passes for another 64 yards and scored three touchdowns, leading the way to a startling 41–20 win.

Sims quickly established a style of running that was a devastating blend of speed and raw power. He was able to elude or demolish defenders, as the situation required. Sometimes, instead of giving a potential tackler the conventional stiff arm, he *kicked the guy's face mask* with his cleats and continued on his way. He could dart like a jitterbug. He could vault over piles of bodies into the end zone. Nobody could do the things Billy Sims could do.

The Lions sprinted to a 4–0 start, their best since 1956. One giddy fan hoisted a banner at the Silverdome that read: IF IT WASN'T FOR THE PRICE OF GAS I'D SWEAR IT WAS 1957. By late September Sims's face was splashed on the cover of *Sports Illustrated*, which anointed him DETROIT'S SUPER ROOKIE. After each win, the roof of the Silverdome rippled from the sound of fans singing along with the song blasting from the public-address system—a home-made version of Queen's hit, "Another One Bites the Dust," recorded by the Lions' tight end David Hill and the defensive backs Jim Hunter and Jimmy "Spiderman" Allen. *"Are you ready, are you ready for this?"* they sang. *"Are you sitting on the edge of your seats? So come on out and watch the Detroit Lions no one seems to beat. And another one bites the dust. And another one, and another one, and another one bites the dust . . ."*

Nothing could dampen the euphoria in Detroit—not even a waterlogged and bumpy playing field. In the latest Silverdome snafu, crews had rolled up the Astroturf in January and loaded twenty-eight rolls onto railroad cars for the trip to a carpet cleaner in Greenville, Mississippi. The turf was unrolled on an abandoned runway at the local airport, where the cleaning was to take place. But torrential rains fell all winter, and the turf never got dry and only half of it got cleaned. When the sopping rolls were shipped north, they weighed six tons more than they'd weighed on the trip south, which helped push the cost of the half-assed cleaning job from $30,000 to $47,000. "The question is why they went to Mississippi," said a mystified Jose Santiago, the city's finance director. "All I can see is that they went out and spent $47,000 and didn't get the turf clean anyway."

Two players suffered knee injuries after tripping over the uneven seams, including the prized rookie Tom Turnure, who had to undergo season-ending surgery. After ten months of rehab, Turnure returned to the Silverdome wearing a massive brace on his left knee, hopeful he could restart his career in the 1981 season. "The field is unbelievably bad," he said. "Something should be done about it." But the city of Pontiac said it couldn't afford the $500,000 needed to replace the threadbare turf. Russ Thomas, though unhappy with the condition of the field, offered a tepid compliment: "This is not the worst conditions we play on."

The Silverdome's turf wasn't the only place where cracks were showing. In the wake of Danielson's and Sims's contract disputes, two stellar defensive linemen were fighting toxic wars with Russ Thomas that had started during training camp. First, Al "Bubba" Baker, a defensive end who'd been named defensive rookie of the year and had made the Pro Bowl twice, demanded a contract extension with a healthy raise. When Thomas balked, as he always did, Baker stayed away from training camp and sat out the season opener in Los Angeles. Baker sent a telegram to Thomas demanding to be traded, even put his house up for sale and started packing. Eventually Thomas, realizing he was about to drive off a star, came around and gave Baker a one-year extension worth $200,000 plus a $50,000 signing bonus. This, too, had a strong whiff of Bill Ford's quiet pressure. Baker got a warm welcome from his teammates when he returned to the locker room.

The veteran defensive tackle John Woodcock was another no-show at training camp. After sitting out the 1979 season while recuperating from back surgery, Woodcock was entering the option year of his contract, which meant the team was required by the collective bargaining agreement to give him a 10 percent raise, to $49,500, far below the average for a player with his experience and skill. At the end of the season, Woodcock would become eligible for free agency. Rather than meet Woodcock's demand for a new contract, Thomas let him twist in the wind, just as he had done with Gary Danielson. Woodcock played, but he kept boiling.

The veteran placekicker Benny Ricardo was also in his option year and was also hoping for a raise above the mandatory 10 percent. He walked out of training camp and started referring to Russ Thomas as "the Ayatollah," a reference to the Iranian leader who was then holding fifty-two Americans hostage in Tehran. When Ricardo's agent and Russ Thomas failed to reach a contract, Monte Clark put Ricardo on waivers. "You've never seen a guy so happy to be cut," Ricardo said. "I talked to [ex-Lions coach] Tommy Hudspeth before I left camp, and he said, 'If you want to get out of Detroit, walk out. When you confront Russ Thomas, you never win.'"

After their 4–0 start, the Lions came back down to Earth, losing three of their next four. The ninth game of the season, against the stumbling San Francisco 49ers, was seen as a must-win to get the Lions back on track to the playoffs. But on the Wednesday before the game, a fed up Woodcock tossed his football shoes into a garbage can, walked out of the locker room for the last time, then drove home to California. "I just can't take it anymore," Woodcock told a reporter shortly before his dramatic departure. "I just can't play for [Thomas]." Unnerved, the Lions came out flat against the 49ers the following Sunday but were saved when Gary Danielson scampered eight yards for a late touchdown that delivered an uncomfortably close 17–13 win. Instead of celebrating after the win, Danielson uncorked his bottled-up frustration over Russ Thomas's handling of player contracts, including his own, as well as the GM's rumored trespasses onto Monte Clark's turf.

"I think it's hurting our team," Danielson said of Woodcock's departure. "Obviously the whole thing is a joke. The guy comes back after an injury. He plays the game tough and strong, and he still can't get anything done on the contract. When [Thomas] starts using the word fair, I start laughing. That's the last thing he is—fair. I know what I had to go through."

Danielson wasn't finished. "A number of guys on the team are frustrated," he went on. "I'm sure this can come back and hurt me, but some things have to be said that the head coach can't say. Too many things are happening in the background—the questioning of game plans, the questioning of personnel moves. I just hope the head coach is making the decisions and not anybody else, [but] I wonder if everyone is pulling in the same direction. It's hurting us. We have 80,000 people at the games. We're selling out. People are begging us to win. There's got to be a better way."

Thomas shot back: "To say I suggested a quarterback change or a change in the game plan to [Monte Clark] is a damn lie."

Woodcock's agent, Howard Slusher, suggested that the general manager failed to notice the sellout crowds at the Silverdome because he was so busy trying to paint Woodcock as a "traitor" who'd tried to "blackmail" management. "It is," Slusher said, "Thomas at his best."

◆

After two costly one-point losses, the Lions wound up tied with the Vikings for the Central Division lead at the end of the season with identical 9–7 records. However, based on their winning percentages against NFC teams, the Vikings qualified for the playoffs and the Lions, once again, were left out. This one hurt the worst. They had come so close—if they had simply tied one of those two close losses, they would have gone to the playoffs. Billy Sims rushed for more than 1,300 yards and was named Rookie of the Year, but the Lions could not escape their fate of being second-best.

They even lost off the field. After the season, Michigan courts awarded sizeable workers' compensation claims to three former Lions whose careers were cut short by work-related injuries: tight ends Charlie Sanders and Jim Mitchell and running back Steve Owens. When the team announced it would appeal the rulings, Sanders told the *New York Times*: "I don't understand why the Lions are appealing my case. There is no question that the injury that cut down my career was sustained in a game for the Lions. They said so in a press release announcing my retirement."

Russ Thomas provided a cold answer: "We appeal all cases like this as a matter of course."

Sanders said he'd heard about his rights under workers' compensation laws "through the grapevine." Those laws, which vary from state to state, require employers, including the owners of professional football teams, to cover medical expenses and make cash payments when a worker suffers incapacitating injuries on the job. The three Lions' successful claims were yet another sign of how the times were changing. "Until now," the *Times* article concluded, "few football players took advantage of this law, but the NFL Players Association has recently launched an educational program, hiring lawyers knowledgeable in workers' compensation to explain it to players."

Sanders then asked the question that would soon come to haunt the NFL: "Has it turned into such a business that our physical well-being is expendable?"

THE AYATOLLAH'S
HUSH PUPPIES

Billy Sims suffered a sophomore slump in 1981. He had some spectacular games, some middling games, and he missed some games due to a painful toe injury. Gary Danielson went out with another injury, this time to his wrist, but his backup, little-used Eric Hipple, was a pleasant surprise. The team finished strong, crushing Minnesota in the penultimate game to set up a dramatic showdown in the season finale against Tampa Bay. The winner would go to the playoffs while the loser would go home for the winter. The largest crowd in team history, 80,444, showed up at the Silverdome to watch the Lions drop a sure touchdown pass, give up a fumble for one touchdown, give up an eighty-four-yard pass for another, and miss an easy field goal. History is destiny, and by now it was in the team's DNA to find a way to lose a game they could have, should have, won. And they did, losing 20–17. Season over.

The next game played in the Silverdome was on Jan. 24, 1982—Super Bowl XVI, between the San Francisco 49ers and the Cincinnati Bengals. Pete Rozelle's earlier quip about ice-fishing came back to bite him. A *Sports Illustrated* reporter named Paul Zimmerman, a man with a gift for pushing people's buttons, went on national television to say that Super Bowl week in Detroit reminded him of the Moscow Olympics with one difference: "the security guards in Moscow were nicer." The area around the Silverdome, he added, was a wasteland of "dirty snow and barbed wire—it's hideous, horrible."

He likened the press headquarters at Dearborn's Hyatt Regency Hotel to being "stuck out here in Siberia." For this, Zimmerman was challenged to a fistfight by a TV cameraman, who snarled, "I'll bet you're from New York."

"No," Zimmerman replied, "I'm from Hamtramck"—the city within the city of Detroit.

It was hard to argue with his central point. The wind-chill factor in Pontiac on game day was 21 degrees below zero, and pregame traffic outside the stadium got so clogged, thanks in part to the motorcade of Vice President George H. W. Bush, that many fans abandoned their cars and trudged to the stadium through the Arctic air. It was like a remake of *Nanook of the North*, minus the walrus hunt. Some fans arrived too late to hear Diana Ross sing the national anthem or watch Bobby Layne perform the coin toss, but once they thawed out they were treated to an entertaining game, won by San Francisco, 26–21.

After the game, a *Sports Illustrated* spokeswoman confirmed that numerous people had called in to cancel their subscriptions after hearing Zimmerman's remarks. "But," she was quick to point out, "people call in to cancel every year after we run our swimsuit issue, too."

◆

Pontiac wasn't the only place experiencing a chill. Whispers were swirling that the NFL Players Association might call a strike when the current collective bargaining agreement expired on July 15, 1982. To add to the chill, Billy Sims announced that he was not going to report to training camp until Russ Thomas lived up to his promise to renegotiate the upcoming option year on Sims's contract. Thomas, true to form, insisted he had made no such promise. Cue the perennial contract wars.

Monte Clark stayed out of the line of fire. Bill Ford, apparently satisfied with his coach's performance despite the blown chance to make the playoffs, gave Clark a new five-year contract worth $1.2 million.

When negotiators for the players and the owners failed to reach a new collective bargaining agreement by July 15, the Lions claimed they were not allowed to negotiate any new contracts—namely Sims's—until a new agreement was signed.

So Sims donned his cowboy hat and cowboy boots and went home to his ranch in Hooks, Texas. When Bill Ford called during the third week of the holdout, Sims was hopeful that a higher power had come to his rescue. But he was in for a disappointment—much like Sam Williams two decades earlier when he'd tried get around the general manager by appealing directly to the owner. After the call from Ford, Sims told reporters: "The conversation was a few minutes and it left me with a feeling he didn't care. He left it up to Russ. He didn't help anything. One of his servants could have called me. He just said his hands are tied."

Sims was learning what Sam Williams already knew: "Bill Ford will not say yes or no to *anything*."

Or as Sims's agent, Jerry Argovitz, put it: "Mr. Ford is afraid to step on anybody's toes. Apparently, Russ Thomas's Hush Puppies are more important than Billy Sims's boots."

Bill Ford responded to this witticism by calling Argovitz "a leech" and "an idiot" and "a Machiavellian con artist of the highest order."

Negotiators for the players and owners agreed to keep talking, which allowed the season to open on schedule, and Sims and the Lions reached an uneasy truce shortly before the opening kickoff. But after the Lions won their first two games over weak opponents, the collective bargaining talks broke down and the NFL Players Association called a strike. In addition to restive players, the NFL owners had another new source of worry: a rival league, calling itself the United States Football League, was opening for business and threatening to siphon off college players and NFL veterans, much as the AFL had done two decades earlier. The strike would drag on for fifty-seven days, into early November, wiping out two months of games. Under the settlement, the players won a seniority-based minimum wage scale, severance pay and $60 million in bonuses, but Ed Garvey, the executive director of the players' union, insisted the strike was primarily a psychological victory. "Management will never again take lightly the threat of the union shutting down the industry," he said. But Garvey had misread the room. The players didn't get the thing they wanted most: free agency, which Curt Flood had helped bring to baseball, the freedom to be worth whatever someone was willing to pay you. The players soon dumped Garvey.

When they returned to action, the Lions were out of sync and lost three straight games, leading Bill Ford to deride his team as "just a rag-tag operation all the way around." But that operation received an early Christmas present. The strike had forced the league to improvise a new playoff format, and it decided that at the end of the nine-game season, eight teams from each conference would qualify for the playoffs. The Lions' 4–5 record was good enough for the NFC's eighth seed—one of a handful of times in league history that a losing team qualified for the playoffs.

Playing against top-seeded Washington, the eventual winner of the Super Bowl, the Lions were exposed for the impostors they were, getting so badly trounced that CBS switched to the St. Louis-Green Bay game during the third quarter. When the final whistle mercifully sounded, the Lions limped off the field on the short end of a 31–7 thrashing. Billy Sims had rushed for just nineteen yards and fumbled twice in the biggest game of his career. He described his season as "mediocre." It was a word that seemed to keep cropping up when people talked about the Detroit Lions.

◆

The Lions opened the following season by losing four of their first five games, but then Monte Clark worked his magic and the team reversed field, winning four of its last five to claim the Central Division title. The Lions had made the playoffs in back-to-back seasons, though the feat merited an asterisk because of the strike.

This year was different, though. The Lions traveled to San Francisco believing they could reach the Super Bowl, and in the divisional round they gave the 49ers everything they could handle. The Lions outgained their hosts 412 yards to 291, Billy Sims atoned for last year's dud by running for 116 yards, catching four passes, and scoring two touchdowns. But San Francisco's quarterback, Joe Montana, engineered a brilliant scoring drive to give the 49ers a one-point lead late in the fourth quarter. The Lions weren't done yet. With five seconds left, Eddie Murray launched a forty-three-yard field goal attempt. It sailed wide by inches. Final score: San Francisco 24, Detroit 23.

After the game, Bill Ford said, "I'm very proud of this team."

Most of the games in 1984 were also close. Unfortunately, most of them were also losses. The brief playoff euphoria and the novelty of Billy Sims had worn off, and Silverdome sellouts were a thing of the past. Team officials blamed the attendance decline on the popularity of the Tigers, who had riveted the city as they stormed to the American League pennant and got ready to take on the San Diego Padres in the World Series. The Tigers, unlike the Lions, were stocked with magnetic stars—Kirk Gibson, Lou Whitaker, Alan Trammell, Jack Morris, and Willie Hernandez, among others—and the crowds were as big and electric as they'd been in 1968.

The fifth game of the World Series was played at Tiger Stadium on Sunday, Oct. 14, the day the Lions hosted Tampa Bay at the Silverdome. Leading three games to one, the Tigers could seize the championship with a win, and more than 51,000 fans flocked to the corner of Michigan and Trumbull, hoping to witness history. They were not disappointed. Kirk Gibson, who'd starred in football at Michigan State, whacked a three-run homer in the bottom of the eighth inning to secure a Series-clinching 8–4 win. Once again there was dancing in the streets of the Motor City.

That day in Pontiac, 44,308 fans showed up for the Lions game, the smallest turnout in Silverdome history. Many of them were gone by the time the Lions scored in overtime for a 13–7 win, and the next day's recap in the *News* read like an obituary: "The Lions clearly have fallen out of favor with their fans. People were leaving in the fourth quarter with the game tied. They didn't care who won." But the real killer was yet to come.

The following Sunday was a day few Detroit Lions fans will ever forget. The Lions took their 2–5 record to Minnesota to play the Vikings, where players likened the Metrodome's artificial turf to a sidewalk. On his first run of the game, Billy Sims set the Lions' all-time rushing record. Then, midway through the third quarter of a tight game, Sims took a handoff and headed to his right. When he planted his right foot to cut back against the grain, his foot snagged in the artificial turf, freezing him. As tacklers arrived, Sims felt his right knee give out. Lying on the field, he recalled later, "I said, 'Wow, I sure thought I had torn something.'"

The Lions' tight end Rob Rubick recalled the scene vividly thirty years later: "I do remember him lying there and like pounding the turf, and . . . I'm thinking, 'We're fucked.' It's like the Curse of the Lions. I'm not a believer in curses, but if there were such a thing, we definitely would have one."

Sims said he had never felt such pain, and he had to be helped off the field. After the game, a team doctor speculated that Sims would have to stay off his knee "two or three days." Sims added, "It's not that bad."

No, it was much worse. An arthroscopy revealed that Sims had sustained severe tendon and ligament damage, and on Tuesday he underwent surgery at Ford Hospital. He would be out, at the very least, for the rest of the season.

WHITE BOY RICK

This was the season when crack cocaine—cheap, smokable, highly addictive and highly profitable little white rocks—began to course through the streets of American cities. In Detroit, "the crack mecca of the Midwest," according to the reporter William M. Adler, this lucrative trade was dominated by a handful of ingenious entrepreneurs, including an unlikely local legend, a baby-faced white teenager known as White Boy Rick, who was destined to become the subject of a Hollywood movie and the recipient of a long federal prison sentence. It was revealed later that while he was moving major quantities of cocaine into Detroit, White Boy Rick was also working a sideline as an FBI informant. His rivals included a family posse from the Arkansas cotton patches, the Chambers brothers, along with Young Boys Inc., Best Friends, Johnny and Leo Curry, and "Maserati Rick" Carter, who was gunned down in his hospital bed while recovering from gunshot wounds suffered in an unsuccessful hit. The dealers were as vicious and colorful as the Purple Gang from the days of Prohibition, and their mastery of vertical integration, production, quality control, distribution and retribution would have made Alfred Sloan and old Henry Ford drool with envy. At their peak, the Chambers brothers ran a four-story crack emporium out of the derelict Broadmoor apartment building that was grossing more a million dollars a week. One reason for the dealers' success, aside from their business acumen, was that they enjoyed a virtually limitless market for their product. There was no shortage of people in this blighted city who were willing to trade ten dollars for a brief ecstatic escape from a life without a job, without hope or purpose, or the prospect of anything remotely approaching ecstasy. Even successful people kept coming back to the Broadmoor again and again once they'd smoked a few of those addictive little white rocks. It was all about repeat business.

The dealers, while no strangers to pressure from the police, enjoyed an exalted status south of Eight Mile Road. Johnny Curry's fiancée, for instance, was Cathy Volsan, a niece of Mayor Coleman Young. When the couple had a child, Young hosted the baby shower at the Manoogian Mansion, the mayoral residence near the Detroit River, a bash that attracted a long line of luxury cars filled with the city's drug lords and their wives and girlfriends. Mayor Motherfucker treated Volsan like a daughter, according to an extensive report on the city's crack trade by the investigative reporter Evan Hughes. "Young sought to protect her," Hughes wrote. "As a police sergeant later testified, as many as four officers monitored Volsan and her mother, the mayor's sister, around the clock at taxpayer expense . . . These police looked on while Volsan socialized with the city's drug bosses, and they tried to keep her out of potentially embarrassing situations." Your tax dollars at work.

Meanwhile, the Motor City was burning again—but not from sparks thrown off by racial friction. Now a uniquely Detroit tradition known as Devil's Night reached its twisted zenith when, on the night before Halloween, arsonists targeted the ample supply of abandoned, boarded-up structures, turning this kindling into more than eight-hundred soaring bonfires. As word of the yearly torchings spread, fireflies came from around the corner and around the world to witness the spectacle. The writer Ze'ev Chafets called it "the fire buff's Super Bowl." If Detroit couldn't get into the real Super Bowl, well, it would create its own bizarre flaming surrogate. Unlike the fires of 1967, which were a response to ingrained injustice, these fires were mere spectacle: pointless, vaguely suicidal. They announced that Detroit was a city on the verge of a nervous breakdown—or maybe the breakdown had already happened. It was mystifying. No one knew what to make of so much mad fire.

◆

For the next few years we can speed up the projector because the Lions' movie rarely changes. Players come and go, fan interest continues to ebb, and what happens on the field is a virtual replay from one year to the next: the team finishes no higher than third place, fails to post a winning record, never makes the playoffs.

Part of the reason was the announcement in the summer of 1986 that after nearly two years of rehab, Billy Sims could still not make cuts with his right knee, an essential tool of his trade. His career was over. In four and a half seasons he had rushed for more than 5,000 yards. A potential Hall of Fame career had been cut short.

Two noteworthy lives were soon cut short. The years of high living finally caught up with Bobby Layne, who was a physical wreck when he died of cardiac arrest at the age of fifty-nine; and Henry Ford II, no stranger to high living, power struggles and the starring role in his own globe-trotting soap opera, died from complications of pneumonia just weeks after his seventieth birthday. Bill was now the last Ford brother standing.

After firing Monte Clark and his nine assistants, Ford had brought in Darryl Rogers, a successful coach at several colleges, including Michigan State, who had no experience in the NFL. Shades of Rick Forzano and Tommy Hudspeth. Given the title of head coach and director of football operations, Rogers, known for his quick wit and relaxed approach, led the team to two straight losing seasons.

The NFL Players Association went on strike again after the fourth week of the 1987 season, which led to the cancellation of one week's games and the hiring of strike-breaking players to keep the turnstiles spinning. A few nights after the Lions' scabs lost to the Seahawks' scabs in front of a handful of fans in the Silverdome, the Lions' defensive coordinator, Wayne Fontes, crashed his car and wound up getting charged with drunken driving and possession of a small amount of cocaine. Fontes kept his job, and the Lions kept foundering.

Late that season, with the team on a four-game losing streak, Rogers began to hear rumors that his job was in jeopardy. One day the beat reporters who covered team practices were surprised to see Bill Ford walk onto the field. He chatted with the sportswriters for a while before announcing that Rogers would definitely be back next season. After practice, when a reporter asked Rogers how he felt about Ford's vote of confidence, the coach quipped, "What's a guy have to do to get fired around here?"

Rogers got his answer when the team got off to a 2–9 start in 1988. After a loss to Tampa Bay in a one-third-full Silverdome, Ford finally put Rogers out of his misery and promoted Wayne Fontes to interim head coach. By then Fontes had pleaded guilty to drunken driving and gotten the cocaine possession charge thrown out on an illegal-search technicality. The team finished with a 4–12 record, tied for last place.

After years of waffling, Bill Ford finally put his foot down and insisted that Russ Thomas adhere to the mandatory retirement age of sixty-five and step down after the 1989 season. To get technical about it, Thomas turned sixty-five on July 24, 1989, so if Ford had been serious about observing the mandatory retirement age, he would have shown Thomas the door *before* the 1989 season. But Ford, the man who could not say yes or no to *anything*, let Thomas take one last lap. It was a way to get rid of him without actually taking forceful action to get rid of him—the ideal solution for a man like Bill Ford, whose indecisiveness and sense of loyalty rendered him constitutionally incapable of making such an unpleasant and long-overdue decision.

At the last draft under the Russ Thomas regime, the Lions caught an unexpected break. They had the third pick in the opening round, and they watched, delighted, as the Dallas Cowboys used the first pick to take future

Hall of Fame quarterback Troy Aikman and the Green Bay Packers used the second pick to take the offensive lineman Tony Mandarich.

It was a stunning blunder by Green Bay—Mandarich would last just four seasons with the team—and it meant that the Heisman Trophy winner from Oklahoma State, a running back destined to become one of the greatest players in the history of the game, was still available. The Lions actually did the right thing.

They drafted Barry Sanders.

THIRD QUARTER

ROCK BOTTOM

(1989-2014)

THE SAVIOR (II)

As the 1989 season approached, Wayne Fontes was given a five-year contract and named permanent head coach. Like his predecessors, he was given control of all football operations. A big, gregarious guy who favored fat cigars, atrocious shirts, and even more atrocious sweaters, Fontes jumped into the job with gusto. He referred to himself as "the Big Buck" because he believed there was a bull's-eye on his back and everyone was gunning for him. One fan referred to him as "a cartoonish goofball."

It was still not known who would be called upon to fill Russ Thomas's outsized Hush Puppies at the end of the season, though there appeared to be two front-runners for the job. One was Chuck Schmidt (no kin to Joe), a CPA by trade who'd started out as the Lions' accountant in 1976 and had risen to become controller, then vice president for finance; the other was Jerry Vainisi, the team's vice president for player personnel for the past two seasons. Vainisi appeared to be the stronger candidate. He was an accountant and lawyer by training who'd spent eleven years as controller and treasurer of the Chicago Bears before becoming the team's general manager in 1983. In that role, working hand in glove with the irascible coach Mike Ditka, he helped assemble the machine that steamrolled its way to three straight Central Division titles and the Super Bowl championship in 1985, but he was fired a year later in a power struggle with team president Michael McCaskey. The NFL, such a fickle mistress. When Vainisi had arrived in Detroit in 1987, he was given the vague title of "in-house counsel," but soon he was doing what he did best—acquiring players—which put him in direct conflict with Darryl Rogers, the director of football operations, and Russ Thomas, the lame-duck general manager.

It was hard to find fault with Vainisi's track record in Chicago or the moves he'd made since arriving in Detroit. His philosophy was simple: coaches coach, scouts scout, and you build champions through the draft, not trades. He promptly drafted four players who had the potential to be foundation stones for long-term success: safety Bennie Blades and linebacker Chris Spielman in 1988, and Barry Sanders and quarterback Rodney Peete the following year. Now it fell to Chuck Schmidt to get Sanders's signature on a contract.

Schmidt had been involved in negotiating player contracts for several years, and he had amassed an impressive track record. All draft picks were signed before training camp had opened in the summer of 1988, an unimaginable achievement under penny-pinching Russ Thomas. But with Sanders the stakes had taken a quantum leap, and Schmidt found himself in a good, old-fashioned alley fight with Sanders's ambitious agents, C. Lamont Smith and David Ware.

To be fair, Schmidt's struggle to sign Barry Sanders was hardly an anomaly. This was known as the Year of the Holdout, when three of the top five draft picks—Barry Sanders, Deion Sanders, and Derrick Thomas—remained unsigned. (The top pick, Troy Aikman, had no reason to hold out; after the Dallas Cowboys offered him an $11 million, six-year contract, his only question was, *Where's the pen?*) Part of the reason for the holdouts may be that all three players believed, correctly, that they were destined for the Hall of Fame and they intended to be rich by the time they got there—and for years afterward. Another factor was that they all hired agents who knew leverage when they saw it and weren't afraid to use it.

C. Lamont Smith and David Ware had an added incentive. They were hungry young Black men trying to break into a game that was undergoing rapid but uneven change. While there were more Black players in the NFL every year, the ranks of owners, general managers, coaches, and agents remained overwhelmingly white. As they set out to woo Sanders, Smith, and Ware were under added pressure because no Heisman Trophy winner had ever been represented by a Black agent. Part of the reason for this, in Smith's opinion, was that most Black athletic prospects had not yet broken free of deeply ingrained illusions. "The difficulty for Blacks in sports management," Smith told *Ebony* magazine, "is getting over the mental block that many athletes and their families have about dealing with other Blacks. So many Blacks still believe that the white man is magic, that his ice is colder."

Barry Sanders's father harbored no illusions about whose ice was colder. William Sanders of Wichita, Kansas, was a roofer by trade, the father of eleven children, a man who knew the meaning of work and who looked at the world through cold, clear eyes. Those eyes could see that his son's talent was the family's ticket to a new way of life, and William intended to see that the ticket got properly punched. When Barry announced his intention to play his senior season at Oklahoma State after winning the Heisman as a junior, his father flew into a rage, screaming at Barry that he was a fool not to grab the iron while it was hot. Eventually Barry caved in and entered the NFL draft a year early. When the elder Sanders agreed to meet the prospective agent Smith at his favorite soul-food restaurant in Wichita, he showed up in a tam-o'-shanter and shades, chewing on his perpetual cigar. Papa Sanders had come to size up this slick guy from Denver. Was he just another hustler, or someone to be trusted? The two men hit it off that day, and after a long courtship, William Sanders told his son to ignore the advice of his college coaches, who wanted him to sign with established agents, and instead go with the two hungry young Black agents. Once again Barry, a dutiful son, obeyed.

After successfully petitioning the NFL to allow Sanders to enter the draft a year before graduation based on his family's economic hardship,

Smith and Ware rolled up their sleeves and started negotiating with the Detroit Lions. They soon hit a roadblock. Its name was Chuck Schmidt.

"He was a numbers guy, a bean counter," Smith recalled in a recent interview. "I don't feel he understood how value is created in professional sports teams—by winning games and drawing people to the stadium. Our position with Barry was always that he's different, he's not going to be put into a running-back box. He's a *franchise* player. Chuck Schmidt's approach was to save a nickel and save a dime rather than increase value. It's hard to negotiate with people who are not moved by logic. Chuck did not want to be moved by logic."

There was a logical reason for this: Chuck Schmidt had learned his craft at the knee of Russ Thomas, the nickel-and-dime master.

The two sides slugged it out for five months while fans in Detroit agonized and Sanders worked out by himself in California. Finally, three days before the season opener, a truce was announced. Sanders agreed to a five-year contract with a complex formula of salary, signing bonus, incentives, and annuities that pushed its potential total value to $9.3 million.

Three days later, Mike O'Hara of the *Detroit News* was in the Silverdome press box getting ready to cover the Lions' season opener against the Arizona Cardinals. Before the opening kickoff, O'Hara saw something he'd never seen before. A Lions coach had set up a blocking dummy in one of the end zones, and Barry Sanders, who'd missed training camp and had practiced with the team just once, was ordered to slam into the dummy, again and again and again. The goal of this unusual exercise was to reacquaint Sanders with physical contact, to quickly get him into what's called "football shape."

Like everyone else in the building, O'Hara spent the first half checking the Detroit bench to see if Sanders was about to get sent onto the field, secretly hoping it would happen. Such a hope put O'Hara in danger of breaking the First Commandment of the NFL press box: Thou Shalt Not

Cheer or Boo or Otherwise Show Favoritism or Disdain for Any Team or Player.

In self-defense, O'Hara says his hope was driven by the reporter's primal itch, not by partisanship. "I was hoping for a good story," O'Hara said recently. "And a good story was him playing."

Sanders remained on the sidelines through the listless first half, which ended with Phoenix leading 6–3. Then, with 5:24 left in the third quarter, everyone—fans and sportswriters alike—had their wish come true.

"When Sanders trotted out to the huddle," O'Hara said, "a buzz started to build."

Sanders was wearing the number 20 on his jersey, the number worn by Lem Barney and Billy Sims. Many fans were surprised to see that Sanders was not particularly big for an NFL running back—just 5'8" tall and a shade over 200 pounds—but he, unlike Lem Barney and Billy Sims, had legs that looked like a pair of pistons.

"When he got the ball the first time, the buzz turned into a roar," O'Hara said. "It was an electrifying moment."

Sent straight up the middle, Sanders sliced through the line, juked to his left and scampered for an eighteen-yard gain, instantly showing off all of his tools: speed, power, timing, and a nearly magical ability to change directions so abruptly that befuddled tacklers were left grabbing at air. On his fourth run, Sanders scored the first touchdown of his NFL career. The Silverdome erupted. When Sanders jogged off the field, Wayne Fontes wrapped him in a bear hug and shouted above the roar, "I love you!" So did the city of Detroit.

After the Lions lost the game on a last-minute field goal, Mitch Albom of the *Free Press* aptly rated Sanders's debut "an Oscar-winning performance in a B-movie." Many sequels were to follow. Though Sanders eviscerated opposing defenses on a weekly basis, the Lions lost their next four games. By then Mike O'Hara, who had watched and written about a small army of brilliant running backs, needed just four words to rate Barry Sanders: "Best I ever saw."

As Sanders's rookie season unfolded, Russ Thomas and Jerry Vainisi were at war with each other. As far as Thomas was concerned, Vainisi was a little too fond of seeing his name in the papers, not always prudent in the politically charged NFL and especially not in the Detroit Lions' front office. Thomas also resented Vainisi's popularity in league circles and with the national media. It was Thomas who had brought Vainisi to Detroit, but they were locked in a bitter feud, barely on speaking terms.

While management feuded, the Lions, led by their rookie running back and a journeyman quarterback named Bob Gagliano, won six of their last seven games, including their last five. Sanders rushed for a staggering 1,470 yards and was the hands-down rookie of the year. Though the Lions finished the season with a 7–9 record and missed the playoffs, they had momentum. And a new savior.

At the end of the season, Sanders gave each offensive lineman a Rolex watch. This tight-knit band of bruisers dubbed themselves "the Road Crew" because they paved the way for Sanders's mesmerizing runs. They considered it noble work, and so did Sanders. Though no one knew it at the time, the rupture of their bond would lead to one of the darkest days in this franchise's dark history.

A ROLLERCOASTER ON STEROIDS

In the last weeks of his long career with the Lions, Russ Thomas gave numerous valedictory interviews, occasionally growing so emotional that he had to swat away a tear with a big meaty hand. One headline described him as THE SADLY MISUNDERSTOOD LION OF WINTER. Thomas defended his record and tried to focus on the good memories, but from time to time he let a hint of petulance slip out. As in: "I'm not sure people want to know when I do something that works out."

Considering his feud with Jerry Vainisi, it's hardly surprising that Thomas pushed for his protégé, Chuck Schmidt, as his successor, and it's even less surprising that Bill Ford listened to his trusted water carrier one last time. But there was a wrinkle. When the changing of the guard was formally announced at a late-December press conference, the longtime general manager's successor was not named the general manager. It was as though the very title had been tainted by Thomas's prolonged overkill of mediocrity.

Instead, Chuck Schmidt was given the title of executive vice president and chief operating officer. He made it clear at his introductory press conference that he had a simple, self-effacing philosophy: "Work hard, keep your mouth shut, and good things will happen." Then, with a fist pump, he added: "Hooray for the bean counters!" Now the Lions would be run by an accountant rather than an accomplished football mind. Schmidt was described in the press as "a loyal soldier" and "a skinny Russ Thomas."

Some saw Schmidt's elevation as the latest episode in the Lions' oldest story—promoting the wrong guy and letting the right guy get away. There was widespread sentiment that the right guy this time around was Jerry Vainisi, and Jerry Vainisi obviously agreed. Five months after Schmidt's promotion, Vainisi resigned from the Lions to help launch the World League of American Football, later called NFL Europe. Vainisi claimed that his departure from the Lions had nothing to do with getting bypassed for the GM's job, but few believed him. He did take a parting shot at Thomas. "The organization is unified now," Vainisi said. "They're all pulling together for a common purpose. It was never the case during the three years I was there." And there was no doubt where Vainisi laid the blame.

◆

Lost in Barry Sanders's pyrotechnics on the field and the warfare in the front office was a revealing glimpse into the soul of the Detroit Lions. It was provided by the retired tight end, Charlie Sanders.

After all his battles with Lions management—the snubbed requests for contract renegotiations, the misdiagnosis of his injuries, the suspicion that he was goldbricking, the team's appeal of his workers' compensation award—Charlie Sanders and the Lions' organization had managed to arrive at a reconciliation. Unable to stay away from the game he loved and still feeling a deep attachment to the only team he ever played for, Sanders swallowed his bitterness and went to work on the team's radio broadcasts. After developing admiration for Wayne Fontes and the staff he was assembling, Sanders asked if he could play a role. Fontes hired him as assistant coach for tight ends in 1989, Barry Sanders's rookie season. To top it off, Charlie Sanders published a memoir in 2005 that papered over any bitter feelings while celebrating the team's colorful history, its camaraderie and occasional triumphs. He even gave Russ Thomas a pass.

Charlie Sanders's journey was a vivid display of the team's yin and yang, its dark side and its light side, its history of bitter partings with star players followed by a long cold war that gives way to a slow thaw and an eventual reconciliation. It had happened with Bobby Layne, who left town in tears for Pittsburgh in 1958 and was welcomed back a quarter-century later to perform the coin toss before the 1982 Super Bowl. It happened again with Charlie Sanders, and it would keep happening with countless other stars. This yin and yang became as much a part of the team's culture as quarterback controversies, contract squabbles, second-place finishes, the revolving door in the coach's office, and an owner who had no clue how to fix any of it.

The long-suffering fans got another dose of disappointment when the team failed to build on the momentum of 1989 and slipped to a 6–10 record the following season. Like Billy Sims before him, Barry Sanders also "slipped" in his sophomore season—running for 1,304 yards, which was fewer than his rookie season but still more than any other NFL running back. It was an indication of just how high he had set the bar.

During the offseason, word came from Naples, Florida, that Russ Thomas had died in his sleep at the age of sixty-six, barely a year into his forced retirement. While few tears were shed by Lions players or fans for one of the most divisive figures in the history of the organization, Chuck Schmidt offered a nimble eulogy for his mentor: "Deep down he was much more sensitive than people could see. He had a very big tender side to him. Very few players ever found it, but when they did they saw a different side of Russ Thomas." The *New York Times* obituary offered a summation of Thomas's career that went a long way toward explaining why the paper was known as the Gray Lady: "He developed a reputation as a tough but fair bargainer, determined to hold down salaries." It was like saying the Lilliputians were determined to hold down Gulliver.

◆

There are many ways to describe the Lions of 1991. Jekyll & Hyde. A Rollercoaster on Steroids. From week to week the team careened from disaster to triumph to tragedy to bliss to crushing disappointment. The wild ride opened with a 45–0 humiliation at the hands of the powerful Washington Redskins, followed by four straight wins. Then—get ready for a little whiplash—a 35–3 thrashing by the San Francisco 49ers followed a week later by a 34–10 thrashing of the Dallas Cowboys, in which the Lions' starting quarterback Rodney Peete suffered a season-ending Achilles tendon injury: trauma and triumph in a single afternoon.

Three weeks later, trauma gave way to tragedy. After throwing a block, offensive lineman Mike Utley landed awkwardly on his head and suffered a severe injury to two vertebrae in his neck. Unable to move from his chest down, Utley was placed on a stretcher, and as he was wheeled off the field he gave his teammates the thumbs-up sign. Shell-shocked, they regrouped to win that game, and then, while wearing stickers on their helmets with Utley's number 60, they rattled off five straight wins to finish the season at 12–4, taking the Central Division title, earning a bye in the wild card round and at least one home playoff game. Linebacker Chris Spielman had a simple explanation how Utley's injury affected the team: "We owe it to him to be our best." The thumbs-up gesture became the team's signature. Utley's football career was over. He never walked again.

The Silverdome was packed and rocking when the Dallas Cowboys came to town for one of two divisional playoff games. This one had star power—it featured the league's top two running backs in Sanders and the Cowboys' Emmitt Smith—and it was proof of C. Lamont Smith's claim that value is created in professional sports by winning games and drawing people to the stadium.

The 80,000 people in the stadium on this day got their money's worth. With the Dallas defense keyed to bottle up Sanders, the Lions' backup quarterback Erik Kramer exploited the thin secondary, throwing for 341 yards and three touchdowns. Sanders, despite the heavy traffic, shook loose for a thrilling forty-seven-yard touchdown burst that put the game away—and sent Bill Ford into a fit of ecstatic screaming.

As the clock wound down on the Lions' 38–6 victory, Ford made his way from the owner's box to the sidelines to savor the moment with his team. When the final whistle sounded, the players did what players were obliged to do for the TV cameras in such moments: they snuck up behind the coach and the owner and doused them with a tubful of icy Gatorade. The elegant, sixty-six-year-old multimillionaire, to his credit, wiped away the icy sludge and laughed himself silly. It was the last time he would be able to laugh with such abandon.

The next test was sterner. To win the NFC championship game—and a ticket to the franchise's first Super Bowl—the Lions had to travel to Washington and beat the team that had demolished them in the season opener. The Redskins were favored to win the rematch by at least two touchdowns. Nobody gave the Lions a chance. Perfect, said the faithful.

The night before the game, the Lions' chaplain Dave Wilson was holding his regular pregame service in the team hotel. "The goal is to win tomorrow," he told the players, "to get to the Super Bowl—"

"You're wrong," said the linebacker Chris Spielman, rising to his feet. "That's not the goal—because the goal is not to get to the Super Bowl. The goal is to *win* the Super Bowl." Then Spielman sat down.

Things did not start well the next day for the visitors. Erik Kramer fumbled on the Lions' second offensive play, and after four minutes the team was down 10–0. But they didn't fold. They trailed by just one touchdown at halftime even though Kramer was mercilessly harassed and Barry Sanders was handcuffed. They believed they still had a chance. But after a Detroit field goal attempt was blocked in the third quarter and the Redskins promptly connected on a forty-five-yard touchdown pass, the air seemed to go out of the afternoon. "Somewhere in the parking lot," Mitch Albom wrote in the next day's *Free Press*, "the Lions' driver started the bus."

The Redskins scored twice more on another long pass and an interception return, and a close game turned into a 41–10 rout.

Snow began to fall after the game. As the tomb-like Lions team bus pulled away from the stadium, Wayne Fontes looked out the window and saw a man and a woman standing across the street, looking like a couple of out-of-towners waiting for a taxi that would never come. Fontes realized it was Bill and Martha Ford. He ordered the driver to stop the bus, then he stepped out into the snow, walked up to the Fords, and suggested they wait for their ride inside the warm bus. Bill Ford declined, saying they didn't want to interfere with the team.

As they made small talk, Fontes began to apologize for the team's play that day. Ford cut him off. "I understand," he said. "Maybe next year. This is the best we've been in years, and it's been a great run."

Then the Fords' car pulled up and drove them off into the snow while Fontes climbed back onto the bus and headed for the airport. It was the closest the Lions would get to the Super Bowl in Bill Ford's lifetime.

ANOTHER SICKENING THUD

Maybe next year didn't happen. Two more tragedies struck in the offseason, adding to the mounting evidence that this team was cursed. The Lions' left guard, Eric Andolsek, one of the blocks of granite in the Road Crew, was killed in a freak accident when a truck ran off the road and struck him while he was doing yard work at his home in Louisiana; and Wayne Fontes's brother Len, the Lions' defensive backs coach, died of a heart attack at fifty-four. Quarterback Rodney Peete wondered, "How much more pain can this team take?"

Not much, as it turned out. The team never recovered, tumbling to a 5–11 finish and last place in the NFC Central Division, even though Barry Sanders, buoyed by a renegotiated contract, surpassed Billy Sims's team rushing record in just his fourth season. While the Lions were missing the playoffs, the Dallas Cowboys, the team the Lions had beaten soundly twice the prior season, were headed in the opposite direction, winning the first of their three Super Bowls during the decade.

That fall, after years of nasty legal wrangling, a federal court ruled that the NFL owners' limited system of free agency, a remnant of the reserve clause known as Plan B, was a violation of antitrust laws. By the end of the year, all twenty-eight owners approved an agreement in principle that would grant players unrestricted free agency after four years of service. A year later, an as-yet-undetermined salary cap would kick in to shield owners from the thing they dreaded most: an all-out bidding war for top talent. A new age had arrived. An NFL player was now worth as much as an owner was willing to pay him. And until the salary cap kicked in, the sky was the limit.

Bill Ford's lifelong sense of noblesse oblige flew out the window that day. "We're going to do whatever you can do, and we're going to do it very forcefully," he vowed. "If it means buy a team, we're going to buy a team."

It didn't work out quite that way. Ford didn't hand Chuck Schmidt a stack of blank checks and tell him to go shopping. But when the coveted free agent guard Harry Galbreath spurned the Lions and signed with the Packers, Ford jumped. "I got on the phone real quick," he said. "I had a very matter-of-fact conversation with Chuck Schmidt. I wanted to make sure we stepped up to the plate in a hurry." Sounding like the Godfather, he added, "I wanted to make offers they couldn't refuse."

Schmidt, able to spend more freely, got busy making offers that were nearly impossible to refuse. He succeeded in shoring up the offensive line with free agents, trading a first-round draft pick for the proven pass rusher Pat Swilling (who would turn out to be a bust), and matching the Cowboys' offer sheet on Erik Kramer, a valued backup quarterback. The club also re-signed the offensive tackle and free agent Lomas Brown, a close friend of Barry Sanders.

Sanders was impressed by Ford's new aggressiveness. "He backed up his talk," Sanders said. "That's something that players really look for in management. They're putting us in the best position to win. I know we're a lot more optimistic."

The revamped Lions, a year removed from the twin tragedies of the previous offseason, responded by reprising their Jekyll & Hyde act in 1993. Hot streaks gave way to cold streaks, the offensive coordinator Dan Henning got axed in mid-season, and starting quarterback Rodney Peete got benched. The Lions capped this schizo season by beating the Bears and Packers to win another Central Division title with a 10–6 record. Even though he sat out the last five games of the regular season with a sprained knee, Barry Sanders rushed for more than 1,000 yards for the fifth consecutive year.

The playoffs opened with a home rematch against the Packers in the wild card round. With Barry Sanders back in action and performing like Barry Sanders, the Lions took the lead with a fourth-quarter touchdown. With the game apparently in hand, they promptly demonstrated that even though they were much improved, they were still their own worst enemy. Late in the third quarter they had given up a 101-yard interception return for a touchdown, an NFL playoff record, and now, with the Packers on a desperate last-minute drive, quarterback Brett Favre lofted a forty-yard pass that seemed to stay airborne for a week. As the ball began its lazy descent, players and fans realized that the Green Bay receiver Sterling Sharpe was all by his lonesome in the end zone, with no defender in the same zip code—thanks to crossed signals among the defensive backfield. Sharpe cradled the pass for his third touchdown of the day, the Packers closed out the 28–24 victory, and another Lions season ended with a sickening thud.

◆

Bill Ford had started moonlighting. After stepping down as vice chairman of Ford Motor Company, he had remained on the board of directors and its powerful executive and finance committees. Always a night owl, he now started showing up at the office late in the day and working into the night as a consultant on the design of a new Jaguar sports car. A lifelong lover of fast cars, especially the British Jags and MGs he'd seen on European trips with his father, Ford was thrilled to get back to one of his first loves, automotive design. Ford Motor Company had bought Jaguar for $2.6 billion in 1989, part of an ill-advised spree of buying up high-end foreign brands, including Land Rover, Volvo, and Aston Martin. At the time, Jaguar was losing $400 million a year, and a new two-seater was seen as a key to a badly needed company revival. Bill Ford was back in the car game, back to the heady days of the Continental Mark II. This time, though, his unerring eye for style and his sense of history would not get sabotaged by his big brother, Ernie Breech, and Bob McNamara. This was his chance for a small measure of redemption, and he seized it.

Chuck Schmidt was also a busy man. With the salary cap set to kick in on Dec. 23, 1993, the Lions signed a flurry of contracts with prized players in order to keep them out of the looming salary-cap calculations. Barry Sanders led the parade with a new $17.2 million four-year contract that included an $11 million signing bonus, which made him the highest-paid running back in the league. Also signing on the dotted line were wide receiver Herman Moore, center Kevin Glover, and linebacker Chris Spielman, the fiercest competitor on the team. Sounding like a Vince Lombardi acolyte, Spielman said, "I've always said I've got to win. That's the whole purpose of my life." As he'd made clear before the playoff game in Washington, he meant winning the Super Bowl.

That summer, an astonishing work of art came to life on an exterior wall of the forty-story Cadillac Tower in downtown Detroit. It was a 170-foot-tall, 100-foot-wide image of Barry Sanders in his Lions uniform, a football tucked under his left arm, his left knee kicking high. The painting was part of a Nike ad campaign, and it announced that Barry Sanders was now literally larger than life, a monumental talent who towered over the heart of the Motor City.

Wayne Fontes had added Tom Moore, a brilliant offensive strategist, to his staff, first as quarterbacks' coach, then as offensive coordinator. The Lions made the playoffs again in 1994, only to lose again to the Packers in the wild card round, 16–12. The box score explained why: Barry Sanders rushed for a total of one *negative* yard.

The following year, Fontes understood that he was coaching with a gun to his head. After the team got off to a 3–6 start, Bill Ford gave another of his ultimatums. "It's got to be the playoffs," he said, adding that anything less would be "unacceptable." Under Tom Moore's guidance, the offense exploded. After pocketing a $5 million signing bonus, the free agent quarterback Scott Mitchell hit his stride, Herman Moore set an NFL record with 123 catches for the season, and Brett Perriman added 108. It was the most potent one-two aerial punch in the league, buttressed by Sanders's 1,500 yards rushing. The team finished the season with seven straight wins, a 10–6 record and another wild card berth.

Today Tom Moore is eighty-four years old and just finished his forty-fifth season in the NFL, currently with Tampa Bay. He recently recalled what it was like to coach a rare talent like Barry Sanders. One day Sanders walked into Moore's office in the Silverdome and said, "Coach, I watch a lot of film, but what I see on that screen and what I see on the field aren't the same thing. Every game starts out really fast, but the more carries I get, the more it all slows down." And the slower the game got, the better Sanders performed—so he wanted to touch the ball twenty-five, thirty times per game. Moore was happy to oblige. "He'd have twelve carries for thirty-eight yards," Moore said. "Then he'd have eighteen for a hundred and eighty-five."

Not always. The brilliance of Sanders, Moore, Perriman, Spielman, and a handful others was not enough to prevent the team's third straight exit from the playoffs in the first round. With Mitchell throwing three interceptions and Sanders carrying the ball just ten times for a paltry forty yards, the Lions absorbed a 58–37 shellacking by the Philadelphia Eagles.

After the season, Bill Keenist, then the Lions' vice president for administration and communications, began hearing rumors that the team was not going to re-sign Pro Bowl offensive tackle Lomas Brown, who was eligible for free agency. Brown and the center Kevin Glover were drafted in 1985, the same year Keenist joined the front office, and Keenist had watched them grow into roles as team leaders. When the Lions drafted Barry Sanders, a wide-eyed kid from Kansas who had never lived in a big city, Brown and Glover took the rookie under their wings. Sanders, a bachelor and a ravenous eater, loved it when the Glovers invited him and

Brown over for some home cooking and the chance to wrestle on the floor with the Glovers' kids.

"There was a genuine bond between those three," Keenist said recently. "Lomas and Kevin were not only teammates to Barry, they not only blocked for Barry, but in many ways they were family to Barry. Big brothers, if you will."

When Keenist asked Chuck Schmidt if the rumors about letting Brown go were true, Schmidt replied that Brown, a veteran of eleven seasons, was now thirty-two years old and probably nearing the end of his run. It was Schmidt's way of justifying the decision not to re-sign one of the team's leaders.

Keenist was appalled. Brown was coming off a first team All-Pro selection and his sixth Pro Bowl season in 1995. Keenist was convinced Brown was a cornerstone of a team that had made the playoffs in three of the previous four seasons. "He was still playing at an elite level," Keenist said.

He believed Schmidt's business mind blinded him to the vital human dimension of every football team. "There's a uniqueness about the football culture," Keenist said. "The locker room, the huddle, the relationships, the brotherhood. Over my years in the NFL and with the Lions, I came to realize that for those with a financial background, one plus one always equals two. That's not a criticism as much as it's just acknowledging a reality I experienced over the years. But in the football culture, one plus one can equal ten—because the value of certain players, like a Lomas Brown or Kevin Glover, is so much greater than any calculation might suggest. Losing Lomas made our whole team a lot less."

It also damaged team morale. "When you see a guy like Lomas Brown not being treated well," Terry Foster wrote in the *News*, "especially a guy who has been through the wars, it sends a bad message." Bill Ford Jr. later acknowledged that cutting loose a solid player and fan favorite like Brown was "a public relations disaster."

To make the disaster even worse, Schmidt's estimation of Brown's future was not shared by other general managers. The free agent lineman was pursued by half a dozen teams, and he wound up signing a three-year,

$9 million contract with the Arizona Cardinals. He won't play much longer? As it turned out, Brown was barely halfway through a career that would run for a total of eighteen seasons and culminate with a Super Bowl title in Tampa Bay. Once again, the Lions let the wrong guy get away, then compounded the mistake by bringing in the wrong guy to take Brown's place: an average player named Ray Roberts, who signed a three-year contract for $9 million. Which ended any speculation that Brown had been cut loose because of salary-cap considerations.

The Lions weren't finished. During that offseason the team waved goodbye to two other free agents who were pillars of the defense—the linebacker Chris Spielman, who was coming off his fourth Pro Bowl season, and the defensive back Bennie Blades. Two years later, with his career flourishing in Buffalo, Spielman looked back on the mass exodus from Detroit. "They let a core group of guys go that obviously still have quite a bit of good years left in them," Spielman said. "I still have a hard time understanding why I wasn't brought back, or wasn't even given an offer to come back and play." He also had a hard time understanding why the Lions replaced him with the free agent linebacker Michael Brooks, who got a $2.7 million contract and was cut after four games. Finally, Spielman admitted: "I'm kind of a little bit bitter about that."

He wasn't alone. The prospect of losing his close friend Lomas Brown distressed Barry Sanders so deeply that he offered to defer some of his salary if the Lions would keep Brown on the roster. The team declined. Already growing tired of the early exits from the playoffs, Sanders now had to wrestle with an unsettling question: if management was willing to give up on so many battle-hardened veterans, how serious could it be about building a team capable of winning the Super Bowl? Angry as he was, Sanders was in for an even more infuriating shock.

PRIVATE PEOPLE

In early 1995, while the Lions were in the midst of their streak of early
playoff exits, thirty-seven-year-old Bill Ford Jr. was named the team's
vice chairman. He started attending league meetings and appearing
in newspaper columns, cementing the decades-old assumption that he
would eventually succeed his father as team owner. At about this time,
Ford Jr. latched onto an idea that turned him into not just your average
dog with a bone; it turned him into a pit bull with a juicy buffalo shank.
Once he got his teeth around it, he wasn't going to let go.

His idea was that the arrival of free agency had turned the Lions' business model from dismal to disastrous. In this age of rising salaries for
players and coaches, the Lions simply could not compete with other teams
as long as they paid $2 million a year in rent but received no revenue from
Silverdome parking, concessions, advertising, or luxury suites. Therefore,
Ford Jr. reasoned, the Lions should renegotiate their debilitating lease at
that dirty cave in Pontiac, and if they failed to win satisfactory concessions
from Silverdome management, the team should pack up and move into a
new, state-of-the art stadium in downtown Detroit. He categorically ruled
out that the team would join the parade of franchises bolting to greener
pastures in another state. The Lions, like the Fords, belonged in Detroit.

The main driver of Ford Jr.'s idea may have been economics, but there
were additional considerations. A piece of the Silverdome roof had collapsed after a heavy snowstorm in March 1985. Luckily, the panels gave

way in the middle of the night when the building was empty so no one was hurt, but it was an unsettling moment and it forced the Pistons to play the rest of their home games at Cobo Arena in downtown Detroit while the Silverdome roof underwent repairs. Soon after the collapse, Pistons owner Bill Davidson announced that the team would abandon the Silverdome and move into a new, privately financed home, a cut-crystal jewel called the Palace just up the road in Auburn Hills.

Now, in the spring of 1996, another item was added to the growing list of the Silverdome's charms. A Pontiac health inspector discovered a large pipe that was discharging human feces, toilet paper, and foul water into the Clinton River. The inspector traced the pipe to the point where it joined a nearby Silverdome sewer line. The Silverdome's plumbing had never been adequate, and when the overtaxed system was unable to handle peak demand—such as during intermission of a sold-out tractor pull—raw sewage backed up from the floor drains in the stadium's concession stands. Managers acknowledged that such backups had happened "numerous" times. So a pipe was grafted to the sewer line, and when the line began to back up a valve was opened so that excess untreated sewage could be diverted into the Clinton River. This may not have been good for the environment, but it had the salutary effect of cutting down on raw sewage backups in the concession stands. No more hot dogs served with a side order of E. coli. It was also learned that workers dumped cooking oils and fats into the sewer lines, increasing the danger of clogs and backups. Elias Brothers, home of the Big Boy and holder of the lucrative concessions contract, could not be reached for comment.

So the Lions had no shortage of reasons for wanting to get out of their lease at the Silverdome. Beyond these considerations, Ford Jr. argued passionately that moving the Lions back to Detroit would be a transfusion for the heart of the city, which, for the first time in decades, was showing blips of life. Ford Jr. had developed a close relationship with Detroit's business-friendly mayor, Dennis Archer. The conciliatory successor to Coleman

Young was trying to heal the city/suburbs rift while aggressively backing casino gambling, the Tigers' plans to build a new stadium downtown, and, in an irony lost on no one in Detroit, General Motors' interest in purchasing the RenCen. There was a vibe that Detroit might actually be on the cusp of a comeback. Against this backdrop, Ford Jr. argued that moving the Lions to downtown Detroit would be seen as a statement about the team's—and the Ford family's—commitment to their hometown, right up there with Uncle Henry II's RenCen.

Bill Ford Sr. was intrigued enough by his son's idea to let him run with it. The team hired the well-connected political operative Tom Lewand to negotiate a more favorable lease with the Silverdome, but the two sides remained far apart. Meanwhile, plans for a stadium in downtown Detroit were gaining steam.

With those balls in the air, Bill Ford Jr. became more active in the Lions' front office. Chuck Schmidt had overseen numerous improvements—a remodeled weight room and players' lounge, a stronger emphasis on marketing, promotions, media relations, and charities, the hiring of a labor lawyer to help with contracts and the salary cap—and now Ford Jr. tried to remake the team's culture from within. To this end he took fifty staffers on a three-day retreat with the goal of getting them to wrestle with a question no one in the front office had ever bothered to ask: "What should we as an organization be doing to win the Super Bowl and have the most satisfied fans in the country?"

That summer, after talks with Silverdome management reached an impasse, the Lions announced that they would move into a $315 million domed stadium in downtown Detroit, next to the open-air stadium the Tigers had agreed to build. The cost of the football stadium would be split about evenly between government and private sources—a departure from the sweetheart government-financed stadium deals in Baltimore, Atlanta, Jacksonville, Cleveland, and other cities. The Ford family would kick in $50 million, while Ford Motor Company agreed to pay $50 million for naming rights for twenty-five years. The NFL offered an interest-free $100 million loan.

And so Ford Field was born.

◆

After the Lions finished the 1996 season at 5–11 and in last place in their division, Wayne Fontes finally got the long-expected ziggy. All of his assistants, including Tom Moore, were also fired. Fontes had compiled a 66–71 overall record in seven-plus seasons—the most wins (and the most losses) by any Lions head coach—and he had guided the team to its lone playoff win since the last championship season way back in 1957. But his freewheeling style had worn out its welcome with some players, many fans, much of the news media and, most importantly, with Bill Ford. Not everyone was pleased by the coach's departure. In his autobiography, Barry Sanders wrote of Fontes: "I thought he deserved another chance."

There is no shortage of theories why the Lions of the 1990s failed to reach the Super Bowl even though they had installed a core of talented players around their superstar Sanders, the first running back to gain 1,500 or more yards in three consecutive seasons. A compelling theory was put forward by John U. Bacon, who noted in the *Detroit News* that there had been eight head coaches since Bill Ford bought the team, and four of them were promoted from the ranks of Lions assistant coaches. Only one, the ill-fated Don McCafferty, had been a winning head coach elsewhere in the NFL. Bacon's conclusion: "Serious national searches for proven head coaching talent simply don't happen here."

Now, as if to rebut Bacon's critique, Bill Ford mounted what he called a "wide-angle" nationwide search for a coach who was a proven winner in the pro ranks—not an untested assistant coach or a college-level mediocrity. For once, the Lions' timing was perfect. A week after Fontes got fired, Bobby Ross resigned as head coach of the San Diego Chargers after a dispute with the team's general manager over personnel decisions. In his five seasons at the helm, Ross had led the Chargers to three playoff appearances, two division titles and one Super Bowl. Ford soon had Ross signed to a five-year, $9 million contract that gave him freedom to choose his assistant coaches and all player personnel.

The hiring of Ross was applauded even by some of Ford's most unforgiving critics. Dean Howe offered this left-handed compliment in the *Ann Arbor News*: "Three cheers for owner William Clay Ford. After thirty-two years he finally made a logical decision. He hired a good football coach."

One observer noted that with Fontes gone, "the country club is over" for Lions players. Ross himself left no doubt that changes were coming. "I want perfect practices," he declared. "Perfect practices make for perfect games."

In addition to more rigorous practices and training camps, Ross instituted weight requirements, curfews, and other strict measures unfamiliar to players accustomed to the country-club atmosphere under Fontes. Ross was determined to get the underachieving Lions back to fundamental physical football played by a versatile team that was not dependent on its one superstar.

That superstar hit the lottery during the offseason. With his contract set to expire at the end of the 1997 season, Sanders's agents got busy negotiating a new deal that would secure his long-term future. The result was a five-year contract with a one-year option that paid $34 million, eclipsing the contracts of star quarterbacks Troy Aikman and John Elway and making Sanders the highest-paid player in the NFL. "The thing that sets this apart," said the agent C. Lamont Smith, "is that we finally broke the glass ceiling for quarterbacks."

When some suggested that Sanders was driven by raw greed, Terry Foster wrote in the *News* that the record-setting contract had to be seen in light of the team's past dealings with top players, including Lomas Brown and Chris Spielman. "Sanders obviously did not trust the organization to do the right thing," Foster wrote. "And quite frankly, I don't blame him."

Sanders responded by delivering the most remarkable performance of his remarkable career. It culminated in the final game of the regular season, when Sanders racked up 184 yards and scored a fourth-quarter touchdown to lead a 13–10 win over the New York Jets. In a throwback to the pretelevision 1950s, Sanders simply flipped the ball to a referee after scoring the touchdown. No dancing for the cameras. No showboating. Why not? Because, he once told a teammate, he *expected* to score the touchdown. The day's work gave Sanders 2,053 yards rushing for the season—just the third time a running back had broken the mythical 2,000-yard barrier—and it moved Sanders past his father's hero, Jim Brown, on the career rushing list. Becoming the most prolific running back in the history of the game was now within Sanders's grasp. To commemorate the moment, he posed for a picture with his big brother Kevin Glover, their numbers—20 and 53—representing Sanders's total yardage for the season.

The win over the Jets put the Lions back in the playoffs as the fifth-seeded wild card, but during the game the Curse paid another visit: Lions linebacker Reggie Brown suffered a severe spinal cord injury and briefly stopped breathing. After he was resuscitated, he was carted off the field on a stretcher. Brown would walk again after extensive physical therapy, but his football career was over.

The Lions' season was soon over, too. The players wore helmet decals with Brown's number 59 when they traveled to Tampa Bay for the wild card game, but this time the talisman conferred no magic. Sanders was held to sixty-five yards rushing, Mitchell completed just ten passes before leaving the game with a concussion, and the Lions lost 20–10, their fourth first-round playoff exit in the past five seasons.

It was going to be a long winter for a frustrated Barry Sanders, who shared the league's MVP honors with Green Bay quarterback Brett Favre. While Favre led the Packers to the Super Bowl, Sanders watched the playoffs from his living room sofa, seething. If Sanders was fed up with losing, he was about to be infuriated by the front office's offseason maneuvers. His good friend and the team's unquestioned locker room leader, Kevin Glover, was eligible for free agency. Glover, now thirty-four, wanted $3 million a year, but the Lions offered him $2 million and started talking with the twenty-six-year-old free agent Jim Pyne of Tampa Bay. Glover had been the victim of some front-office shenanigans a year earlier, when the Lions designated him their "franchise player," which meant no other team could vie for his services. Shortly before the designation was set to expire, the Lions lifted it—after other teams had already done their shopping. Glover was forced to accept a one-year contract, which helps explain why Terry Foster defended Barry Sanders's distrust of the organization. Now Glover, also disinclined to trust the Lions, signed a three-year, $8.1 million contract with Seattle. The Lions promptly signed Pyne to take his place. Glover insisted he harbored "no hard feelings" about how his thirteen-year career with the Lions had come to an end. But on that day something died inside Barry Sanders.

◆

During the 1998 season, for the first time in his career, the soft-spoken Sanders started venting his pent-up displeasure. After the team committed fourteen penalties while getting throttled by Minnesota and falling to 2–5 midway through the season, the usually taciturn Sanders made it clear that the thrill was long gone. "I just sort of come here to work," he said after the game. "I show up and play with the guys who are out there. But the fact of the matter is that we just made some errors that, God, you don't see 'em make in junior high or Pop Warner games. It's like, wow!" The sloppiness was even more perplexing because it came from players coached by Bobby Ross, known as a detail-oriented perfectionist.

A picture in the *Oakland Press* showed Sanders sitting on the bench late in the Minnesota game, his right shoe gone, his glazed eyes searching the upper reaches of the stadium for answers to unknown questions. The caption read: DETROIT'S BARRY SANDERS SOUNDS LIKE HE'S GETTING TIRED OF ALWAYS LOOKING UP AT OTHER TEAMS IN THE STANDINGS.

Sanders admitted that he missed Lomas Brown and Kevin Glover, but he insisted that their departures weren't the main problem. What was?

"The Jekyll-and-Hyde aspect," he replied.

Meanwhile, Lomas Brown was missing Barry Sanders—and the city of Detroit. The week after the loss to Minnesota, the Lions got ready to host Brown's new team, the Arizona Cardinals. In the run-up to the game, Brown said, "Since I put in most of my time in Detroit, it's home for me. A lot of my friends are still there. I miss the guys. I miss everything about Detroit and the organization. Still to this day, I still miss those guys."

It's remarkable that a player could miss everything about an organization that had treated him so shabbily. This speaks to the magnetic pull Detroit and its storied football team exert on players and fans alike. This bond explains why veteran players such as Lomas Brown, Kevin Glover, Chris Spielman, Bobby Layne and many others remained loyal to the team and the city even after they were sent packing.

The game was changing, and old-school franchises like the Lions ignored the changes at their peril. The NFL historian Michael MacCambridge has noted that the league's new system of free agency with a salary cap, though revolutionary, was not the most significant aspect of the latest collective bargaining agreement. "The agreement," MacCambridge wrote, "accomplished something that would prove even more important: by establishing a sense of proportion that guaranteed players almost two-thirds of every dollar the NFL made, it made the players partners of the owners in more than rhetorical terms."

This was especially true of the elite players—with at least one notable exception. Larry Lee, an offensive lineman with the Lions in the 1980s who joined the front office in 1993 and was now vice president of football operations, had a close-up view of the interactions between Lions players and ownership. "The Ford family are good people, they really want to win,"

Lee told the *Free Press*. "But today's sports are not an employee-employer kind of a profession anymore—pro football isn't. They're business partners. The top players, the key players and the owners now are business partners. And the Fords have just been a private family that just won't let players get that close to them like that. . . . Barry's talking to his fellow guys and seeing how they're being treated . . . and [the Fords] weren't like that. Not because the Fords were evil or mean people or nothing. They're just private people. With that being the case, I think that's been a part of the lack of championships around here."

This lack of a sense of partnership with the Fords helps explain what Barry Sanders was looking for in the upper reaches of the Silverdome after that lopsided loss to Minnesota. He was looking for an exit sign.

SICK OF IT

While the Lions were in San Francisco to play the 49ers in the closing weeks of that season, Lions publicist Bill Keenist was spotted conversing with a man who was well known in league circles. The guy had won four Super Bowl rings playing linebacker for three different teams, including the 1991 Washington Redskins who had so rudely denied the Lions their lone shot at the Super Bowl. Since his retirement from playing he had become a polished and highly respected broadcaster. He knew the game and he knew the players and the coaches. He was articulate and personable. Everyone liked him. He would make the dream-come-true, can't-miss general manager, Keenist believed, the man who could take the Lions, at long last, to the Promised Land. Several other teams shared the assessment, and they were pursuing him.

His name was Matt Millen.

A few days after the Lions returned to Detroit following their loss to the 49ers, the story broke in the Detroit papers that the Fords were talking with Millen about an unspecified job in the team's front office, possibly as general manager. Millen's lack of management experience was not seen as a liability, according to the *Oakland Press*: "That Matt Millen has been a broadcaster rather than a team official since retiring as a player after the 1991 season is being viewed as a plus by the Lions." Bill Ford Jr., an ardent advocate of hiring Millen, said, "We need someone to inject life into this organization."

Millen played down his contact with the Fords as "just talk," but it was more than that. It was history doing what history tends to do: repeat itself. Now we travel back in time to Jack Kennedy and Bob McNamara in that Georgetown townhouse in 1960; we travel back to Bill Ford and Dick Morris in that suite at the Plaza Hotel in 1963. This time around it's Bill Ford and Matt Millen in Detroit in late 1998. After Ford mentioned the GM's job, Millen, like Morris and McNamara before him, demurred. "Mr. Ford," Millen said, "I really appreciate this, but I'm not qualified. I've had no training. I know the game of football, but there's a lot more to [the job] than that."

"You're smart," Ford replied. "You'll figure it out."

After thirty-five years, Ford had barely changed his tune from *Oh, you can handle it with your left hand.*

Despite his demurral, Millen told a reporter that he was eager to get out of the broadcast booth and back into the action. Then he added a swipe—possibly inadvertent, possibly not—at the Lions' chief operating officer, Chuck Schmidt. Sounding a lot like a man auditioning for a job, Millen said, "I see accountants who have been crunching numbers for years put in charge of a football team. I've been around football for thirty-five years. I have passion for the game and understand what it takes to win. I know players and I know coaches and I know what it takes. Football is what matters. This is the National Football League, not the National Accountant League."

The Fords may have been interested in Millen, and Millen may have been interested in a top job with the Lions, but there was a fly in the ointment. Bobby Ross's contract gave him control over all player personnel moves—drafts, trades, cuts, and free agent signings—which are customarily part of a general manager's purview. Something had to give.

A week later, it did. After making an offer that Millen was expected to accept, Bill Ford Sr. suddenly reversed himself and withdrew the offer. It soon came out that Bobby Ross had threatened to quit if any of his power was taken away and given to a new GM—just as he had walked away from the San Diego Chargers after his authority was diluted. Ever-loyal Bill Ford backed away at the last minute and stuck with Ross. In an effort to save face for Ford, Millen claimed that he was withdrawing his candidacy because of "family considerations."

One headline laid out the truth: FORD SR. KILLED MILLEN DEAL.

Bill Ford Jr. was said to be livid over his father's last-minute reversal. Though he swallowed his anger when talking to the press, his disappointment and sense of resignation were impossible to miss. "I think it's a shame," said Ford Jr., who had just been named chairman of the board at Ford Motor Company. "But this is my father's team, and I really have no impact. I have my hands full at Ford. Whatever happens from here on is really my father's decision."

Meanwhile, cracks in team morale were beginning to show. No one outworked Bobby Ross, who showed up at the office before dawn and worked late into the night. Barry Sanders observed that Ross "seemed to have very little fun in football," implying that his players weren't having much fun either. Some of those players were having so little fun that they wanted to get out of town. Cleveland had been granted a new franchise to replace the Browns, and now each established team had to expose five players to the expansion draft that would stock the Cleveland roster. After one year with the Lions, Jim Pyne, the lineman who had supplanted Kevin Glover, asked the Lions to make him available in the expansion draft because playing in Detroit was, in Pyne's opinion, "a bad situation." The team obliged, and the Browns plucked Pyne with their first pick. Same old story: the Lions let a Pro Bowler and team leader get away in favor of a player who was itching to flee after one mediocre season.

"Pyne is typical of the decisions that led to the Lions' collapse," the *Free Press* wrote. "Ross signed him to replace the former Pro Bowl center Kevin Glover, although Pyne had played guard—not center—in his four NFL seasons at Tampa Bay. As it turned out, Pyne had an extremely difficult season. He didn't fit well into the blocking schemes, and the entire offensive line suffered."

No one knew more about the offensive line's struggles than Barry Sanders. As his long winter of discontent dragged on, sportswriters began to suggest that the Lions owed it to Sanders to trade him to a competitive team so he would at least have a chance to win a Super Bowl ring in the waning years of his career—a virtual impossibility in Detroit. Such a trade, the thinking went, would yield a bushel of draft picks and would jump-start another rebuild. Then the rumors started.

There were whispers that Sanders was so fed up with losing that he was considering early retirement. Given the fact that he would probably need just one more season, two at the most, to gain the 1,458 yards needed to surpass Walter Payton and become the top running back in the history of the game, the rumors at first seemed preposterous. How could an athlete walk away when he was at the peak of his powers and on the threshold of greatness? But Sanders vanished after the 1998 season, avoiding the press and failing to return Ross's phone calls or answer his long letters. After Sanders failed to show up for a mandatory minicamp that spring—to the loud displeasure of the un-fun Ross—Mike O'Hara of the *News* reached Barry's father by phone at his home in Wichita. When O'Hara asked if there was any substance to the rumors, he got an earful.

"He's sick of [the Lions]," William Sanders told O'Hara. "He's sick of losing. He's sick of the whole situation." Sick enough to retire? "He is really considering it. . . . I wouldn't blame him if he walks away from the game. The whole city ought to be sick of it."

In the next day's *Free Press*, William Sanders seemed to back off from his earlier remarks. "He's not going to leave the team," he predicted. "I'm almost sure he's going to fulfill his contract, but that don't mean he's not displeased with the way things are going."

Asked if his son was seeking a trade, William said, "He's too loyal to ask to be traded. He'll suffer through it again, like he has the last ten years, with a grin on his face like nothing's wrong." Besides, fitting Sanders's fat contract under another team's salary cap would have been nearly impossible. Then Papa Sanders closed with a zinger: "The Ford family is great, but there's no way in the world Mr. Ford would hire some of the guys to run his company like they run his football team. If he did, he wouldn't sell a car."

◆

Father, it turns out, was only half-right. His son did not ask to be traded, but on July 27, 1999, Barry Sanders stunned the football world when he sent a fax to his hometown newspaper, the *Wichita Eagle*, announcing that he was retiring from football. It began: "Shortly after the end of last season, I felt that I probably would not return for the 1999-2000 season. I also felt that I should take as much time as possible to sort through my feelings and make sure that my feelings were backed with conviction. Today, I officially declare my departure from the NFL."

The short fax went on: "I have no regrets [and] I leave on good terms with everyone in the organization."

But *why* was he walking away?

"The reason I am retiring is simple: My desire to exit the game is greater than my desire to remain in it."

Sanders promptly flew to London. Four years would pass before he expanded on that overly simplistic reason for his departure. As he wrote in his autobiography: "My retirement letter didn't even hint at my frustration, because I didn't want to take shots at people as I left. . . . Management had let quality players slip away. We'd been losing for years. Now we were right back where we were when I arrived. . . . I didn't see what good there was in hanging around when the organization wasn't trying to put together a winning team. . . . I didn't think we were as serious about winning as our competitors."

Then Sanders took a belated shot: "The man with whom I had the most trouble was Chuck Schmidt. He was basically a businessman who came from a very traditional background. He had his favorites who he'd pay and others who he didn't want to pay." There's no doubt Sanders was comparing Scott Mitchell's $5 million signing bonus to the ignominious departures of Sanders's two best friends.

Bill Keenist, the team's publicist, put it succinctly: "I firmly believe that the departures of Lomas Brown and Kevin Glover were the first dominoes to fall that would lead to Barry's decision to retire."

Through bad decisions, subterfuge, and lack of commitment, the Lions had accomplished something almost beyond imagining: they had chased away one of the greatest players in the history of the game just as he was about to obtain immortality. If this team truly was cursed, it was beginning to look like the Curse was largely self-inflicted.

◆

On the first day of training camp that summer, Bobby Ross was mobbed by reporters who bombarded him with variations on the same question: Is it your fault that Barry Sanders is gone? Is this the result of how you communicate with your players? Are you a leader? Are you in command?

The barrage infuriated Ross. With his face red and his eyes ablaze, he vented to Thomas George of the *New York Times*: "I have coached football nearly all of my life, and to have to answer those kind of questions about my character and my motives, it's insulting. You'd think I just rolled out of bed today and have no history with coaching and with players. It's nonsense the way this is happening, how I'm being crucified for a guy that just doesn't want to play football anymore."

The team, surprisingly, improved that season. Their record was mediocrity itself, 8–8, and even though they lost their last four games they managed to slip into the playoffs as the sixth-seeded wild card.

The website Football Outsiders ranked them "one of the worst playoff teams ever," and they lived up to the billing with a convincing 27–13 first-round loss to the Washington Redskins.

By now it was apparent to everyone, including Bobby Ross, that Bobby Ross was not the answer to the Lions' prayers. His players saw him as too regimented, too conservative, too old-school in how he perceived the relationship between the head coach and a new generation of players who were accustomed to the perks and power of free agency. Despite this widening gap, the team got off to a 5–2 start in 2000—then hit a wall. They got trampled by the Colts in Indianapolis, then lost to Miami at home, 23–8. The players looked indifferent, and the 77,000 paying customers in the Silverdome did not appreciate the lackluster effort. They cheered when quarterback Charlie Batch lay motionless on the field after suffering a serious head injury, then booed him when he wobbled off the field under his own power, suffering from a concussion. Several players expressed outrage over the fans' behavior.

In the locker room after the game, Bobby Ross was close to tears. "It's one of the most embarrassing losses I've ever had," he said. "I obviously failed." Then he dissected the source of his failure: "You want your team to be a model of who you are and what you are. I expect us to fight, I expect us to compete. But we never fought back, we never competed. We need to ask ourselves some questions this week. Are we going to fight, or are we going to sit there and take it?"

Ross hinted that he was ready to quit, but Bill Ford talked him into going home and sleeping on it. The next day, after asking himself some hard questions, a burnt-out Ross pulled a Barry Sanders and quit with a year and a half left on his contract. Bill Ford Sr. tried again to talk Ross into staying, but it was no use. "He had nothing else to give," Ford said, conceding defeat. "His gas tank was empty."

There was no time for a wide-angle nationwide search for a seasoned NFL coach, so Ford reverted to form and immediately named Gary

Moeller, a Lions assistant and former University of Michigan coach, as Ross's successor. Ford gave Moeller a contract through the rest of the season plus two more. When Drew Sharp of the *Free Press* asked Ford why anyone should think he was capable of hiring the right coach, Ford bristled. "I'm not saying they should or shouldn't have any trust in me," he snapped at Sharp. "I don't really worry about what others think. I have to do what I feel is best for my team. And this is my team, and it's my decision." Then he ended the conversation. "What do you want me to do—fire myself? I'm not going to do it."

Moeller led the Lions to a winning record of 9–7 that season, but a loss to the lowly Chicago Bears in the regular-season finale knocked them out of the playoffs. After making the postseason six times during the 1990s, the team had begun its agonizing journey to the bottom.

THE WIZARD OF ARRRGH

Now entering the twilight of his life, Bill Ford's interests ranged far beyond Ford Motor Company's stock price and the Lions' latest drama. He had extensive real estate holdings in Detroit, California, Florida, and New York. He was still devoted to his family, still loved bird hunting, driving fast cars, and roaring out onto Lake St. Clair in his powerboat *The Sea Lion*. His Achilles injuries had turned him into an avid golfer, a sport that makes fewer demands on the body than tennis or skiing, and he became so passionate about the game that he developed a seaside course in partnership with his buddy Bob Hope and the famed golf course architect George Fazio.

It was there, at his exclusive Jupiter Hills Club in Tequesta, Florida that Bill Ford had a late-life reunion with his former PR guy Dick Morris. The two had remained in touch over the years, chatting on the phone occasionally and exchanging Christmas cards, and one day around the time Bobby Ross walked off the job in Detroit, Ford invited Morris to join him for a round of golf at Jupiter Hills. After the game, Morris noticed that Bill Ford was getting ready to drive off in a sparkling blue Jaguar XKR convertible, the fruit of his nighttime consulting work a decade earlier, a clear echo of the revered XKE. The Jag allowed Ford to pretend he was back on the test track in Dearborn in his little speedster, the throttle stuck as he roared around the oval at a hundred miles per hour, as alive as he'd ever been. When Morris remarked that the Jag was a beauty, Ford said, "I need to get rid of it. You can have it if you want it."

Morris, assuming he was joking, mumbled that he couldn't afford such a car.

"If you want it," Ford replied, obviously not joking, "drop off a check with the housekeeper at Hobe Sound. I'll leave the keys in the ignition."

Realizing Ford was serious, Morris asked, "How big a check?"

"I don't know. Ten grand?"

And so Dick Morris, a septuagenarian widower who knew a good investment when he saw one, became the unlikely owner of a sporty blue bullet that was easily worth $35,000 and turned heads wherever he drove it. Every time he slid behind the wheel, Morris thought back to that day when he had watched Bill Ford "ingest" a Degas sculpture in New York without bothering to ask the price. He also thought back to Gene Bordinat's remark about Bill Ford from those long-ago cocktail hours at the Dearborn Inn: *When it came to big stuff, man, he was generous.* Or maybe, Morris thought, this was Bill Ford's way of making amends for stiffing me on that bonus back in 1969. Once again, Morris couldn't figure it out.

◆

Not long after he gave away that Jaguar, Bill Ford engineered one last grandiose disaster that would haunt him to his grave. With the downtown stadium nearing completion, Ford tried to woo the legendary general manager Bobby Beathard out of retirement, but Beathard wasn't interested. Ford then revived his son's idea of giving control of all football operations to Matt Millen. This time, with Bobby Ross out of the picture, the deal went through without a hiccup and Millen was named the team's president and chief executive officer in early 2001.

Despite Millen's lack of any front-office experience, one writer praised his hiring as "the smartest thing William Clay Ford Sr. has ever done." But others pointed out that the emperor was stark naked. "Let's not get carried away in thinking that the Lions' savior has arrived," cautioned Rob Parker in the *Free Press.* "Saviors usually come with track records. Millen has none."

So Millen got busy creating a track record. He fired Gary Moeller and his staff and accepted Chuck Schmidt's resignation after twenty-five bumpy years with the organization. Then Millen tried to woo a pair of coaching legends, Bill Parcells and Joe Gibbs, but they turned him down. So Millen settled for San Francisco's offensive coordinator, Marty Mornhinweg, giving him a five-year, $5 million contract. Among those swept away in the purge was the highly regarded director of player personnel, Ron Hughes, who was given much of the credit for putting together the competitive 1990s teams that kept going to the playoffs but coming home empty-handed. So Hughes was gone. Clearly, this was not just a new century. This was a new era.

◆

As the Matt Millen era got under way, the Lions had to address a little housekeeping chore. Their lease at the Silverdome ran through 2004, and if the Lions bolted for Ford Field in 2002, as planned, the nice people in Pontiac wanted to be compensated for the revenue they would lose without their anchor tenant. They pegged the potential loss at $112 million, while the Lions contended it would be closer to $8 million. Bring in the lawyers.

While the lawyers haggled, the Silverdome managers made life unpleasant for their wayward tenant. To keep the team from practicing in the stadium, the staff blasted loud music and blew air under the Astro-Turf, causing the field to ripple and making practice impossible. It was a reprise of US troops blasting Guns N' Roses' "Welcome to the Jungle" to smoke Manuel Noriega out of the Vatican Embassy in Panama City a decade earlier. Mornhinweg adjourned practices to the bubble adjacent to the Silverdome.

But it soon became apparent that practice was not making perfect. The Lions got hammered by Green Bay in their season opener, then the league postponed the next Sunday's slate of games in deference to the 9/11 terrorist attacks. Pete Rozelle had let the games go on the Sunday after President John F. Kennedy's assassination in 1963, and he later stated that he came to regret the decision. His successor, Paul Tagliabue, was not going to repeat that blunder.

So at least the Lions didn't lose the second week of the 2001 season. They did lose the following Sunday, however, falling 24–14 to the expansion Cleveland Browns, who had won just five games in their first two years of existence. The Lions' backup quarterback, Ty Detmer, threw seven interceptions and the team committed fifteen penalties, a breathtakingly inept performance. As omens go, this one was not good.

Meanwhile, the Glass House was boiling with turmoil that actually outdid the turmoil inside the Silverdome. In a power struggle with CEO Jacques Nasser, Bill Ford Jr., with an assist from his father, persuaded Ford Motor Company's board of directors to fire Nasser and name Ford Jr. CEO, in addition to his duties as chairman of the board. Fixing the mess Nasser left behind would prove to be a full-time job, and Ford Jr. became far less visible around the Lions' operation.

Lucky guy. The team kept losing, and after five weeks they were the only winless team in the league. By the time the lawyers reached an agreement on a Silverdome lease buy-out in late November, the Lions' record was a frightful 0–10. Their bad record inspired even worse jokes. Here's one:

"Knock, knock."

"Who're there?"

"Owen."

"Owen who?"

"Owen Ten."

That immaculate record had also caught the attention of the comedian Jay Leno, who turned the Lions' woes into a running gag during his monologues on *The Tonight Show.* As in: "The Lions were banned from practicing at the Silverdome because Pontiac is suing them over breaking their lease. Isn't that amazing? The Lions practice?" Or: "Later this month, Britney Spears is playing in Detroit. She's a two-touchdown favorite over the Lions."

The settlement with the Silverdome called for the Lions to pay $26.2 million for the privilege of leaving the building, but it did nothing to stanch the bleeding on the field. The Lions lost their next two games and were now in realistic danger of making history as the first team in league history to go 0–16 in a season. Then the football gods showed a little uncharacteristic mercy. The Lions' luck turned in their thirteenth game, and they held on to squeak past Minnesota, 27–24. The players and fans reacted as though they'd won the Super Bowl, and in the euphoria after the game, Lions' wide receiver Johnnie Morton hurled his helmet into the air and shouted, "Tell Jay Leno to kiss my ass!"

The next night Leno jumped right back on the one-win Lions. "The nice thing is they won before the home fans," he began. "In fact, there were over twenty-eight people in the stands." He added, "I think the Vikings are on suicide watch today."

Morton soon found himself appearing remotely on *The Tonight Show* from the Silverdome while Leno welcomed a donkey draped in a Detroit Lions blanket onto the set in California. Leno asked Morton if the empty seats behind him were in the Silverdome. When Morton replied that they were, Leno said, "Looks like a home game." Then Leno gave the donkey a kiss.

◆

For the first time in a life of uninterrupted success, Matt Millen began to realize he had set himself up to fail. The job of running a football team was a different world from playing the game of football. "It was too big for me," Millen said of the GM job. "I felt bad for Marty. I couldn't help him. I was just trying figure [everything] out." He also admitted that he'd hired the wrong guy: "Marty is an excellent play-caller, but he's not a head coach."

After finishing Millen's and Mornhinweg's first season with a 2–14 record, the Lions opened a new $35 million practice facility in suburban Allen Park and baptized their new domed stadium in downtown Detroit with an exhibition game against the Pittsburgh Steelers late in the summer of 2002. The Lions lost the game, but no one seemed to notice or care. Everyone was too busy gushing about the new stadium, though it would soon become apparent that Ford Field, like the Silverdome before it, was not a magical cure for the Lions' many ills.

It was also apparent that Ford Field was a major upgrade. The sightlines were better, there were glass walls that let in sunshine and gave the place the feel of a big, airy room. The concessions were vastly improved, the concourses were spacious, and there was a sufficient number of bathrooms with toilets that actually flushed. A former J.L. Hudson's warehouse had been converted to luxury suites, giving the stadium a physical link to its surroundings. Downtown Detroit was now on the rebound, and it offered far more enticing entertainment options than the parking lots of Pontiac.

Even the playing surface got rave reviews. Players loved the forgiving, two-and-a-half-inch-thick FieldTurf, a composite of sand, synthetic grass blades and recycled tire crumbs (Firestones, naturally). Everyone agreed it was a major improvement over the Silverdome's notorious AstroTurf. "We played on some brutal fields," Matt Millen said, "like a frozen Chicago stadium or the rug put over concrete in Pittsburgh. You hated to go out there because you knew the field would punish you. This stuff is much better. Your foot won't stick in it; it feels like a lawn. We wanted the best, and we got it."

After the inaugural loss to the Steelers, an ebullient Bill Ford Sr. rode an elevator down from his luxury suite accompanied by a familiar antagonist, Drew Sharp of the *Free Press*. "This stadium makes you feel like you're a part of everything," Ford enthused. "What it has is a personality. What we had there in Pontiac was basically just concrete and steel that had a certain feel to it that was, uh, what's the word . . ."

"Sterile?" Sharp offered.

"Yes, sterile. That's the description I've been using. But there's a warmth to this facility that's evident from the very first day. It's only been open for one day, but it already has a familiar, lived-in feel to it."

"But," Sharp pointed out, "familiarity isn't exactly a good thing for this franchise in some respects."

"Yeah," Ford said with a laugh, "that's true, isn't it?"

◆

The team's first-round draft pick that year was Joey Harrington, a highly regarded quarterback from Oregon who would come to symbolize the Lions' dysfunctional drafting practices under Matt Millen. An astute assessor of talent, Millen claims he wanted to draft a defensive player or trade the team's first-round pick for additional draft choices that would fuel the rebuild. Mornhinweg advised the team to draft a defensive player or trade down instead of taking Harrington, while claiming that Millen actually favored drafting Harrington. Bill Ford Sr. wanted to draft Harrington, and so did the quarterbacks coach, Kevin Higgins, and director of player personnel, Bill Tobin. The team drafted Harrington and promptly signed him to a six-year, $36.5 million contract. It was a case of he said, he said, he said, he said. It was also another bad omen.

When Harrington stepped off the plane at Detroit's Metro Airport the day after the draft, a fan approached and congratulated him for landing one of the two toughest jobs in Detroit; the other was playing goalie for the Red Wings. Then the guy slapped Harrington on the back and said, "We haven't had a quarterback since Bobby Layne. Good luck!"

With Harrington sitting on the bench, the Lions lost the first two games of the season by big margins, including a 31–7 gift to the Carolina Panthers, who were coming off an even worse 1–15 season and were led by thirty-six-year-old retread quarterback Rodney Peete, a former Lion who hadn't thrown a pass in the previous two seasons. The two losses led the *News* to dub the Lions "the NFL's worst team." This was also the first drumbeat in what would soon become a deafening cacophony. FIRE MILLEN NOW, NOT LATER, urged a headline in the *Oakland Press*. The accompanying article contended that Millen "has been nothing shy of a disaster."

But Millen wasn't the only target of the city's rising ire. Some began to blame his prime advocate, Bill Ford Jr. "This was his first opportunity to prove that the son had indeed learned from the sins of the father," the *Free Press* stated, "but the Millen move is blowing up in his face, and it is casting doubt about his ability to find the right people to run the team."

Joey Harrington was pressed into service as the starting quarterback for the third game of the season, the team's home opener against the Packers and their legendary quarterback, Brett Favre. Though Harrington acknowledged it was a "thrill" to get his first start in the first regular-season game at Ford Field, he added: "I had a gut feeling that it would have been best for me to sit for a year and learn."

Two months later, with the Lions at 3–7 and sinking, Millen did himself no favors when he went on a Chicago radio show before a home game against the Bears and said, "I have a guy right now who I believe is a devout coward." He then speculated that this unnamed Lion did not possess "testicles." The locker room erupted.

"It's derogatory toward the player, and it's negative for the team," said cornerback Todd Lyght. "We don't need to promote negativity around here."

"Where's the love?" an unnamed player added. "Ripping us [to Chicago fans] and then we're supposed to go and play them? Where's the loyalty? There is none."

"We're supposed to be together, and he's attacking us," said a third player. "That's not right."

The papers pounced, running a picture of Bert Lahr in his furry costume and asking, WHO'S THE COWARDLY LION?" Millen was dubbed "the Wizard of Arrrgh," and one writer offered a suggestion: "Maybe Matt should ride his Harley up the Yellow Brick Road and sing, 'If I only had a brain!'" Most of the articles about the radio show pointed out that Millen was unavailable for a comment because he was paying his weekly visit to his family at their farm in eastern Pennsylvania. The family had refused to move to Detroit, fueling the rap that Millen was a carpetbagger without a deep commitment to Detroit or its football team.

The lowlight of Marty Mornhinweg's tenure as head coach came in the midst of the eight-game losing streak that turned the 2002 season into a 3–13 debacle. The Lions were playing the Bears again, this time at the University of Illinois' Memorial Stadium on a blustery day. The game ended in a tie, and when the Lions won the coin toss before the sudden-death overtime session, Mornhinweg ignored the NFL coaching Bible and elected to kick off so his team would have the wind at its back for a potential winning field goal. When the Lions forced a fourth down with eight yards to go on their own thirty-five-yard line, Mornhinweg's strategy appeared to pay off, as the Bears would likely punt rather than attempt a fifty-two-yard field goal into the teeth of the whipping wind. But when the Bears were called for holding on the third down play, Mornhinweg, instead of declining the penalty and forcing the punt, accepted the penalty and gave the Bears another third down, this time with eighteen yards to go. They gained a first down and eventually kicked the game-winning field goal into the wind. As botch jobs go, this one was a masterpiece.

It was also the end for Marty Mornhinweg. After compiling a 5–27 record, he got the ziggy at the end of his second season. But this team's troubles had only just begun.

THIS CULTURE OF LOSING

Millen's quest for a new coach took him back to the well in San Francisco, where he reached down and pulled up Steve Mariucci, who was coming off a successful six-year run as head coach of the 49ers that ended, as these affairs so often do, in a clash with the team's owner.

The hiring of Mariucci resembled the hiring of Bobby Ross, resembled it so closely, in fact, that many Detroiters experienced a sense of déjà vu. As head coaches, both had compiled impressive records with their previous employers but failed to win a Super Bowl and eventually fell out of favor. Both were highly regarded around the league—one report went so far as to call Mariucci "the most sought-after coach in the market." And both were destined to get sucked into the black hole that had awaited every head coach of the Detroit Lions since 1957.

Though Mariucci was a native of tiny Iron Mountain in Michigan's Upper Peninsula, deep in the heart of Green Bay Packers country, he was initially welcomed by Detroit's fans and media. But by hiring a new head coach without interviewing at least one minority candidate, the Lions had run afoul of the NFL's new diversity policy, and Millen was slapped with a $200,000 fine. Another unsettling omen.

It was a minor setback compared to the dark clouds that were bunching on the horizon. The jury was still out on erratic Joey Harrington, but the verdict would be swift on Millen's first-round draft pick in 2003, the Michigan State wide receiver Charles Rogers, who signed six-year contract for $55 million, including a $14 million signing bonus. Rogers suffered a broken right collarbone during his fifth game of his rookie season and was knocked out for the year. He broke the same collarbone on the third play of the 2004 season and was again out for the year. When he showed up for training camp in 2005, his once-blazing speed had slipped to "average," according to Millen. During the season Rogers received a four-game suspension for violating the league's substance abuse policy. After that season the Lions let him go, and he would spiral into drug and alcohol addiction and die at thirty-eight. Rogers is now considered one of the biggest draft busts in league history.

"Straight up," Rogers admitted after the Lions released him, "I choked."

Meanwhile, Joey Harrington was undergoing struggles of his own in his second season. After the Lions lost five of their first six games, grumbling was heard in the locker room. "I think teammates started getting pissed," Harrington recalled years later. "It was like, 'They're paying you a heckuva a lot of money to be playing better than you are.' And that was the truth. There was also this culture of losing that I did not want to subscribe to, and it created a bit of a rift. Looking back, I could have handled it in a different way. My continued insistence that we can get better if we keep working didn't sit well with people."

That upbeat attitude won Harrington the disparaging nickname "Joey Blue Skies" from his teammates. The discord was enough to lend credence to Bill Ford's assertion way back in 1963 that offering a "ridiculous" contract to the untested rookie quarterback Pete Beathard would disrupt the team's morale. Forty years later, Joey Harrington was proving him right.

As far as Matt Millen was concerned, Harrington, for all his talent, lacked one critical ingredient. "Joey had all the tools," Millen said in a recent interview. "He had the arm, he understood the system, he was a sweet kid. But he didn't have *it*. *It* is something you can't define. A player's got *it* or he doesn't. Joey was a good kid and a hard worker, but he didn't have *it*."

In Mariucci's first season, the team went 5–11 for its third straight last-place finish in the division. In the following year's draft, Millen used the first-round pick on another wide receiver, Roy Williams of Texas. Williams was an improvement over Rogers, which wasn't saying much. He set a team rookie record for receiving, but he had a fundamental flaw. "Roy didn't like to work," Millen said. "I had him in my office all the time." Williams's repeated trips to the principal's office didn't do him or the team much good. The Lions got off to a 4–2 start and appeared ready to contend for the NFC North title in 2004, but a five-game losing streak snuffed that fantasy. The team finished with a barely improved 6–10 record that was not good enough make the playoffs but did get them out of the divisional cellar, which was taken over by the Chicago Bears.

It was a small consolation to Joey Harrington. "Three years of coming close," he said at the end of the season. "I'm tired of it."

So were most players and fans. Apparently, Bill Ford Sr. was not. After Matt Millen compiled a lackluster four-year record of 16–48, precisely one win per four games, Ford gave him a contract *extension*—$5 million a year for five more years, an inexplicable vote of confidence that made Millen one of the highest-paid GMs in the league. Maybe Ford believed that one out of four ain't bad. Or maybe Ford, who announced he was stepping down from Ford Motor Company's board of directors after fifty-seven years, was overcome with a spirit of generosity. Whatever his motivation, as far as most fans and sportswriters were concerned, Millen's contract extension was loyalty taken to a nearly pathological extreme.

Millen's Waterloo came on draft day before the 2005 season. After deep research, Millen and the team's coaches and scouts were in unanimous agreement that they would use their first-round pick on DeMarcus Ware, a promising linebacker from Troy State. When the Lions' turn came around, however, they were hit with a surprise: the coveted wide receiver Mike Williams from Southern Cal was still available.

(Also still available was Aaron Rodgers, a quarterback out of California who could have fixed the Lions' Joey Harrington problem. The Packers took Rodgers with the twenty-fourth overall pick, and he would earn league Most Valuable Player four times and lead the team to a Super Bowl title in 2011.)

Now a debate raged in the Lions' draft room. The prevailing sentiment was to change course and draft Williams, even though the team had drafted wide receivers the past two years. Millen wanted to stick with the plan, but as the clock ticked down and the pressure ratcheted up, he caved in. His twenty-four-year-old son Matt Jr. was in the room that day, and he exploded when the team picked the wide receiver instead of the linebacker.

"Dad," Matt Jr. roared, "you graded DeMarcus Ware yourself and said he'll be an All-Pro—and then you took *Mike Williams*!? Why did you do that?" Then he punched his father in the stomach and stormed out of the room.

"What happened was I didn't trust my gut," Millen Sr. said recently, which may help explain why his son's punch landed where it did. "For somebody who has strong opinions about everything—namely me—I gave more credit to guys who've been in the business longer. I should have stuck with my gut. I should have trusted myself, and I didn't. Like an idiot."

Fire Matt Millen had by now become a mantra in Detroit, a panacea for every species of woe. The poor man had been reduced to a punching bag and a punch line. The Lions suck again this season? *Fire Matt Millen.* Mayor Kwame Kilpatrick's a crook? *Fire Matt Millen.* Car won't start? *Fire Matt Millen.* The sad thing about it was that Millen was a decent, well-meaning man, liked by just about everyone who had personal dealings with him. But if he had no enemies, he also had no business running an NFL team—and he freely admitted his mistakes. He didn't work the job year-round, the way he needed to. He didn't travel enough, didn't spend enough time on the phone, didn't build relationships with other executives, didn't attend enough college games. As a player, he'd wanted coaches to tell him what to do and then get out of the way and let him do his job; as a GM, he realized, too late, that he needed to guide his coaches. And make smarter draft picks.

When I reached Millen by phone recently at his home in Bucks County, Pennsylvania, he came across as a man at peace with his past. He understands that his success as a football player, which led to his success at explaining the game to radio listeners and television viewers, did not prepare him for success as an NFL general manager. It was a simple—and inarguable—case of miscasting by Bill Ford and his son. Millen has come to accept the fact that he had no business running the business of a professional football team, and he has not let himself be defined by his one failure in a life full of success.

"That job is not about X's and O's," Millen told me. "After you get the right pieces of the puzzle in place, it's more a managerial job." Millen's problem was that he never managed to get the right pieces of the puzzle in place—thanks to those bad draft picks and countless personnel mistakes.

Steve Mariucci proved to be one of those mistakes. When the team put on a pitiable show in a 27–7 loss to Atlanta on Thanksgiving Day in 2005, dropping their record to 4–7, an angry Millen wanted to fire Mariucci on the spot. Instead he spent the weekend cooling off and fired him the following Monday. Mariucci, barely halfway through his five-year contract, had compiled a 15–28 record.

Some players were dismayed by Mariucci's abrupt firing, and the finger-pointing began in the locker room. Harrington was a prime target. "We're all at fault," said cornerback Dre Bly, "but I just feel like Joey has been here four years, and being the number three pick in the draft, he hasn't given us anything."

Millen named defensive coordinator Dick Jauron interim coach for the rest of the season, which ended with a 6–10 record, nowhere near the playoffs. In the offseason Millen hired Rod Marinelli, an assistant coach at Tampa Bay who had helped guide the team to a Super Bowl title in 2003 but had no head coaching experience. Marinelli was, in the words of *Sports Illustrated* writer Michael Rosenberg, "a good man who was well-liked by his players but was not meant to be a head coach." In short, a classic Detroit Lions head coach.

The torturous Joey Harrington experiment came to an end when the Lions traded him to Miami in the offseason. He had compiled an 18–37 record as a starter, and he was an emotional wreck. "The confidence I had that was brimming when I left Oregon was completely gone when I left Detroit," Harrington said. "It created a whole lot of issues for me that went beyond performance because I was dealing with depression and anxiety."

◆

Joey Harrington wasn't the only person in Detroit suffering from depression and anxiety. Bill Ford Jr.'s tenure as CEO of Ford Motor Company was turning into a train wreck that was turning him into an emotional wreck. Gone was the quick smile he'd worn when he took over from Jacques Nasser in 2001. At that time the company's stock—the major source of the Ford family's fabulous wealth—was trading at $16 a share. Now its value was less than half of that, and falling fast. The board of directors was beginning to doubt the wisdom of giving the reins to such a young and untested executive, even if his name was on the building. Like his father and his football team, the son seemed to have no clue how to turn the car company around.

In desperation, the company and the Ford family engaged in a dance that would indirectly lead to a reversal of the Lions' fortunes several years down the road. Ford Jr. brought in his brother-in-law, Steve Hamp, as his chief of staff and ordered him to work with chief financial officer Don Leclair and outside investment bankers to explore all possible ways to save the company. Hamp was an odd choice for such a high-stakes mission. He was married to Ford's older sister Sheila, and he'd spent the past twenty-seven years as an administrator at the Henry Ford Museum, where he rose to the presidency and oversaw the reconstruction of Greenfield Village and the acquisition of the Montgomery, Alabama, bus on which Rosa Parks helped launch the civil rights movement. In that world, Hamp was insulated from the warring fiefs inside Ford Motor Company. Predictably, he was stunned by the magnitude of the company's internal problems.

The options Hamp and his group looked into included a possible alliance with Renault, Nissan or General Motors, selling off Ford's foreign brands, taking the company private again, selling pieces of the company to private equity firms, even filing for bankruptcy.

The options were all unappetizing to Bill Ford Jr., who finally admitted that he was in over his head and needed help. The board of directors reached outside the company, outside the auto industry, all the way to the Pacific Northwest for a man who had overseen the turnaround of a large manufacturing company. His name was Alan Mulally, and he had saved Boeing from ruin in the wake of the 9/11 terrorist attacks. Though he knew little about the auto industry, it was hoped Mulally could now use his managerial wizardry to save Ford Motor Company.

Mulally understood that he would have to dismantle the company's byzantine bureaucracy and remake its entrenched culture, which fostered internecine turf wars instead of collegial cooperation. To that end, Mulally insisted on direct contact with his lieutenants, without the buffer of a chief of staff. Bill Ford Jr. resisted, but after some vigorous hand-wringing he acquiesced and informed his brother-in-law that he would have to go.

Hamp's ouster left a bitter taste in the mouths of some family members. It's likely that no one was more bitter than Sheila Ford Hamp, the wife of the deposed chief of staff. Her bitterness would eventually turn into a blessing for the Detroit Lions.

◆

Before Rod Marinelli coached his first game, his defensive line coach made the wrong kind of headlines. Late that summer, Joe Cullen pulled his SUV up at the drive-thru window at a Wendy's in Dearborn and ordered a burger, fries, and a drink. The manager behind the window noticed something out of the ordinary: Cullen, as the manager put it, was "butt naked." He called the police. In a separate incident a week later, Cullen was charged with drunken driving. Later in the season he was suspended for one game and fined $20,000 by commissioner Roger Goodell for "conduct detrimental to the league." Cullen, who claimed he had no memory of the nude trip to Wendy's because he had blacked out from drinking, kept his job but had to go through the league's out-patient treatment program for alcoholism.

After that unnerving prelude, the Lions lost their first five games under Marinelli and took a 2–8 record into their Thanksgiving Day showcase against the Miami Dolphins. The game started well for the Lions, with Dan Campbell, a recent free agent acquisition at tight end, catching a touchdown pass, followed by a field goal. The Lions would not score again. Miami's new backup quarterback, the one and only Joey Harrington, picked the Detroit defense apart, throwing three touchdowns passes that fueled a 27–10 win. The comeback did wonders for Harrington's depression and anxiety. As the game began slipping away, chants of "Fire Millen!" rained from the stands. The chants were no longer confined to Ford Field; they were also heard at Pistons and Red Wings games, in newspaper columns and letters to the editor, at office water coolers, on every sports talk show in town. Newfangled things called websites had popped up, fanning the flames of the Fire Millen movement and winning comparisons to a "mob mentality." Images of a fan being removed from the Ford Field stands while holding a FIRE MILLEN sign were played repeatedly on ESPN. Detroit's local agony had become a national comedy.

Marinelli's inaugural season ended with a 3–13 record. With the second overall pick in the 2007 draft, the Lions drafted the promising wide receiver

Calvin Johnson, whose speed, power, and leaping ability quickly won him the nickname Megatron, after the ferocious gladiator in the Transformers franchise. The team got off to a 6–2 start in Johnson's rookie season before fading to a 7–9 record and yet another no-show in the playoffs. By now it seemed that everyone in the state of Michigan was calling for Matt Millen's head.

Unfortunately, Bill Ford Sr. had still not gotten the memo.

THE GHOST OF GROSSE POINTE

Dick Morris, Bill Ford's former PR guy and the could-have-been general manager of the Detroit Lions, died on Oct. 25, 2008, at the age of eighty-six. My brother and sisters and I, operating in that fugue state common to siblings after a parent's death, divided up duties in preparation for the funeral. It fell to me to notify friends and relatives about our father's death, and after several tries I found myself on the phone with Bill Ford at his home in Grosse Pointe. He sounded genuinely saddened by the news, though of course that could have been wishful thinking on my part—or it could have been that Ford, then eighty-three, had been getting a lot of these calls lately and they always made him wonder: Am I next?

By then I had stopped following football so I was unaware that there may have been a very different reason for the sadness I heard in Bill Ford's voice that day. A month earlier, after the Lions lost their first three games of the season, Ford had finally fired Matt Millen. His reason—"It just didn't work out"—made him sound a lot like big brother Henry II when he gave Lee Iacocca the ax.

Drivers honked their horns in glee when they passed the Lions' practice facility, and the papers made it sound like the entire city of Detroit had been released from a life sentence in a maximum-security prison. Yet Millen's firing did little to mollify the many fans who were irate that his ineptitude had been tolerated so long and that he was leaving town a very rich man.

The blogger Sean Yuille offered a typical rant: "Matt Millen was the worst GM in the NFL and maybe even in sports as a whole. Despite that, he made $35 million in his time with the Lions and will make $15 million more for doing nothing at all."

Millen's long-overdue departure did not fix the Lions. Under Marinelli and interim GM Martin Mayhew, they kept losing. And losing. And losing. Once again the losses climbed into double digits without a win, and once again there was talk that the team might finish the 2008 season without a single victory. Each week, the punch line to the knock-knock jokes got less funny: Owen Ten became Owen Eleven, then Owen Twelve . . .

Marinelli's postgame press conferences had turned into a verbal contact sport. He had hired his son-in-law Joe Barry as defensive coordinator, and the Lions' defense was hands-down the worst in the league. After a typically lopsided 42–7 loss to the Saints that left the Lions one game away from a winless season, Rob Parker of the *News* had a question for the head coach. Claiming he was trying for a humorous note, Parker asked Marinelli: "Do you wish your daughter would have married a better defensive coordinator?"

Marinelli didn't see the humor. Neither did Fox football analyst Terry Bradshaw, who called Parker "a total idiot." When Parker tried to apologize the next day, Marinelli rejected the gesture. "Any time you attack my daughter, I've got a problem with that," he said. "In a room of stink . . . I think there was something wrong with that, yeah."

Marinelli declined to answer questions from reporters as to what he meant by "a room of stink."

Parker's bosses were not amused, either. Managing editor Don Nauss called Parker's question "inappropriate and unprofessional." After the Lions lost in Green Bay to complete the first 0–16 season in NFL history, Parker resigned from the *News*. It would have been funny if it weren't so sad.

◆

The Matt Millen fiasco did have an upside. After hitting rock bottom in 2008, the Lions got to pick first in the ensuing draft and they snagged Matthew Stafford from Georgia, the Promised Land quarterback they'd been seeking since the day Bobby Layne left for Pittsburgh half a century earlier. Fans inclined to look for celestial signs of deliverance took note that Stafford, Layne, and Doak Walker all graduated from Highland Park High School in Dallas. It could not possibly be a coincidence. The stars had finally aligned. The Curse, surely, was doomed.

Stafford lived up to his advance billing. Not since Bobby Layne did the Lions have a quarterback who could engineer so many heart-stopping late drives. With athletic Calvin Johnson as his primary target, Stafford ran a pass-happy offense that put an end to the team's twelve-year playoff drought in 2011, when Stafford threw for more than 5,000 yards and the team scored more than 400 points. Their 10–6 record earned them a playoff berth, but, as usual, they lost in the wild card round on the road, this time to New Orleans.

That playoff loss was Bill Ford's last rodeo. He stubbornly clung to ownership of the team in the final years of his life, watching from afar as Stafford and Johnson tried to carry mediocre teams coached by Jim Schwartz, who compiled a 29–51 record in five seasons. All the while, Bill Ford ignored pleas to sell the franchise.

What do you want me to do—fire myself? I'm not going to do it.

His loyalty and tenacity now seemed like mulishness, a stubborn refusal to admit that he was wrong—wrong in the people he hired, wrong for his misplaced loyalties, wrong for clinging to ownership of this cursed franchise. And so, after giving this witty, classy gentleman a pass for decades, the fans began to turn on him. In the penultimate year of his life, *Sports Illustrated* acknowledged that the city's passion for the Lions had morphed into widespread hatred of Bill Ford. After stating that Matt Millen's 31–84 record was "one of the worst executive performances in American sports history," the article added that Ford was "a good man who has been an awful owner . . . a man who is beloved by those who know him and reviled by those who don't." The article, a sort of advance obituary, concluded: "[F]ans would like him if they didn't hate him so much."

Among those who knew Bill Ford and loved him were his players, including some who'd had bitter dealings with management. Joe Schmidt, Sam Williams, Jon Morris, Charlie Sanders, Lomas Brown—to name just a few—all had high praise for Ford. It's not as illogical as it might seem. Ford created the stage that allowed them to play in the big time, and he truly loved his team. By washing his hands of such day-to-day concerns as contract negotiations—or claiming to—he was able to deflect much of the players' displeasure onto management. Even Lomas Brown, who was brutally discarded after eleven stellar seasons with the team, came to the defense of the "cool dude" Bill Ford. "We all knew that Mr. Ford knew football," Brown wrote in his memoir, "but the information he was getting was filtered through guys like Chuck Schmidt or Russ Thomas . . . Once management convinced Mr. Ford that I wasn't as important as in years past, I was toast as a Lion." Yet Brown continues to sing Bill Ford's praises to this day.

In the face of such heated hostility from the fans, however, Ford had become virtually invisible late in life, no longer attending owners' meetings, rarely showing up for games at Ford Field, largely absent from the locker room and the newspapers. After taking over the Lions' beat for the *Free Press* in 2010, Dave Birkett says he hardly ever saw Ford and never interviewed him. Bill Ford, once a loquacious quote machine, had become the ghost of Grosse Pointe. It may be that shame played a part in his late-life invisibility—shame for having disappointed so many people for so many years. Including himself?

Detroit was grappling with far more serious problems than the Lions' ongoing woes. In the summer of 2013 the city, facing $18 billion in debts and no realistic way to pay them off, filed for Chapter 9 bankruptcy, the biggest municipal bankruptcy filing in US history. By then, barely half of the city's streetlights worked, and more than half of the parks had been closed because of budget cuts. The city's population, after peaking at 1.8 million in 1950, had shrunk to 700,000 residents, more than 80 percent of whom were Black. In announcing the bankruptcy filing, Rick Snyder, the white Republican governor, said, "This is a difficult step, but the only viable option to address a problem that has been six decades in the making." The city would emerge from bankruptcy a year a half later after rebuffing attempts to sell off the heart its patrimony to satisfy debts. Among the treasures spared by the so-called "grand bargain" were the Diego Rivera murals at the Detroit Institute of Arts commissioned by Edsel Ford.

◆

Bill Ford's last act was the belated hiring of the Lions' first Black head coach, Jim Caldwell. The end finally came two months later, on March 9, 2014, when Ford died of pneumonia in his Lake Shore Road mansion, surrounded by his family. He was five days shy of his eighty-ninth birthday.

The obituaries were generally kind, focusing on Ford's courtly manner, his colorful and opulent life, his tight-knit family, his philanthropy, and his deep ties to a quintessential American industry. But without fail the obituaries also mentioned Ford's half-century of nearly constant futility as owner of the Detroit Lions. AUTOMAKER WILLIAM CLAY SR. COULDN'T MAKE LIONS HUM read one typical headline.

Now that he was gone, everyone in Detroit wondered what was next for the Lions. They didn't have to wait long for the answer.

ON THE ROAD TO REDEMPTION

(2014-2024)

QUINNTRICIA

The obituaries noted that Bill Ford was to be buried at Detroit's Woodlawn Cemetery, near the graves of his parents and brother Benson and many other Motor City royals, including the civil rights activist Rosa Parks and the Motown star David Ruffin. Four years later they would be joined by the Queen of Soul, Aretha Franklin. (Henry Ford II was cremated, and his ashes were scattered on the Detroit River.)

The day after Bill Ford died, even before the funeral, his widow Martha Firestone Ford held a press conference to announce that her late husband had left a succession plan for the Lions in place. It killed any hopes that the family would sell the team. Martha was taking over as principal owner and chairwoman, and her four children would serve as vice chairpersons. It was still widely assumed that Bill Ford Jr., after orchestrating the construction of Ford Field and taking a more visible role in team affairs, would soon succeed his eighty-eight-year-old mother as principal owner.

Jim Caldwell coached the team to an 11–5 record in his first season, good enough for a wild card playoff date in Dallas. With the Lions holding a narrow lead late in the fourth quarter, a referee called pass interference on Dallas, which would have given the Lions a crucial first down. Then the referees mysteriously reversed the call, the Lions had to punt, and Dallas scored a late touchdown to win the game 24–20, sending the Lions to their eighth straight playoff loss since 1991. The Curse appeared to be alive and well.

Martha Ford soon made it known that she, unlike her late husband, had no patience with business as usual. After the Lions got off to a 1–7 start the following season, she fired the two holdovers at the top of the organization, president Tom Lewand and general manager Martin Mayhew. Coming in mid-season, it was the sort of swift, forceful shakeup her late husband had been loath to make. Martha decided to retain head coach Jim Caldwell, but it was understood that he was now skating on thin ice.

The team rallied but still finished with a losing record and missed the playoffs. At the end of the season, future Hall of Famer Calvin Johnson, his spirit broken by the team's failure to win a single playoff game in his nine seasons—which included the winless nightmare of 2008—announced that he was retiring at the age of thirty. Years later Megatron explained his reason for following Barry Sanders's lead and walking away from the team while still in his prime. "You got me on offense," Johnson said, "you've got Stafford, you got Ndamukong Suh on defense. You've got some beasts all around the team in key positions that you should be able to have a winning team. We just didn't have the winning culture though. There's a lot more that goes into it than having those key players." Like Sanders, Johnson was headed for a rocky postretirement relationship with the team.

Martha Ford had promised to conduct a thorough national search for a new president, but she needed just two weeks to locate her man. And she didn't have to scour the nation to find him. In fact, she didn't have to look beyond the city limits of Detroit or even beyond the snug confines of the Ford family circle.

Rod Wood, the team's new president, was not a football man. He was a former bank executive who'd spent the past eight years running Ford Estates, a private company that advises family members on investments, tax planning, and other financial matters. Though Wood's duties would be confined to the team's business operations, the hiring of a family intimate with no football experience gave off an unsettling whiff of business as usual, even cronyism. "The Lions," as the *Free Press* put it, "never learn from prior mistakes."

Wood, to his credit, admitted that he was out of his depth when it came to conducting a search for the general manager of a professional football team, so he and Martha brought in Ernie Accorsi to guide them. Accorsi had worked on Pete Rozelle's staff, and he'd also been general manager of the Cleveland Browns, Baltimore Colts, and New York Giants. More recently he'd helped several teams vet and hire successful GMs. His hiring by the Lions was rated "a coup" by one reporter, and it helped temper some of the skepticism over the hiring of Wood.

In January 2016, the Lions offered the general manager's job to Bob Quinn, the director of pro scouting with the New England Patriots. It was a plausible hire, but it had come from outside, not from within. This would prove to be a fatal flaw.

The Lions finished 9–7 that year and made the playoffs, losing again in the first round, this time to Seattle. Caldwell's second straight 9–7 finish the following season was not good enough to make the playoffs. Though Caldwell had a 36–28 record after four seasons—making him the Lions' first winning coach since Joe Schmidt—Quinn, like all general managers, yearned to put his personal stamp on the team. So he persuaded Martha Ford to let Caldwell go and replace him with the Patriots' defensive coordinator, Matt Patricia, a personal friend of Quinn's. The idea was to import some of the "Patriot Way" pixie dust from New England, winners of five recent Super Bowls under former Lions' assistant coach Bill Belichick and quarterback Tom Brady.

It sounded like a fine idea to Martha Ford.

◆

Shortly before Patricia's hiring was announced, the Big Muffin was back in the news. After the Lions had decamped in 2001, a Canadian billionaire named Andreas Apostolopoulos had bought the Silverdome for $538,000, almost exactly a penny on the dollar, but his big plans for turning a profit failed to bear fruit. And so Apostolopoulous announced that he would implode the building that had hosted Elvis, the Pope, a Super Bowl, and the Lions' only playoff victory since the Eisenhower administration.

On Sunday, Dec. 3, 2017, an expectant throng showed up for the big bang, but they were disappointed when the charges were fired, puffs of smoke shot out of the sides of the building—and nothing happened. The Big Muffin refused to fall down. It was forgotten, but not quite gone. This, of course, inspired much online merriment.

"Once again angry people leave the Silverdome after a disappointing ending," said one podcast.

"The Lions now still have as many successful stadium implosions as they do Super Bowl trophies," said another.

"It was a dud," chimed in a third, "just like many of the Lions' performances there."

The next day, after the faulty wiring was repaired, the implosion was a success. The Big Muffin was now a pile of twisted steel, concrete, and mostly bad memories.

◆

Thirteen minutes into his introductory press conference, Matt Patricia planted a No. 2 pencil above his right ear. It would become his trademark, designed to announce that he was a serious student of the game. He'd played football and earned a degree in aeronautical engineering at Rensselaer Polytechnic Institute—some sportswriters called him "the rocket scientist"—but he had never played professional football and he had never been a head coach. In other words, he was yet another perfect candidate for the Lions' head coaching job.

Before Patricia coached a game for the Lions, the *Detroit News* broke the story that the team had missed something during its background checks of the half dozen candidates for the head coach's job. While he was a student at RPI in 1996, Patricia had spent a spring break at South Padre Island, Texas. One night Patricia and a teammate on the RPI football team visited the hotel room of a female college student they'd met at the beach. What happened in that hotel room remains in question, but after Patricia and his buddy left, the woman went to the police, claiming the two friends had sexually assaulted her. Later that night, after the woman identified them, Patricia and his teammate were charged with sexual assault and released on bond. Eventually they were indicted on aggravated sexual assault charges by a Texas grand jury, but the charges were dismissed when the woman said she could not handle the stress of testifying in open court. When the story broke in Detroit twenty-two years afterward, at the peak of the #MeToo movement, an indignant Patricia said he found it "incredibly unfair, disappointing and frustrating that this story would resurface now with the only purpose being to damage my character and reputation. I firmly maintain my innocence, as I have always done." The Lions stood by their new coach—after all, a man's innocent until proven guilty—but Martha Ford's first head coach hire was already under a cloud.

Things went downhill from there. Seeking to assert himself, Patricia adopted an authoritarian approach from the opening day of training camp. He banned music in the locker room and forbade jersey swaps with opposing players after games. He cursed and belittled his players. Before a game against the Carolina Panthers, Patricia showed a video of Carolina defensive back Cam Newton doing a gleeful dance after intercepting a pass. The intention was to show the players that this kind of showboating was not the Patriot Way, not the Patricia Way. But the players were delighted by Newton's celebration. When Patricia shut off the video, the safety Quandre Diggs shouted, "No, we like that, coach! Keep that running!" Message sent, message not received. Patricia even replaced the team's longtime chaplain, Dave Wilson, with a "character coach" because that, too, was the Patriot Way.

The Lions lost that game to Carolina and nine others, tumbling to a 6–10 record and a last-place finish. The only bright spot was a moral victory over

Patricia's former mentor, Bill Belichick and his New England Patriots, but moral victories don't go very far in the NFL, especially when the atmosphere in the locker room is toxic. While the players were cleaning out their lockers at season's end, someone produced a bottle of champagne and some orange juice and mixed a round of mimosas in Solo cups. The players cranked up the music and merrily toasted the end of the season—at least they wouldn't have to listen to Matt Patricia for a few months.

Patricia softened his approach somewhat in his second season but it didn't do any good. Matthew Stafford was lost for the year after suffering broken bones in his back in a Week 9 loss to the Oakland Raiders, and without him the team went into a nosedive, losing its last nine games and finishing with a 3–12–1 record, even deeper in the cellar. Fans now arrived at Ford Field with paper bags over their heads, ashamed to show their faces in public—not unlike Bill Ford in the last years of his life. Some fans scrawled SAME OLD LIONS on their paper bags. Others wore T-shirts emblazoned with the plea SELL THE TEAM alongside a picture of Martha Ford in her trademark black sunglasses—a clear sign that fans believed the source of their years of suffering was the Ford family.

The fans, predictably, started calling for the heads of Quinn and Patricia, who were now regarded as a joined-at-the-hip entity called Quinntricia, a Detroit wrinkle on the slightly more glamorous Hollywood couple known as Brangelina.

Martha Ford wasn't ready to perform the decapitation(s) just yet. At the end of the 2019 season she summoned daughter Sheila and Rod Wood to meet with a select group of reporters and explain why ownership was giving Quinn and Patricia one more chance to prove themselves. During that half-hour briefing, Sheila did most of the talking. "[Changing coaches] would have been the popular choice, the popular decision, and we knew that," she told the gathered reporters. "But as I say, we're doing what's right for the organization."

Dave Birkett, the beat reporter for the *Free Press* and an astute student of the game, is not easily impressed. But as he left Wood's office that day, Birkett had to admit to himself that he was impressed. "In her first lengthy interaction with reporters since taking a more prominent role as the team's most visible vice chair," he wrote, "Ford Hamp came off as smart, strong and decisive, someone well aware of how Tuesday's decision will be received publicly but confident enough to make the call anyway—or urge her mother to, at the very least. Just as Bill Ford Jr.'s fingerprints were all over the Matt Millen hire years ago, Ford Hamp's are both on the decision to keep Patricia and Quinn now and to give them what essentially amounts to a playoffs-or-bust mandate in 2020."

Though no cries from suffering fans and no number of paper bags or T-shirts were going to convince the Fords to sell the team, it turned out that this tradition-bound family was still capable of surprises. When Martha Ford announced that she was stepping down as principal owner in the summer of 2020, she stunned the Lions organization and the rest of the NFL by naming Sheila, not Bill Jr., as her successor.

Family history and chemistry came into play here. When Bill's and Martha's kids were growing up, the Ford household was a "hypercompetitive" place, in Bill Jr.'s telling, where everything was a cutthroat competition, from dinner table conversations to cards, trivia, pool and video games and, of course, sports. While Bill Jr. excelled at hockey, Sheila became a Michigan state junior tennis champion at seventeen, and she played varsity tennis at Yale, where she was a member of the first class of women admitted to her father's alma mater. Her interest in sports seeped into the classroom at Yale, where she was one of two women enrolled in a sports writing seminar conducted by the Pulitzer Prize–winning columnist Red Smith of the *New York Times*. (In a column, Smith dubbed Sheila "a knockout"!) After graduating from Yale she earned a master's degree in early childhood education from Boston University and taught for a while before raising three sons in Ann Arbor and becoming active in youth soccer.

But she was no soccer mom cheering from the sidelines. She coached for more than ten years.

Sheila had come of age during the flowering of the women's liberation movement, and she had never been at peace with patriarchal codes. In her early years it was a given that no Ford woman would ever serve on Ford Motor Company's board of directors, certainly not as chairman of the board, and it was rare for any woman to reach the upper floors of the Glass House.

(There have been at least two recent exceptions to this rule. Elena Ford, a granddaughter of Henry II and a self-proclaimed "car freak," climbed the corporate ladder and is now the chief dealer engagement officer. And one of Bill Jr.'s daughters, Alexandra Ford English, was elected to the board of directors in 2021, the year after her aunt Sheila became principal owner of the Lions.)

Until Sheila's mother assumed the Lions' top spot after her father's death, the team's front office had not been much more welcoming to women who were not secretaries. That may have been acceptable when Bill Ford Sr. had bought the team a half-century earlier, but this was now the twenty-first century and the old ways of running companies and sports franchises like extended boys' clubs were no longer acceptable to Sheila Ford Hamp. Or, apparently, to her mother.

In his book about Alan Mulally's turnaround of Ford Motor Company, former *Detroit News* business columnist Bryce G. Hoffman addressed this friction between brother and sister. "In a family like the Fords," Hoffman wrote, "the usual sibling rivalries sometimes escalate into business battles. That was certainly the case between Bill and Sheila."

An early battle followed Bill Jr.'s acquiescence to Mulally's demand, back in 2006, that chief of staff Steve Hamp had to go. "Friends said Sheila resented this," Hoffman wrote, "just as she resented her exclusion from the family's football franchise, which Bill ran with his father. [The friends] suggested this made her a more vocal critic of her brother, and that criticism increased after Hamp joined the company as Bill's chief of staff in late 2005."

After their father's death, these resentments may have spurred Sheila to become more active in the family business, and since that business was now run by a woman, she found she was welcomed more warmly in the Lions' front office than she had been in years past. Signs of Sheila's rising influence were there for the reading. She had run the briefing with reporters to explain the decision to give Quinntricia one last chance. She'd started traveling to road games and was a regular presence on the sidelines. She attended league meetings with her mother and was named to the Super Bowl and Major Events Committee. Her growing visibility, coupled with Bill Jr.'s diminishing role, should have left little doubt who was now the top lieutenant.

The precise thinking that led Martha Ford to elevate her daughter instead of her son is unknowable because the Fords, as noted, are private people who are disinclined to air their business in public. (Both Sheila Ford Hamp and her brother Bill Ford Jr. declined requests to be interviewed for this book.) So the best one can hope for is informed speculation, which leads to the conclusion that Martha Ford must have found something wanting in her son, who bore some responsibility for the Matt Millen debacle and, for good measure, had seen Ford Motor Company stock plunge so sharply on his watch as CEO that he had to bring in an outsider to save the company. Then he had let that outsider talk him into firing a member of the family, his own brother-in-law. For reasons known only to her, Martha came to believe that her smart, strong, decisive—and fiercely competitive and hungry and tough—daughter was more likely to lead the Lions back to relevance. Martha may have believed that boys' clubs tend to produce soft boys. There's evidence that her assessment was shared by at least one other player in this succession drama. After his introductory meeting with Bill Ford Jr. in the summer of 2006, Alan Mulally had jotted down his terse first impression of the scion who was then running Ford Motor Company: "Not tough enough." Ford Jr. admitted as much to a vice president: "I've never turned around anything."

Maybe Martha agreed with these assessments. If so, it should not have come as a shock when she picked daughter over son to run the Lions. Ford family watchers claim that the daughter takes after the decisive mother while the son tends to follow the lead of the less forceful father. Proof of the validity of this theory arrived almost immediately. Midway through her first season at the helm—Quinntricia's playoffs-or-bust last chance—the Lions got shut out by the middling Carolina Panthers, then embarrassed by the equally mediocre Houston Texans on national television in their Thanksgiving Day game. The back-to-back losses left them with a 4–7 record and only the slimmest mathematical chance of making the playoffs. During the game, Sheila, wearing a mask in keeping with Ford Field's COVID protocols, was visible in her suite burying her face in her hands, unable to watch what was taking place on the field.

Two days later she fired Quinn and Patricia.

In his two and a half seasons, the departing head coach had compiled a 13–29–1 record, which made him the fourth losingest coach in Lions' history. That's no small achievement. Lions players, past and present, rejoiced at the news of his firing. So did most fans.

Now Sheila Ford Hamp faced her make-or-break moment. Would it be business as usual, or would she make a clean break with the team's—and the Ford family's—old way of doing things?

"WE'RE GOING TO BITE A KNEECAP OFF"

As she set out to hire a general manager and a head coach, the new principal owner of the Detroit Lions decided that since the Ford family's old ways of doing things had produced just one playoff win in fifty-six years of ownership, it was time to try something daring and new. The conventional path was to hire a general manager and let him select a coach who, in turn, would build a staff of assistant coaches. Sheila Ford Hamp had a different idea.

As she began her quest, she had to take into account an unwelcome new development. Matthew Stafford, the team's Promised Land quarterback since 2009, was now thirty-two years old and beginning to ask himself the questions every NFL veteran must eventually confront. How long will my body hold up to the weekly punishment? What are my chances of winning a Super Bowl with my current team? Is it time to move on? The answers, in order, were: not much longer; slim to none; and yes. Rumors began to circulate that Matthew Stafford wanted to be traded to a contender.

Sheila Ford, Rod Wood, and chief operating officer Mike Disner, an expert on contracts and salary cap, acknowledged that trying to import the Patriot Way via Quinn and Patricia had been a disaster. The answer was to build a *Detroit* Lions team from the ground up. So one of their first moves after the firing of Quinntricia was to bring back the quintessential Detroit Lion, Chris Spielman—the warrior linebacker who had played his final season as a Lion with a painful and debilitating torn pectoral muscle but didn't miss a single game, the guy who had stood up on the eve of the team's lone conference championship game in 1991 and corrected the team chaplain, telling him that the goal was not to win the NFC Championship, the goal was to win the Super Bowl. That was the mentality they were looking for. Spielman's bitterness over being exiled to Buffalo had faded with time. His love for Detroit and the Lions had not. His would be a critical voice in the search for a general manager and coach, as well as the ensuing rebuild.

Hamp kicked off each GM candidate interview by stressing that the goal was nothing less than a teardown and reconstruction of the team's culture. She always used the word "collaboration," which was, curiously, the essence of the systems Alan Mulally had installed at Boeing and Ford Motor Company when he'd set out to smash the warring fiefs inside both corporations and remake their cultures. After Hamp finished her remarks, the others jumped in for a freewheeling conversation. Then they independently graded each candidate in twelve categories, on a scale of one to five, and loaded the results into a spreadsheet. The goal was to create an egoless, collaborative organization with everyone pulling in the same direction. No finger-pointing, no turf wars, no power grabs. Therefore, if a potential GM wanted authority to pick his coach and control all facets of the operation, he was cut from the list.

Before long, one name stood out: Brad Holmes.

Then serving as director of college scouting with the Los Angeles Rams, Holmes had been captain of the North Carolina A&T football team that won the Historically Black Colleges and Universities national championship in 1999. After graduation he got a job as a PR intern with the Rams and doggedly worked his way up the scouting ladder. He was regarded as a master assessor of talent, shrewdly using the draft to help build a roster that had turned a perennial doormat into a team that went 13–3 in 2018 before losing to New England in the Super Bowl. The Rams' quarterback was Jared Goff, who they'd drafted with the No. 1 pick in 2016. Since the

Lions were determined to rebuild through the draft, Holmes's strengths were seen as a perfect fit.

All the while, the search crew had been looking at possible head coaches. They kept coming back to Dan Campbell, then assistant head coach to Sean Payton in New Orleans. In his ten-year playing career, Campbell was a tight end used mainly as a blocker. He looked the part: 6'5", 265 pounds, with a bull neck and legs like oak trees. He'd made it to the Super Bowl early in his playing career, and his last season was with the winless Lions in 2008. So he had been to the top of the mountain and to the bottom of the basement, and he understood, firsthand, what Detroit's players and fans had been through. But he brought more than empathy to the table.

In his ten-year coaching career, Campbell had served as interim head coach of the Dolphins for a dozen games in 2015 after Joe Philbin was fired mid-season. And Spielman, who'd spent years working as a television analyst, had many opportunities to watch Campbell interact with players. It was obvious to Spielman that Campbell had earned their respect. When Spielman called Campbell's boss in New Orleans to find out more, Payton sang his assistant's praises for an uninterrupted half hour. Deal closed.

"He's known as a coach who gets what he asks from his players because he speaks and interacts with them from a place of shared personal experience," Nick Baumgardner wrote in *The Athletic*. "And in that way, he's the opposite of Patricia." And for that reason, he was perfect for the Lions' rebuild.

The Lions announced the hiring of Holmes as GM on Jan. 14, 2021, and named Campbell their new head coach the following week. The two met for the first time after they were hired. At his ninety-minute introductory press conference, Campbell delivered a mad-dog monologue that lit up the football world and has since become embedded in Detroit lore. It's worth quoting at length: "This place has been kicked, it's been battered, it's been bruised, and I can sit up here and give you coach speak all day long. I can give you, 'Hey, we're going to win this many games.' None of that matters, and you guys don't want to hear it anyway. You've had enough of that shit, excuse my language."

Now he cranked it up a gear.

"Here's what I do know, is that this team is going to take on the identity of this city. And this city's been down and it found way to get up. It's found a way to overcome adversity. So this team's going to be built on: we're going to kick you in the teeth, all right, and when you punch us back, we're going to smile at you and when you knock us down, we're going to get up, and on the way up, we're going to bite a kneecap off. And we're going to stand up and then it's going to take two more shots to knock us down. And on the way up, we're going to take your other kneecap, and we're going to get up and then it's going to take three shots to get us down. And when we do, we're going to take another hunk out of you. Before long, we're going to be the last one standing. That's going to be the mentality."

What the fuck was this? Had the Lions hired a foam-at-the-mouth Texas lunatic? Or was this a refreshing break from the tight-ass conventions of head coach introductory press conferences, with their pablum "coach speak" that Campbell so clearly scorned? Could this be a breath of fresh air? Nobody knew what to think.

Meanwhile, Holmes learned after he was hired that Matthew Stafford did indeed want to be traded. A lot of novice GMs would have panicked at the prospect of losing their franchise player. Holmes took the news coolly. He was smart enough to see it as an opportunity.

◆

Half a dozen teams were interested in Matthew Stafford, and the Carolina Panthers made a tantalizing offer that included their first-round draft pick, which meant the Lions could pick seventh and eighth and snag two blue-chip players for an instant jump-start. But the Los Angeles Rams made an offer that was more enticing to Holmes: the proven quarterback Jared

Goff along with a third-round draft pick this year and first-round picks the next two years. Holmes was in this for the long haul, not the quick fix, so after less than a month on the job he dropped his first bombshell: he was trading Matthew Stafford to the Rams.

It was a seen as a bold move, but a win for both sides. The Rams had soured on Goff since their Super Bowl loss, and in Stafford they were getting a proven star who'd languished on mediocre teams and now had the chance to take a solid Rams team over the top. For their part, the Lions were getting a twenty-seven-year-old quarterback with Super Bowl experience—a player Holmes still believed in—plus a stack of bricks that could become the foundation of their long-haul rebuild.

With his first NFL draft still a month away, Holmes was confronted with another major decision—and a test of his commitment to the collaborative culture the team was trying to build. The gifted but oft-injured receiver Kenny Golladay was going to be eligible for free agency, but Holmes decided not to protect him with the designation of franchise player. Kenny Golladay, as far as Holmes was concerned, was more concerned with the future of Kenny Golladay than with the future of the Detroit Lions. After a sparkling performance against Jacksonville during the Bob Quinn regime, Golladay had written to Lions' management on Instagram: "This shit gone cost you! Don't let that go over y'all head." After Holmes let him go, the New York Giants signed Golladay to a four-year contract for $72 million. He bombed in New York—"the most overpaid player in the league," in the estimation of one sportswriter—and after two seasons the Giants released him. The episode would make Holmes look like a genius.

Now it was time for his first NFL draft, time for Holmes to start mixing the mortar and laying the bricks. When the Lions' No. 7 pick came in the first round, Holmes didn't merely pick; he pounced on the offensive tackle Penei Sewell from Oregon. Holmes moved so swiftly that league officials urged him to slow it down before making future picks. He ignored them. Though the highly touted quarterback Justin Fields from Ohio State was still available, Holmes had faith in his own recently acquired quarterback, Jared Goff, and he saw Sewell as something bigger than a brick—a 335-pound cinderblock who could anchor the all-important offensive line for years to come.

Holmes's decisiveness was not lost on Sewell. "There are clips that I see online of that pick when it happened," Sewell told *The Athletic*. "To see him react like that to pick me, I was like, 'Oh, it's on.' If he asked me to go swim 200 miles, I'd swim 200 miles. I'd go as far as he wants me to go."

Sewell has indeed proven to be a cinderblock, but Holmes's most inspired moves may have come later. Many GMs treat the later rounds as a time to throw darts and hope they hit something. Not Holmes. He used the No. 75 overall pick on defensive tackle Alim McNeill and the No. 112 pick on wide receiver Amon-Ra St. Brown. Both would have an immediate impact, and St. Brown would make the Pro Bowl in his second season and be named All-Pro in his third. To top it off, Holmes signed the free agent linebacker Alex Anzalone, another brick for the defense.

Meanwhile, Campbell had put together a solid coaching staff, including guys who had other offers but wanted to work with him. Though impressive, these building blocks did not translate into overnight success. In the first season of the Holmes/Campbell regime, the Lions lost their first eight games before managing a tie against the Steelers, followed by two more losses. A 0–10–1 start is not exactly a confidence builder with fans who'd grown weary from listening to new GMs and coaches promise them the world, only to flame out. There were groans that these were—after all, yet again, *oh please no!*—the Same Old Lions.

◆

It was at about this time that I hatched the idea of writing a history of the Ford family's ownership of the Detroit Lions. I'd been thinking about my late father, Richard Morris, and the hours we had spent at his home in Athens, Georgia, in 1995, tape-recording his reminiscences from the first seventy-three years of his life. I remembered that during those taping sessions my father had talked extensively about his seventeen years at Ford Motor Company in the 1950s and '60s, and he'd gone into vivid, often hilarious, sometimes touching detail about his working relationship and friendship with William Clay Ford. When I listened to those tapes again a quarter-century after we'd made them, it struck me that, yes, they contained a seed that might be made to blossom into a book.

Over the years I'd followed the Lions in a very casual way, the way many grown men maintain a tenuous connection to their boyhood passions. I occasionally checked the Monday papers for the previous day's NFL scores and the current standings, usually shaking my head that the Lions seemed to have a magical gift for being unable to get out of their own way. General managers and coaches and players came and went, owners came and went (though they were always named Ford), *stadiums* came and went—but the Lions kept losing. Such perennial failure could not be an accident. I asked myself: why did it keep happening? What was the source of the Lions' chronic failure?

My father's stories contained a possible answer. All organizations, including sports teams, are shaped from the top down, and beginning in that suite in the Plaza Hotel in late 1963, the culture of the Lions began to be shaped by the upbringing, character, and personality of one man: William Clay Ford. Here, I told myself, was that rare American thing—a story of futility. It went against the nation's worship of success stories, and for that very reason it was irresistible to me. When a working title popped into my head, I was on my way.

I would call the book *Natural Born Losers.*

◆

The halftime ceremony during the home game against the Baltimore Ravens in the third week of the 2021 season was supposed to be a joyous occasion. After a protracted cold war, the Lions and the newly minted Hall of Famer Calvin Johnson had arrived at an uneasy truce. At the halftime ceremony, Megatron would wear his golden Hall of Fame blazer onto the turf of Ford Field, where he would be presented with his Hall of Fame ring. But when Sheila Ford Hamp started to speak, she was drowned out by thunderous boos from 50,000 fans. Johnson had to flap his arms to quiet the crowd so she could finish her remarks. It was a jarring display of how the fans felt about the Ford family. Some even expressed outrage over the WCF patches the players had been wearing on their jerseys since William Clay Ford's death. The patches were an "abomination," declared a blogger called weaselpuppy. "The fact that the Ford family wants it there only shows their cluelessness."

The fans' displeasure with the Fords had been smoldering for decades, of course, so the team's war with Calvin Johnson merely added fresh fuel to a very old fire. This particular war had begun the day after the end of the 2015 season, when Johnson broke the news to coach Jim Caldwell that he was retiring. Caldwell immediately started contacting Ford family members and team officials to break the news. When the team's new president Rod Wood spoke with Johnson, he wasted no time firing the first shot in a war that would drag on for years.

As Johnson recalled: "I knew there was going to be a problem once Rod talked to me and the first thing out of his mouth was like, 'Did you earn all your bonus?' I was like, 'Oh, shit.' I knew right then that this was going to be a problem. I was like, 'All right, I see how this is going to be.'"

Johnson saw, correctly, that this was going to be ugly. NFL teams are entitled to recoup prorated shares of signing bonuses when players retire before their contracts expire, though most make exceptions for star players who have made extraordinary contributions to the team. Consider the Indianapolis Colts. When their franchise quarterback Andrew Luck shocked them by announcing during training camp in 2019 that he was retiring at twenty-nine, with three years left on his six-year, $139 million contract, the team took this gut punch in stride. Considering Luck's nine stellar seasons, the team allowed him to keep $12.8 million of his signing bonuses and another $12 million bonus. This largesse hurt the team's salary-cap math, but it was the Colts' way of saying thank you. The Lions under Chuck Schmidt had shown no such gratitude to Barry Sanders, and now under Rod Wood they were showing none to Calvin Johnson. He had signed an eight-year contract in 2012, and the Lions demanded that he refund a prorated share of his signing bonus, $1.6 million. It made the team look appallingly picayune and cheap.

Johnson paid back the money but developed a festering bitterness toward the Lions' front office. Barry Sanders, after paying back a share of his own signing bonus, had reconciled with the team and taken on a role as a handsomely paid ambassador in 2017—eighteen years after his retirement and thirteen years after his induction into the Hall of Fame. In the NFL, hard feelings tend to have a long shelf life.

(Alex Karras provides further proof of this. Despite his highly praised performance over a dozen seasons, he wasn't inducted into the Hall of Fame until 2020, eight years after his death, a snub most attribute to his lack of contrition over his gambling suspension. The profusely apologetic Paul Hornung, on the other hand, entered the hall in 1986. Turns out the high priests of the NFL have thin skins and long memories.)

Before the Lions' Mike Disner got involved in the hiring of Brad Holmes and Dan Campbell, he had begun working behind the scenes to bring a thaw to the cold war between the team and Johnson. With Johnson's eligibility for the Hall of Fame approaching in 2021, the Lions offered to pay him $500,000 a year for three years to make appearances at training camps and various sponsor events, plus a one-time $100,000 payment to his charity. The offer equaled the $1.6 million Johnson had repaid the team, but Johnson rejected it as "not serious." He wanted his money back because he felt he had earned it, period. When it was announced that he would be inducted into the Hall of Fame that fall, Johnson revealed his plan for his trip to Canton. "If I pass Rod Wood," he said, "I'm going to keep moving."

Yet Johnson agreed to take part in the halftime ceremony at Ford Field a month after he was inducted into the Hall of Fame, a sign that a reconciliation had begun. It did little to mollify the fans. Their boos had to sting Sheila Ford Hamp, and the team's mounting losses in the following weeks did little to salve the sting. But when the Lions finished the 2021 season in last place with a 3–13–1 record, she didn't flinch, didn't panic. She knew this was going to take time. Holmes, though discouraged by the losing, was convinced that they were building something. Most of the losses were close. Three came on field goals as time expired. The coach still had the players 100 percent behind him, still ready to bite off kneecaps when they picked themselves up after getting knocked down. Everyone in the building was gaining confidence. Late in the season there were glimmerings of a turnaround as the team won three of its last six games. Not earth-shaking, but respectable, something to build on. Maybe, just maybe, better things were on the way.

Just wait, Holmes kept telling himself, *just wait*.

ONE ASS CHEEK
AND THREE TOES

The wait, as it turned out, was not short—even though Holmes outdid himself during his second draft. With the second overall pick he took the defensive end Aidan Hutchinson, who'd grown up in metro Detroit rooting for the Lions, then starred at the University of Michigan. Later in the first round, Holmes added the flashy wide receiver Jameson Williams from Alabama. In later rounds he picked up the defensive end Josh Paschal, defensive back Kerby Joseph and linebacker Malcolm Rodriguez, who would all make immediate contributions. The team was coming together, brick by brick, from the ground up.

The Lions' rocky 2021 season had won them the dubious honor of appearing on the long-running HBO series, *Hard Knocks*. Camera crews followed the team through the sweaty rigors of training camp, which were leavened by Aidan Hutchinson doing a rendition of "Billie Jean," plus cameo appearances by Eminem and Barry Sanders and a river of unforgettable quotes from Dan Campbell, including this motivational gem: "It doesn't matter if you have one ass cheek and three toes, I'm gonna beat your ass."

One ass cheek? Three toes?

The show was a hit with fans across the country, most of whom knew little about the Lions other than their perennial futility and the annual Thanksgiving game that showcased it in front of a national audience. Suddenly the Lions had the look of league darlings.

Before the 2022 season began, Campbell made another move that would pay dividends. He elevated Ben Johnson to offensive coordinator and gave him play-calling duties. Johnson, who'd played quarterback and studied computer science at the University of North Carolina, was gaining a reputation as a brilliant offensive strategist, an innovator willing to break rules and take chances. He set about rebuilding Jared Goff's wobbly ego, which had taken hits when he was benched in L.A., and then performed erratically during his first season in Detroit. It didn't help Goff's ego that the Rams, behind an inspired performance by Stafford, beat Cincinnati in the Super Bowl that year while the Lions were finishing last in their division. Johnson and Goff, a couple of self-proclaimed "math nerds," two guys obsessed with numbers and probabilities, got to work rehabbing the quarterback's sagging career.

Despite Campbell's magnetic presence and Holmes's savvy drafts and free agent signings, the young Lions were still suffering from growing pains. After losing badly to the Cowboys in Dallas in late October, the team's record slipped to a league-worst 1–5. Holmes and Campbell now owned a dispiriting 4–18–1 record in a season and a half, and fans' patience was beginning to wear thin. Was it time for the team to cut its losses? Time to start over with a rebuild of the rebuild?

Sheila Ford Hamp showed up at the Lions' practice facility in the middle of the week after the loss to Dallas. Reporters perked up, hoping for a quote or two. They were in for a surprise.

"I know this is difficult," Hamp said, launching into an impromptu monologue as reporters crowded around her. "Our rebuild is hard. We really believe in our process, we really believe in—we're going to turn this thing around the right way, through the draft. It requires patience. It's frustrating. Am I frustrated? Absolutely. Are the fans frustrated? Absolutely. . . . But I think we really are making progress. You know, you've seen it. It's just—this was a huge teardown and then turnaround, you know? And we really—we're only a third of the way through the season. We've got eleven more games to go."

She wasn't finished.

"So, I just don't want everyone to push the panic button and give up the ship because I think we've got the right people in place to pull this off. And I truly believe that, and I wouldn't say that if I didn't believe it."

This would prove to be the turning point.

It was becoming apparent that there was a critical difference between the way Hamp operated and the way her father had operated. While Bill Ford stuck with people—usually the wrong people—out of misplaced loyalty, indecisiveness, inertia, or all of the above, there was something steely and steadfast about Hamp's faith in Holmes, Campbell, and the rest of the staff. I believe it comes down to this: she believes in them because she believes in herself.

Even when her father hired the right people, such as Joe Schmidt, he micromanaged them until they were climbing the walls. To flip the coin, he didn't believe in them because he didn't believe in himself. Sheila, on the other hand, borrowed a page from Alfred Sloan's playbook—much as her Uncle Henry II had done when he set out to save Ford Motor Company from ruin at the end of the Second World War. She made a very Sloan-esque vow on the day her mother named her principal owner: "I don't plan to meddle, but I plan to be informed." She proceeded to walk the walk, hiring people she believed in, then getting out of the way and letting them do their jobs—while keeping a sharp eye on their performance. She was frustrated, but she had faith that she'd hired the right people and was seeing tangible signs of progress—*and I wouldn't say that if I didn't believe it.*

Hamp's remarks gave everyone in the building a shot of confidence. Chris Spielman, the man who hates losing more than anyone on the planet, had started seeing something in the film room. "The film was talking to me: *It's coming,*" Spielman said. "I know it's hard to believe, but it's coming. You could see it."

Campbell, meanwhile, made a comment that would prove prophetic: "I'm not going to get down. I don't get frustrated like that. I mean, yeah,

I'm upset. But I also—as a coach and player—I've just seen it too many times. You get a little momentum, things will turn in a hurry, and then you could be the hottest team going."

After the Lions lost their next game by four points, Holmes traded one of the team's best players, the tight end T. J. Hockenson, to Minnesota for future draft picks. He insisted he wasn't throwing in the towel on a lost season. He was doing what he always did: building for the long haul through the draft.

Then, as with Monte Clark's 1–6 team in 1978, something clicked with these 1–6 Lions. Jared Goff's work with Ben Johnson began to pay off, and he started playing with the confidence and poise of a top draft pick who had been to the Super Bowl. Young players began to mature. Instead of beating themselves in the fourth quarter, the team began closing out close games. They won three in a row, lost by three points to Buffalo, then reeled off three more wins. Some of the wins were blowouts. By Christmastime, the *New York Times* dubbed the Lions "one of the ex-doormats with playoff hopes." All of a sudden they were, as Campbell had foreseen, one of the hottest teams going.

They rode their hot streak to frigid Green Bay for the regular-season finale on national television. They'd won seven of their last nine games, and their 8–8 record gave them a slim shot at the playoffs. Though the Lions learned shortly before kickoff that they'd been eliminated from the playoffs by Seattle's victory over the Rams, they scrapped and clawed all night, still biting off kneecaps even though they were now playing only for pride. With Jared Goff and running back Jamaal Williams leading the way, the Lions scored a late touchdown for a thrilling come-from-behind win that eliminated the despised Packers from the playoffs. As the Lions celebrated on the field, TV cameras panned to the stands, where thousands of blue-clad Lions fans leaned over the railing to touch their heroes. The sight of so many Lions fans so far from home was destined to become a staple in the upcoming season.

The Lions had their first winning record since 2017. They'd started 1–6 and finished 9–8, a breathtaking turnaround. Jamaal Williams broke Barry Sanders's team record for rushing touchdowns in a season, and Goff became just the seventh quarterback in league history to throw 300 passes without an interception. Since the Lions had two first-round picks in the upcoming draft, they were already being anointed the early favorites to win their division in 2023. The victory at Lambeau Field, Dave Birkett speculated in the *Free Press*, just might go down as "a torch-snatching" in the NFC North.

None of it would have been possible if Sheila Ford Hamp had not stuck to her beliefs when the team bottomed out in mid-season. There was a sense in the jubilant Detroit locker room that the storm had passed. This team had taken its medicine, and now, at long last, it was time for the fun to begin.

A JOYOUS DIN

As the new season approached, the buzz surrounding the Lions went into the stratosphere. For the first time in the twenty-one-year history of Ford Field, the team sold out every home game before the start of the 2023 season. Once again, Holmes's hoarding of draft picks paid dividends. He snatched two immediate-impact players in the first round, the running back Jahmyr Gibbs and linebacker Jack Campbell, and in the second round he landed two more, tight end Sam LaPorta and safety Brian Branch. Holmes also signed free agent David Montgomery, a rugged, reliable running back in his four seasons in Chicago. As the 2023 season approached, it was widely acknowledged that Holmes, through the draft and judicious free agent acquisitions, had assembled one of the youngest, deepest, and most talented rosters in the league.

No more "Hard Knocks" for these Lions. Their strong finish in 2022 won them a slot in the NFL's splashy season opener against the defending champion Kansas City Chiefs. The nationally televised game would be played in Arrowhead Stadium, one of the most hostile venues in the league, on the night when the hosts would hoist their championship banner. For the Lions, the game had all the trappings of an ambush disguised as a coming-out party. They did have one thing working in their favor: the Chiefs' star tight end, Travis Kelce, who had recently started dating the pop supernova Taylor Swift, was sidelined with a knee injury. It's unlikely the Lions joined in the right-wing speculations that Taylor Swift was a "psyop" for the

Pentagon or that the romance between the tight end and the pop superstar was a plot by the NFL and the Democratic Party to whip up interest in a possible Swiftian endorsement of President Joe Biden's reelection bid. The Lions' defenders were just relieved that on this night they would not have to deal with Travis Kelce, who was a certified handful.

Rather than wilting in the national spotlight, the Lions turned the game into a statement of just how far they had come. With chants of "Let's go, Li-ons!" audible from the thousands of blue-clad Detroit fans in the stands, Goff led a ninety-one-yard touchdown drive to open the scoring. After the Chiefs' Patrick Mahomes threw a pair of touchdown passes, the Lions' rookie safety Brian Branch intercepted a Mahomes pass and raced fifty yards for the game-tying touchdown. It was the first time since Lem Barney in 1967 that a Lions defender had scored a touchdown in his NFL debut. It was also the first interception Mahomes had thrown in a season opener in his career. After the Chiefs scored two field goals to take a 20–14 lead in the fourth quarter, the Lions responded with a seventy-five-yard drive, most of it via the legs of running backs Jahmyr Gibbs and David Montgomery, with Montgomery smashing into the end zone to cement the Lions' 21–20 win. Much of the NFL was stunned that these upstarts had toppled the defending champs. Dan Campbell was not. In the locker room after the game, he said, "We expected to win this game."

The week after that statement win, the Lions unveiled an eight-foot-tall bronze statue of Barry Sanders outside Ford Field. This time Sheila Ford Hamp did not hear any boos.

◆

In early October, after the Lions had won three of their first four games, I drove my 1999 Ford Crown Vic from my home in New York City to Detroit to attend my first game at Ford Field. On the crisp, sunny morning of the game against the winless Carolina Panthers, I drifted through the parking lots behind the Fox Theatre where fans were playing games of cornhole, tossing footballs, and drinking breakfast beers as smoke from grilling bratwursts perfumed the air. On the wall of a nearby office building, a crew was painting a towering portrait of a local artist known as Bakpak Durden. It wasn't Barry Sanders, but it had a majesty of its own. The vibe in the parking lots was festive, upbeat. There was a sense that this was a good day to be a Detroit Lions fan, and more just like it were on the way.

I came upon a burly guy stirring a pot of chili on a gas burner on the tailgate of his pickup truck. This was Dave Tremblay, a retired GM pipe fitter from Windsor, across the Detroit River, who's been attending Lions games since the 1990s and became a season ticket holder in 2003, when the paint on Ford Field was still wet. His enormous hands earned him the nickname Thumbs in high school, and it stuck.

"People have waited a long time for the team to show up, and now the fans are responding," Tremblay said, jerking a thumb at the throng of fellow tailgaters. It wasn't always this way, he added. Like so many Lions fans, he was eager to display his battle scars, including memories of the 0–16 season and the man who made it happen.

"Matt Millen drafted some of the worst players, guys who never panned out," Tremblay said, "and the trades he made were awful. He really brought the team down. During that 2008 season you could hear a pin drop in Ford Field—there were maybe ten thousand people there." Stirring the chili, he let out a rueful chuckle. "It's a lot louder now. Everybody's on the bandwagon."

After sampling one of Tremblay's cocktail wieners wrapped in bacon—a tasty little sponge to sop up those breakfast beers—I walked the four blocks to Ford Field and gave myself a pregame tour. I was impressed. The atmosphere was electric, and the place felt both spacious and intimate, almost cushy, a temperature-controlled bubble that was a world away from the rusting I-beams, frozen concrete, and bone-numbing cold I remembered from late-season games at Tiger Stadium. There would be snowball barrages at Ford Field.

I rode an elevator to the top floor and approached two female employees who were squealing at a video screen by the door that led to the press box. I asked what the commotion was about, thinking I'd missed the kickoff. "Look!" one of the women cried, "It's Eminem!"

"Slim Shady," her friend confirmed, nodding.

And there he was in a luxury box, wearing his trademark black hat and hoodie, just another Detroit homeboy getting ready to watch this reborn version of his beloved Lions.

In the press box shortly before kickoff I introduced myself to Dave Birkett of the *Free Press* and told him, truthfully, that I was an admirer. He did the legwork, then reported what he'd learned in clear, unfussy prose. And he had a deep understanding of the game. A boyish-looking guy with close-cropped hair, Birkett has been covering the Lions since 2001, and he joined the *Free Press* in 2010, shortly after the end of the Matt Millen era. He has seen his share of horrors, but he told me that in the middle of the 2022 season he began to see genuine progress—though his Midwestern reserve and reporter's instincts prevented him from over-egging the team's turnaround. "I think they'll make the playoffs this year, probably get a home playoff game," Birkett said, adding that he didn't believe the team was Super Bowl caliber—yet. He gave Sheila Ford Hamp credit for hiring the right people and then sticking with them when the team was flailing in 2022. I'd been thinking along the same lines, but hearing it from Birkett gave the notion a jolt of credibility. I thanked him for his time and left him to his pregame meal.

The Lions showed inventiveness on offense and discipline on defense as they throttled the Panthers that day. The din in that big room was ferocious, relentless, *joyous*. The Lions scored a touchdown the first time they touched the ball and never looked back, harassing the Panthers' rookie quarterback, Bryce Young, and seeming to score at will. The final score was 42–24 and it would have been even more lopsided if the Panthers hadn't been gifted some dubious penalty calls. But there were no complaints from the 63,648 paying customers as they filed out of the stadium. The festive vibe I'd sensed in the parking lots that morning had given way to a serene sense of accomplishment. The surprising thing to me was that no one seemed surprised by this one-sided victory. This was what they *expected*.

◆

I spent the following week in the Detroit Public Library, scrolling through newspaper microfilm and poring through boxes of files on the Lions. I learned that during the depths of the Depression, the struggling Portsmouth (Ohio) Spartans of the fledgling National Football League were forced to relocate. Before they left town, one of the fans at their rudimentary stadium perched above the Ohio River was a five-year-old girl from a prominent Akron family, Martha Firestone. On April 3, 1934, George A. Richards, owner of WJR radio in Detroit, wrote a check for $7,952.08 (about $150,000 in today's money) to the Portsmouth National Football League Corporation, and the Portsmouth Spartans became the Detroit Lions. The following year, ten-year-old Bill Ford Sr. and his father and brothers were in the stands at the University of Detroit stadium to watch as the Lions, led by future Hall of Famer Dutch Clark, crushed the New York Giants to win their first NFL championship.

Beyond such colorful details, I was searching for a very specific needle in this historical haystack. Before I reached my teenage years I'd become an avid daily reader of the *Free Press*, and for years I'd carried a dim but persistent memory of a headline from the early 1960s, something about the Lions roaring. I liked the way that vivid verb brought the Lions (and the headline) to life. The team was having a rough season at the time, as I recalled, and they had traveled to the West Coast and scored a smashing victory. It seemed hopeless that I would happen upon the headline on those miles of microfilm.

On my third day in the library, the headline swam onto the screen of the microfilm reader.

It was on page 1-D of the Nov. 4, 1963, edition of the *Free Press*. It shouted that the Lions had demolished the San Francisco 49ers the previous day: LIONS FINALLY ROAR, 45–7! The subhead added, 'MORRALL TO BARR' WORKS MAGIC. This was the Lions' much-maligned quarterback Earl Morrall, who on that day threw four touchdown passes. "It may be too late to matter," began the accompanying article by George Puscas, "but those sick and sore Lions finally took on the look of a first-rate football power Sunday . . ."

Amazing. I had carried a fuzzy memory of a headline for sixty years almost to the day, and here it was in front of my eyes, in black and white. The serendipity of this discovery deepened when I connected the dots. In early November 1963 I was in fifth grade at Holy Name School, George Plimpton was busy writing *Paper Lion*, Bill Ford had just dropped his "bombshell" offer to buy the Lions for $6 million, and President John F. Kennedy would soon travel to his doom in Dallas.

That headline spoke to me for another reason. Given the Lions' strong finish to their 2022 season, given what I'd witnessed at Ford Field the previous Sunday, and given the Lions' 4–1 record and all the talk that they were likely to win their division this year—and maybe push deep into the playoffs—it had begun to occur to me that I needed to rethink my book's working title. *Natural Born Losers* did not fit this new version of the Lions. Maybe my title was on that scratchy microfilm: *Lions Finally Roar*. Time would tell.

BAPTISM OF A FAN

Three weeks after my return to New York, the Lions hosted the Raiders on *Monday Night Football* and I arranged to watch the game with a Michigan native named Will Johnson at Bailey's Corner Pub, a neighborhood bar on the Upper East Side of Manhattan. After a long-standing Lions bar on the West Side had gone out of business, Johnson approached the owner of Bailey's, Sean Cushing, before the start of the 2023 season and asked if he would be willing to tune the bars' TV sets to Lions games on Sunday afternoons. Given the buzz surrounding the team, Johnson promised a healthy weekly turnout. Cushing was amenable, so Johnson got the word out on social media. As he'd expected, the response was immediate, and on the unseasonably steamy night of the season opener against the Chiefs, Bailey's was bursting with Lions fans. The credit card machine proceeded to crash, then the ATM crashed. The air-conditioning wasn't getting the job done, and by the fourth quarter the place had turned into a sweaty, rambunctious sardine can. It reminded Johnson of going to games at the Silverdome. "Things never go according to plans when you're watching the Lions," he'd told me on the phone after the game against the Chiefs. "This was the perfect stress test."

Shortly before kickoff of the Monday night game against the Raiders, I slid onto a barstool next to Johnson at Bailey's. He was keyed up but cordial in that unaffected Midwestern way, and as the teams warmed up, his eyes were locked on one of the TV screens behind the bar. "There's something happening here," he said, sounding like a Buffalo Springfield song. "There's excitement that this team might be turning the corner—maybe not the Super Bowl this year, but just the normal success every other sports franchise has experienced." Normal success, of course, was a foreign concept to most living fans of the Detroit Lions.

Johnson told me he grew up in Lake Orion (pronounced OAR-eon), fifteen miles north of where the Silverdome once stood. He was born in 1991, the year the Lions won their only playoff game since 1957, so at thirty-two years old he's too young to remember Barry Sanders but old enough to remember the nightmare of the Matt Millen era, the agony of Joey Harrington, and the glorious but ultimately futile aerial displays put on by Matthew Stafford and Calvin Johnson. When he was ten years old, Will Johnson attended his first Lions game. It was their final season at the Silverdome, and the Marty Mornhinweg–coached team entered that game with a sterling 0–12 record. Miraculously, they managed to beat the Vikings, 27–24. That was the victory that inspired the Lions' receiver Johnnie Morton to fling his helmet and invite Jay Leno to kiss his ass. On that day, Will Johnson was baptized a lifelong Lions fan. Welcome to hell.

"Since then it's been decades and decades of frustration," Johnson said, "and suddenly it's exploding. Did you see the game in Tampa Bay two weeks ago? I was there—and it was a takeover party. We Lions fans took over that stadium. That was another moment when it felt like we were going in the right direction. It felt like we had arrived."

Most of the Lions' away games during the 2023 season turned into takeover parties—tens of thousands of blue-clad fans traveling hundreds, even thousands of miles, often drowning out the home team's fans and giving the Lions an incalculable boost. The parties started during the season opener in Kansas City and kept rolling to Green Bay, Tampa Bay, Baltimore. After those peripatetic blue-clad fans helped secure a close win over the Saints in the Superdome, New Orleans' GM Mickey Loomis was both surprised and displeased. "We're not used to having that volume of visiting fans at our games," Loomis said. "Our stadium's sold out on a season basis. That's disappointing to have that many tickets that are resold and, you know, given to visiting fans."

Loomis wasn't expecting such noisy houseguests. "I was a little caught off guard by the volume," he admitted after the game. "That was unusual and, look, I understand it, but that doesn't mean I have to like it."

The Lions' coaches and players loved it. "Most of our away games have been home games to a degree," said Ben Johnson, the offensive coordinator. Dan Campbell added, "I think we kind of thrive off of that. I mean, seriously, this is pretty awesome."

By kickoff on that Monday night, Bailey's was a miniature takeover party, full of fans in Honolulu-blue jerseys. I noticed that the favorites were Matthew Stafford's No. 9 even though he now toils in Los Angeles, Aidan Hutchinson's No. 97, and the No. 20 worn by—take your pick—Barry Sanders, Lem Barney, and Billy Sims.

As I sat at the bar watching the Lions build a 16–7 first-half lead over the Raiders, an unsettling thought came to me. Maybe I'd been operating under a faulty assumption all along. By focusing on the drawbacks of having a team owner like Bill Ford who'd been born into immense wealth, I seemed to be implying that self-made men made superior owners of sports franchises. This, I realized as I gazed at the TV screen, was not always the case. And the Raiders were proof.

Though they now play in Las Vegas, I still think of them as the *Oakland* Raiders, the original badasses, the Hells Angels of pro football from the wrong side of San Francisco Bay. But under Al Davis, their pugnacious Brooklyn-bred coach and part owner, the Raiders had abandoned the rough-edged town that gave them their identity, hopscotching from Oakland to Los Angeles, then back to Oakland and finally to Las Vegas after Davis's death. This self-made man's mercenary behavior was hardly unusual. Other self-made team owners, many of whom had moaned that player free agency was going to bankrupt them, began treating whole franchises like free agents, holding cities hostage for sweetheart stadium deals and then bolting when local governments and taxpayers declined to pony up, or some other city made a better offer. For this very reason, Robert Irsay moved the Colts from Baltimore to Indianapolis under cover of night in 1984. To fill the vacuum, Art Modell moved the venerable Cleveland Browns to Baltimore in 1996 and rechristened them the Ravens. Carroll Rosenbloom's widow had moved the Rams from Los Angeles to Anaheim and then to St. Louis before the team made a U-turn and returned to Los Angeles in 2016.

But no owner, born rich or self-made, could out-sleaze Dan Snyder. He got his start leasing jets to ferry college students to spring-break destinations, then built a fortune that enabled him to buy a majority share of the Washington Redskins in 1999 for $800 million. He proceeded to destroy one of the most beloved franchises in American sports. Under Snyder, the team sued its own fans for backing out of season ticket contracts during the Great Recession. Among the defendants was a seventy-two-year-old grandmother who'd been a season ticket holder since the 1960s. That's called bad optics. It soon came out that the penny-pinching billionaire owner was selling beer that was months past its freshness date and peanuts acquired from an airline that had gone bankrupt a year earlier. But stale beer and peanuts were, well, peanuts compared to charges by a dozen female employees that Snyder and top team executives had sexually harassed them. After the league fined Snyder an unprecedented $60 million for sexually harassing a former cheerleader and withholding $11 million in revenue that was supposed to be shared with the other thirty-one teams, a movement arose among fellow owners to force Snyder to sell the team.

"We have to act," said Jim Irsay, who'd inherited the Colts and a fortune from his father—and had done right by Andrew Luck when the star quarterback abruptly retired. "[Snyder] needs to be removed."

(This was doubly delicious. After Jim Irsay pleaded guilty to operating a vehicle while impaired—he had the painkillers oxycodone and hydrocodone as well as the anti-anxiety drug alprazolam in his bloodstream, along with more than $29,000 in cash in his vehicle—he blamed his arrest on one of life's glaring inequities: "I am prejudiced against because I'm a rich white billionaire." He was also a graduate of more than a dozen rehab facilities that treated his drug and alcohol addictions. After his guilty plea on the driving while impaired charge, the league suspended him for six games and fined him $500,000.)

Yet this rich white victim of prejudice had gotten the attention of his fellow owners when he expressed the need to get rid of Snyder. Rather than face possible banishment, Snyder preemptively sold the Washington team, recently renamed the Commanders, for $6 billion. Here was living proof that just as no good deed goes unpunished, no bad deed goes unrewarded.

Yes, the Ford family had moved the Lions to the suburbs and then back to downtown Detroit, but they treated their employees decently, developed a fiercely loyal fan base (and sold them fresh beer and peanuts), abided by the league's revenue-sharing rules, and never tried to gain leverage by threatening to move the Lions to another city or state. For all their failings, the Fords were loyal to their hometown, and their fundamental decency put them a sizable cut above some of the self-made owners of NFL teams, including Al Davis, Robert Irsay, and Dan Snyder.

I was jolted from my reverie. The fans around me were growing loudly jubilant as the clock ticked down on the Lions' workmanlike 26–14 victory over the Raiders. The win gave the Lions a 6–2 record, good for first place in the NFC North. Once again, the fans around me acted like they expected this to happen. Yes, I thought as we filed out into the New York night, Will Johnson's right. There's something happening here.

◆

The Lions kept winning. As Dave Birkett had predicted, they clinched the NFC's North Division with a Christmas Eve victory over the Vikings, then lost by a point to Dallas on a controversial call when the referees disallowed a two-point conversion by the Lions after a late touchdown. A victory would have given them home-field advantage throughout the playoffs, but rather than dwelling on what could have been—or dredging up the shopworn Curse—giddy fans were inclined to revel in the Lions' turnaround. Their final 12–5 regular-season record matched the Eagles and 49ers for best in the NFC, the division title was their first in thirty years, and they would host their first home playoff game since 1991.

Now, as the Lions got ready for the playoffs, fans started thinking the unthinkable. Was it possible that these Lions were about to repeat—or even outdo—the history of 1991?

R-E-S-P-E-C-T

Everyone in the city of Detroit, including its sportswriters, seemed to be hyperventilating the week before the first playoff game ever played in Ford Field (not counting the 2006 Super Bowl between Pittsburgh and Seattle). This wild card game would pit the third-seeded Lions against the sixth-seeded Los Angeles Rams, the teams that had swapped quarterbacks in 2021. So Matthew Stafford, the former Lion, would finally appear in a playoff game in Detroit—against his former team and the Rams' former quarterback Jared Goff.

Detroiters were generally understanding and supportive when Stafford requested the trade that sent him to a Super Bowl contender. And when he won the Super Bowl during his first season in Los Angeles, those fans were gracious enough to applaud him—in that bittersweet Detroit way. It hurt to see him succeed so quickly in another town, but most fans retain abiding affection for Stafford and all the thrills he produced during his dozen years in Detroit. I thought of all those No. 9 Stafford jerseys I'd seen in Bailey's Pub and at Ford Field. But this was different. This was a playoff game against Stafford and his Los Angeles Rams. It was so different that one bar near the stadium, Thomas Magee's Sporting House, announced it would deny entry to anyone who showed up on game day wearing a Honolulu-blue No. 9 Stafford jersey. "It's our first home game in thirty years," the bar said on its Facebook page. "Use some common sense." One fan had enough common sense to put black duct tape over the name Stafford when he showed up at Ford Field in his No. 9 jersey.

Yes, this game was going to be different.

"It's just a beautiful piece of poetry, sent to us from beyond the cosmos," Carlos Monarrez rhapsodized in the *Free Press*. Actually, it seemed less like a piece of poetry than the handiwork of a Hollywood scriptwriter with a taste for melodrama, especially that switch-the-quarterbacks plot twist. Whatever you wanted to call it, Monarrez concluded that this game was both an end and a beginning: "We have finally reached the end of the Road to the Playoffs and have begun a new journey: The Road to Redemption."

Traveling that road, as it turned out, was not going to be cheap. The Lions-Rams game became the most expensive wild card game on record, according to TickPick, an online marketplace for event tickets. The average purchase price was $801, more than double the previous most expensive wild card ticket for the 2022 game between Tampa Bay and Dallas.

Of course there were ways to cut corners. Dave Tremblay, the chili-cooking season ticket holder since 2003, sold two of his four upper-deck seats for the bargain price of $750 apiece. "Got to pay for next season's tickets somehow," Tremblay said with a chuckle, noting that the team's sudden success had bumped the cost of his four tickets from $3,400 in 2023 to $5,200 in 2024. Tremblay also noted, dryly, that the Lions didn't offer any refunds during their 0–16 season in 2008.

Ann Morris, a cousin of mine who married a native Detroiter named Mark Sutter, sagely decided to buy tickets to the wild card playoff game as soon as they went on sale online, long before the Lions had clinched a playoff spot. She paid $700 apiece.

"We got a tip to bring earplugs," she said, "and I'm glad we did because I've been to loud shows, including the Foo Fighters, but the minute you walked into Ford Field you heard the roar. When the Lions had the ball, the screen said, 'Quiet, offense at work.' When L.A. had the ball, it was *'Make noise!'* There was no shame in wearing earplugs when the Rams had the ball."

The game was a scintillating slugfest between two teams playing at their peaks, and it went down to the wire with the Lions holding the ball and a one-point lead late in the fourth quarter. Games like this are usually won by the team holding the ball at the end, so everyone in the house was standing, roaring, pleading with the Lions to hold onto the ball and not give the Rams a shot at a game-winning, soul-crushing field goal, an ending Lions fans knew all too well. When Goff completed a pass to Amon-Ra St. Brown for a first down with two minutes left on the clock, the realization began to spread through the stadium that the Rams had used their last time-out. The Lions could run out the clock. This thing was over.

"When it became clear that they had the game won, the crowd went ballistic," Morris said. "The place was pandemonium, blue and white confetti coming down. People couldn't believe it. Men were crying, strangers were high-fiving us. Then they started playing Aretha Franklin's 'Respect.' That was the moment of redemption."

So Carlos Monarrez knew what he was talking about.

Ann Morris wasn't the only person in the building that day who noticed something unusual before the kickoff. Peter King, the veteran *Sports Illustrated* writer and NBC Sports commentator, said on his podcast, "Seventy-five minutes before the game, even before I get to the field, there's this buzz, this noise that you never hear that long before a game. I couldn't believe the fans were already totally, ridiculously into that game."

By day's end, he was even more impressed. "That is a special place right now," he said. "I've been doing this for forty years, and that is among the top five combinations of atmosphere and game that I've ever seen covering football."

Mark Sutter, Ann's husband, was born in Detroit in the spring of 1958, when the Lions were reigning NFL champs. Like many Detroiters, he grew up following all of the city's teams—the Lions, Tigers, Red Wings, and Pistons. As a teenager, Sutter was in the stands at Tiger Stadium on the day Chuck Hughes collapsed and died on the field.

"I've been to a lot of sporting events in Detroit," Sutter said after the win over the Rams, "but I've never seen people so freaking happy. I felt like I knew all these people because we've all shared this long, long experience. These are hard-core fans who've suffered for years. Finally, the cork has been released. It was so joyous."

His next thought brought to mind Dan Campbell's kneecaps press conference.

"It's a parallel to Detroit itself. We've all shared the experience of Detroit being a great city that had a decades-long decline. We've put up with disrespect from people who know nothing about Detroit. Now we're on the rise. We've never stopped being Lions fans. It's in your DNA to be a Lions fan and a Detroit fan."

His thoughts turned to the two quarterbacks at the center of the day's drama.

"Everybody in Detroit likes Stafford, but Goff has become one of us. He was disrespected and discarded—and now he's become the face of this team. When people started chanting 'Jar-ed Goff! Jar-ed Goff!' he really became a Detroiter. And this team is a reflection of Detroit. There are no big stars, but they're a team, they believe in themselves and they find ways to work together. That's the genius of Sheila Ford Hamp. She got the right people with the right approach—and then she got out of the way and trusted them and stuck with them."

He was starting to sound like Dave Birkett—and a lot of other people.

Though the game was standing room only, there was one empty seat in the house—Section 100, Row 18, Seat 14 by the tunnel, Donnie "Yooperman" Stefanski's old seat. On this day, his daughter Megan turned the seat into a shrine, draping her father's old No. 44 Lions jersey on it along with his hunting cap with its Lions logo and a silver-and-blue urn containing his ashes. "All he wanted was to see something like this," Megan told the *Free Press* before kickoff, noting that in all his years of driving down from the U.P. her late father never witnessed a Lions playoff game in Detroit. "I felt like he still deserved to be here for it."

By the time the game ended and the confetti started to flutter down, Megan was hoarse from hours of screaming. "A dream come true," she rasped. "It was the best night in my life."

◆

Next up were the fourth-seeded Tampa Bay Buccaneers in the divisional round, with the winner advancing to face the top-seeded San Francisco 49ers for the NFC championship and a ticket to the Super Bowl. Once again, Ford Field was a typhoon of noise long before kickoff.

This game unfolded like a heavyweight boxing match, each punch answered with a counterpunch. The fighters were tied at 3 after the first quarter, at 10 at halftime, at 17 after three quarters. Somebody had to blink. Early in the fourth quarter, the Lions' Jahmyr Gibbs took a handoff and took off on a thirty-one-yard touchdown gallop. For the first time all day, Tampa failed to land a counterpunch, and the Lions quickly capitalized with another touchdown on a nine-yard pass from Goff to St. Brown. This time Tampa Bay responded with a touchdown, and when the Lions were forced to punt on the ensuing possession, Tampa Bay got the ball back with two minutes left and one last chance. The old familiar dread began to tighten its screws. But the Lions intercepted a Baker Mayfield pass and, just like that, they'd won again. Final score: 31–23.

Now another witness to forty years of football was in for a surprise. Bill Keenist, the Lions' former publicist and team historian, was at Ford Field that day working the game as part of the NFL's broadcast department. "It was beyond surreal," he said after the game. "The emotions carried over all week from the Rams game. Walking out of the stadium after the Tampa Bay game you could feel the unadulterated joy. It was like a spiritual experience. More than that, it was love. I saw tears, I heard screams of joy. Everyone who left the stadium that evening was part of the same joyous family."

LIKE A SNOWMAN
IN THE SAHARA

The Lions were set to play the 49ers in San Francisco in the NFC Championship game on Sunday evening, Jan. 28, with the winner advancing to the Super Bowl. On page A-20 of that morning's *Free Press*, the opening chapter of this book, "The Last Hurrah," appeared in its entirety. My account of the Lions' last championship victory in 1957 was accompanied by a picture of Bill Ford and a bigger picture of Bobby Layne hugging Tobin Rote in the Lions' locker room. Rote is shirtless, smoking a cigarette, beaming. There was also a picture of this book's planned cover. In light of the 2023 team's playoff run and the imminent chance to win a trip to its first Super Bowl, the working title had been changed again, amped up to *Miracle in the Motor City*. Was this hyperbole? I would know by the end of the day.

◆

Will Johnson knew Bailey's Corner Pub was going to be a madhouse on the night of the NFC Championship game, so he showed up six hours before kickoff to make sure he got his favorite stool at the bar. It's safe to say that the emotions racing through Johnson—anticipation, dread, hope, high anxiety—were racing through millions of people across the country, from his fellow old-school Lions fans to the countless newcomers who had adopted this team as the lovable underdogs with an impossibly tortured history and a long-overdue shot at redemption. It seemed that everyone in the football universe east of San Francisco was pulling for the Lions to finally exorcise their demons, much as baseball fans once rooted for the Boston Red Sox to lay the Curse of the Bambino to rest. In a snub to the Dallas Cowboys, the *New York Post* dubbed the Lions THE REAL AMERICA'S TEAM. A color-coded map created by BetOnline, based on social media posts, showed just how strong the team's support had become on the eve of the two conference championship games. Five western states (plus Alaska and Hawaii) were red, designating supporters of the 49ers; four states in the middle of the country were red for the Chiefs; Maryland and Virginia were purple for the Ravens; and the other thirty-seven states were blue for the Lions. If that map of fan sentiment reflected voter sentiment, its sea of blue would spell a landslide reelection for Joe Biden. But back to football.

Will Johnson's six-hour wait was finally over. As soon as the Lions received the opening kickoff, Johnson felt he had slipped into a dream. On the fourth play of the game, with less than two minutes gone, the wide receiver Jameson Williams took a handoff from Jared Goff and sprinted forty-two yards for a touchdown. After the 49ers missed a field goal, David Montgomery ran for another touchdown late in the first quarter for a 14–0 lead.

Will Johnson had to pinch himself. "I couldn't believe what I was seeing," he would say later. "Knowing the Lions, though, I didn't get too excited."

He soon got excited. After the 49ers mounted a long touchdown drive, the Lions responded with an interception and another lightning touchdown, then added a field goal shortly before halftime, which sent them into the break with a shocking 24–7 lead. But Johnson was wise enough to keep his excitement in check. "I knew the 49ers were going to counterpunch," he said. "I knew this wasn't going to continue."

What he didn't know—what no one knew—was that a sixty-six-year-old script was about to get flipped. Back in 1957, in the days before playoffs and Super Bowls, the Lions had to travel to San Francisco for a rare playoff game against the 49ers after both teams ended the regular season tied atop the Western Division with 8–4 records. The winner would go to the NFL title game against the Eastern Division champion Cleveland Browns.

The 49ers bolted to a 24–7 halftime lead that day behind three touchdown passes by Y. A. Tittle. Through the thin walls in the Kezar Stadium locker room, the Lions could hear the 49ers whooping it up, mocking their opponents, debating how they were going to spend their championship money. They seemed to have forgotten that there were still thirty minutes of football to play. Infuriated, the Lions emerged from their locker room with a murderous determination to make the 49ers pay for their premature celebration.

The 49ers booted a field goal to extend their lead to twenty points. It was the last time they would score. Now came the avalanche. Lions running back Tom Tracy raced for two touchdowns, Tobin Rote revived the offense while the defense shut down the San Francisco attack, including a vicious tackle that broke the jaw of San Francisco running back Joe Perry. The Lions took a one-point lead early in the fourth quarter after another touchdown, and the magic suddenly abandoned Y. A. Tittle. After playing so brilliantly in the first half, he coughed up a fumble and threw three interceptions in the disastrous fourth quarter. The Lions added a field goal that put the icing on an impossible 31–27 comeback victory.

Sixty-six seasons later, in January 2024, it was the 49ers who were fuming in their locker room at halftime. The players weren't angry at their opponents; they were infuriated by their own poor play. "We were just pissed off," 49ers coach Kyle Shanahan said. "Guys were extremely pissed. That first half, it wasn't just that we were down seventeen, it was the way we were down. They were kind of having their way in the run game, we weren't getting much in our run game either, and we didn't want to go out like that. That would've been a real rough way to end it if we couldn't play better."

What happened next was a nearly verbatim flip of the script from the 1957 playoff game between these two teams, a reversal so precise that it went beyond uncanny, all the way to surreal.

The 49ers opened the second half with a long field goal that did little to unsettle Will Johnson or the rest of the Lions faithful inside Bailey's and beyond. They still led by two touchdowns with twenty minutes left in the game.

Now came the avalanche.

After a long drive, the Lions faced fourth down with two yards to go at the San Francisco twenty-eight-yard line. Rather than kicking a longish field goal, Dan Campbell, known for his gambling style, went for the first down. But a pass from Goff to Josh Reynolds fell incomplete, and the Lions turned the ball over on downs.

Now the football gods went to work. San Francisco quarterback Brock Purdy heaved a fifty-yard pass that Lions' cornerback Kindle Vildor appeared to break up when the ball bounced off his face mask and into the air. But the 49ers' receiver Brandon Aiyuk leaped and snatched the ball just before it touched the ground, giving the 49ers a freakish first down at the Lions' four-yard line.

When Aiyuk caught that pass, Will Johnson got a sickeningly familiar feeling. "That," he said, "was when I turned from worried to stressed out. That was the moment when, as a Lions fan, I thought, 'Uh oh, we're going to lose this game.'"

Even after the 49ers scored on a short run, the Lions still led 24–17 with five minutes left in the third quarter. They just needed to settle down, regain their poise, work the clock with their potent running game.

It didn't happen. On the first play from scrimmage, the Lions rookie Jahmyr Gibbs fumbled. The 49ers recovered, then scored the inevitable touchdown four plays later. The game was now tied at 24–24.

Even a cold-eyed realist like Will Johnson didn't expect this. "What I didn't expect," he said, "was for the Lions to melt down."

They were melting like a snowman in the Sahara—but it was about to get worse. After a wide-open Josh Reynolds dropped a pass that would have given the Lions a critical first down, the Lions were forced to punt and the 49ers responded by kicking a thirty-three-yard field goal to take their first lead with ten minutes left in the game.

Now Campbell made a second decision that would lead to copious second-guessing. Facing fourth down and three at the San Francisco thirty-yard line, Campbell again rejected attempting a field goal that would have tied the game and instead went for the first down. Goff's pass fell incomplete, and the 49ers met little resistance as they marched up the field for another touchdown. They had now scored twenty-seven unanswered points. Meltdown complete. The snowman had been reduced to a puddle.

Goff was finally able to lead the Lions on a long drive that produced a touchdown with one minute left, but it was too little, too late. The final score of 34–31, nearly identical to the score in the 1957 playoff, matched the greatest comeback—or the greatest collapse, depending on your allegiance—in NFC Championship history.

Bailey's Corner Pub had fallen silent, fans struggling to process what they'd just witnessed. Eventually a woman jumped up on a table and said everyone should offer their thanks to Sean and the staff at Bailey's. There was heartfelt applause, then the place cleared out in a hurry.

Will Johnson lingered, unable to let go. "To be that close to the Super Bowl—which I didn't ever think was conceivable—and then to blow it . . ." He left the sentence unfinished. After a moment he went on: "I'm worried that this was as close as we'll ever get. They will never again have that big a lead in an NFC Championship game."

But then his disappointment gave way to the realization that it had been an unforgettable ride, and he started listing the people who made it happen. "I think Chris Spielman had a huge impact," he said, "but I think the most important hire was Brad Holmes. He built that team through the draft. And Dan Campbell—who I was originally lukewarm on, big rah-rah guy—but they needed a guy who could get rid of the demons. Campbell knew that if he could get the right guys to buy in, they could get rid of those demons."

And last but not least: "Where I give Sheila Ford Hamp credit is when she fired Quinn and Patricia, she said she had to do something different. That didn't happen under her parents. I think Sheila got under the hood and talked to a lot of people who've been through the wringer with the Lions, and she found a way to get out of that rut."

Nothing left to say. On his way home, Johnson texted his girlfriend: That's the worst loss I ever felt as a sports fan.

◆

Great expectations can be a setup for the most devastating disappointments, and Detroit, after such a giddy rise and such a brutal fall, was in a state of shock after the game. "The mood in this city on Monday was like a relative had died," said Bill Dow, sixty-nine, a Detroit native and lifelong fan and freelance historian of the city's sports teams. In his many years of following and writing about those teams, Dow has witnessed his share of heartbreak, but he puts the loss to San Francisco in a class by itself.

"I think this was the worst loss in Detroit sports history," Dow said two days after the game, still in a fog. "They're up by seventeen points with thirty minutes to go, with a chance to go to their first Super Bowl ever—*and they lose!* The Lions through their history have shot themselves in the foot many times, but to lose like this was . . ." It took him a moment to locate the word. "This was cruel."

It's a matter of perspective, Dow went on. With his encyclopedic knowledge of the city's sports history, he can rattle off some of the more heartcrushing moments suffered by each team. The Tigers losing the pennant on the last day of the 1967 season, then losing the clinching playoff game to Oakland in 1972. The Pistons losing to San Antonio in Game 7 of the

NBA Finals in 2005. The Red Wings losing to Pittsburgh in Game 7 of the Stanley Cup Finals in 2009. He could go on.

But Dow pointed out that all of those teams had enjoyed recent success before they got their hearts ripped out—with the exception of the Tigers, who hadn't won a World Series in twenty-three years when they fell short on the last day of the 1967 season. But they quickly atoned by winning the World Series the following year.

The Lions, on the other hand, seem to have been lost in the desert forever. "They haven't won a championship in sixty-six years," Dow said, "and their playoff losses weren't this bad. When they got blown out by the Browns in 1954, they'd just won back-to-back championships. When they lost to Dallas 5–0 in the 1970 wild card game, they were just thirteen years from their most recent championship. And after their lone playoff win in 1991, they lost to a better Redskins team in the NFC Championship game. But this," he said, returning to the present, "this was cruel."

Then, like Will Johnson, he brightened.

"What Sheila Ford Hamp did was, unlike her father, she hired people who know football—Chris Spielman, Brad Holmes," Dow said. "And Dan Campbell is obviously a players' coach. What's remarkable is how she turned the team around in such a short period of time—and she's put the franchise in a position to be successful for some years to come. That disappointing loss in San Francisco could inspire the team to come back and finish this thing off. The Tigers did it in '68 after losing the pennant on the last day of the '67 season. The fans are already getting revved up for next year."

There were few people in Detroit inclined to disagree with him. Once the shock from the meltdown in San Francisco began to fade, people were able to put things in perspective. The Lions' fourteen wins in 2023, including the two playoff games, are the most in a season since the team moved from Portsmouth to Detroit ninety years ago. The team won its first division title in thirty years. Dan Campbell and Ben Johnson were, respectively, finalists for Coach of the Year and Assistant Coach of the Year. After excoriating Campbell for passing up two field goals on fourth downs in the 49ers game—two field goals that would have tipped the outcome—many fans came to admit that it was Campbell's let-it-all-hang-out style that got the team so deep into the playoffs, and there's no fault in sticking with a winning formula. Shortly after the loss in San Francisco, Ben Johnson and defensive coordinator Aaron Glenn turned down head coaching offers from other teams so they could stay in Detroit and take care of unfinished business. Sam LaPorta, with a rookie record eighty-six catches, and Jahmyr Gibbs were finalists for offensive Rookie of the Year. The team fell four points shy of its first Super Bowl. And in just her fourth season as principal owner, Sheila Ford Hamp had doubled the number of playoff wins her parents had managed in fifty-six years.

In its power rankings for the 2024 season, *The Athletic* dubbed the Lions "everyone's favorite underdog" and pegged them at No. 3 behind Kansas City and San Francisco, the contestants in the most recent Super Bowl. "Every significant offensive contributor [on the Lions] remains under contract on a team that finished fifth in the league in scoring," *The Athletic* noted, adding that the surprise return of Ben Johnson and Aaron Glenn will lend stability as Dan Campbell strives to take the team to the next level in 2024.

Clearly, there's something happening here. Despite the cruel ending to the 2023 season, this team is for real, stocked with young talent and built for the long haul. The turnaround, given all the history and all the misery that came before it, was beyond an astonishment. It was very nearly a miracle. And it looks like this team will be back for more.

Hard to believe, but it's true: the Lions finally roared.

NOTES

FIRST QUARTER: Going Down (1957–1973)

The Last Hurrah

p. 3   *It's noon on Sunday:* SI, Jan. 6, 1958; youtube.com/watch?v=n5J4aQrFaFU; DFP, Dec. 30, 1957.

p. 4   *The man pacing the press box:* This description of William Clay Ford comes from my personal memories of seeing him at Lions games.

p. 4   *Buddy Parker, the coach who led:* Bleacher Report, Oct. 12, 2016.

p. 5   *After the charges were dropped:* Vintage Detroit, Feb. 16, 2014.

p. 7   *He'd gotten word that Joe Schmidt:* DFP, Sept. 9, 2017.

p. 8   *The party is already at full roar:* Ibid.

Birth of the Curse

p. 9   *Coach George Wilson criticized both:* DN, Oct. 6, 1958.

p. 9   *The Monday morning after that game:* Bleacher Report, Oct. 12, 2016.

p. 10   *When he was in his prime:* Plimpton, *Paper Lion*, 247–248.

p. 11   *Carol tried to soothe him:* DN, Oct. 7, 1958.

p. 11   *"It's just one of those things:* Ibid.

p. 11   *"It makes me sick:* Ibid.

p. 11   *On his way out the door:* Bleacher Report, Oct. 12, 2016.

p. 12   *Layne traded to the Steelers:* DFP, Oct. 7, 1958.

p. 12   *The Pittsburgh papers:* PPG and PP, Oct. 7, 1958.

p. 12   *What a Mess!:* DFP, Oct. 8, 1958.

p. 13   *Bill Ford took note:* Interview with Dick Morris.

p. 13   *If the coach was free to engineer:* Ibid.

Born Under a Bad Sign

p. 14   *One source of the palace intrigues:* SI, Feb. 6, 1961.

p. 14   *The star of this particular soap opera:* DN, Jan. 9, 1966.

p. 14   *At the time of the sale:* NYT, Jan. 16, 1948.

p. 14   *As conservative as they were:* Bak, *Henry and Edsel*, 129.

p. 16   *Ford also gave a clunky quote:* NYT, Jan. 6, 1961.

p. 16   *Since taking over the unpaid post:* DFP, Nov. 24, 1963.

p. 17   *Occasionally Ford took select players:* DFP, Nov. 3, 2013.

p. 17   *"We had a real close team:* Ibid.

p. 17   *Ford's historic offer:* Forbes, Aug. 30, 2023.

p. 18   *When the Lions' co-owners gathered:* DFP, Nov. 23, 1963.

p. 18   *On the way, Ford turned:* Interview with Dick Morris.

p. 18   *John F. Kennedy had once enjoyed:* presidency.ucsb.edu.

p. 18   *"It turned into a sad, terrible day:* mlive.com, May 9, 2014.

p. 19   *Fifty years after that awful:* vintagedetroit.com, Nov. 22, 2013.

A Degas Bronze and a Job Offer

p. 20   *A few days before Christmas 1963:* Interview with Dick Morris.

p. 21   *The Fords, like many wealthy families*: Ibid.; Collier and Horowitz, *The Fords*, 286.

p. 22   *Bill Ford and Dick Morris walked*: Interview with Dick Morris.

p. 22   *Or did they talk about something*: NYT, Dec. 15, 1963.

p. 23   *Those reactions, while not inaccurate*: Aldrich, *Old Money*, 80.

p. 24   *"That kind of money is ridiculous,"*: DFP, Dec. 4, 1963.

p. 24   *It's good riddance*: DN, Dec. 4, 1963.

p. 24   *The players had hanged Anderson in effigy*: AP photo, Jan. 16, 1961.

p. 25   *And, Morris added with a chuckle*: Interviews with Dick Morris and Jon Morris.

p. 25   *Coinciding with Ford's recent takeover*: NYT, Jan. 25, 1964.

The Long Lost Weekend

p. 27   *The Lions provided a perfect pretext*: Interview with Dick Morris.

p. 27   *Unlike big brother Henry II*: Ibid.; Lasky, *Never Complain, Never Explain*, 98.

p. 27   *And he would drink anything*: Collier and Horowitz, *The Fords*, 315.

p. 27   *The joke went like this*: Ibid.

p. 27   *His wife Martha learned*: Interview with Gene Bordinat.

p. 27   *It all went back to that spring day*: For a brief history of this ill-fated car, see "Continental Mark II: Ford's Fallen Star" in *Collectible Automobile*, June 1986.

p. 28   *Operating on a wing and a prayer*: Interview with William Clay Ford.

p. 29   *And there sat Bill Ford's eldest brother*: Ibid.

p. 31   *The Ivy League Look*: NR.com, Jan. 7, 2019.

p. 31   *Drinking rituals evolved*: Interview with Gene Bordinat.

p. 33   *Dick Morris traveled widely*: Interview with Dick Morris.

p. 33   *When Henry II traveled to Paris*: Collier and Horowitz, *The Fords*, 287.

p. 33   *In his biography*: Lasky, *Never Complain, Never Explain*, 167.

p. 33   *Dick Morris was no stranger*: Interview with Dick Morris.

p. 34   *A plump target for the laughter*: Interview with Gene Bordinat.

p. 34   *Back in 1955 Walker had been anointed*: *Time*, Nov. 4, 1957.

p. 35   *Pathetic was a shibboleth*: Aldrich, *Old Money*, 76.

p. 35   *On the night before the executive committee*: Interviews with Gene Bordinat and Dick Morris.

p. 36   *That evening at the Dearborn Inn*: Interview with Gene Bordinat.

Sportsman of the Year

p. 38   *On January 10*: NYT, Jan. 11, 1964.

p. 38   *Meanwhile, in an unassuming house*: George, *Where Did Our Love Go?*, 28–49.

p. 39   *NFL Commissioner Pete Rozelle announced*: NYT, March 17, 1964.

p. 39   *"Everything was tied together,"*: SI, Aug. 6, 2021.

p. 40   *While playing at the University of Iowa*: Ibid.

p. 40   *There's compelling evidence*: Interview with Bob Whitlow.

p. 41   *"On any given Sunday,"*: WP, Jan. 29, 2023.

p. 41   *They engaged in an ugly slugfest*: Izenberg, *Rozelle*, 43–50.

p. 42   *Unfazed, Rozelle, who saw himself*: Ibid., 67–79; SI, Jan. 6, 1964.

p. 43   *Dick would stroll into the bar*: Interview with David Jackson. There are countless conflicting accounts of this legendary barroom brawl. I have decided to rely on my interviews with David Jackson, who married Jimmy Butsicaris's daughter Liz and worked for many years as a doorman at the Lindell AC Jackson's account comes from several people who were eyewitnesses and/or participants in the big bout.

p. 43   *The Lions' training camp*: Plimpton, *Paper Lion.*

p. 43   *Karras called Rozelle*: SI, Aug. 8, 2021.

p. 44   *Hornung, on the other hand*: Maraniss, *When Pride Still Mattered*, 341.

p. 44   *Lombardi, the Packers' coach*: Ibid., 339.

p. 44   *"Compliance," he said*: SI, Jan. 6, 1964.

p. 44   *When Ford paid off Karras's fine*: DN, Nov. 20, 1963.

p. 44   *One December night in 1963*: fornology.blogspot.com, Nov. 25, 2020.

p. 46   *A month after the reinstatements*: NYT, May 1, 1964.

p. 46   *Four days before Christmas*: DFP, Dec. 22, 1964.

p. 46   *Now the spotlight swung*: NYT, Dec. 24, 1964.

The Snowball Sendoff

p. 48   *It was Erickson who suggested*: DFP, Nov. 3, 2013.

p. 49   *For two and a half hours, in his own telling*: AP, Jan. 8, 1965.

p. 49   *In announcing the hiring*: DFP, Jan. 8, 1965.

p. 49   *Dismayed by the lack of change*: Interview with Dick Morris.

p. 52   *In fairness, there were numerous problems*: SI, June 21, 2017.

p. 52   *The popular linebacker Joe Schmidt*: DFP, March 11, 1966.

p. 53   *"Joe," Looney said*: SI, June 21, 2017; Plimpton, *Paper Lion*, 73.

p. 53   *The turning point came*: Interview with Dick Morris; Collier and Horowitz, *The Fords*, 351.

p. 54   *"You want a messenger boy,"*: SI, June 21, 2017.

p. 54   *"I never saw a game*: SI, Jan. 3, 1972.

p. 54   *I was in the stands that day*: In addition to frigid temperatures, Detroit was hit with five inches of snow the day before the Minnesota game, which provided ample ammunition for Harry Gilmer's photogenic sendoff.

p. 55   *"At least they didn't put rocks in the snowballs,"*: DFP, Dec. 12, 1966.

A Cocoon of Privilege

p. 56   *A typically vicious rebuke*: Bak, *Henry and Edsel*, 132–133.

p. 57   *Instead, strings were pulled*: Nevins and Hill, *Ford: Decline and Rebirth*, 250–252.

p. 57   *Henry's wife and Edsel's widow*: Ibid., 268.

p. 57   *It's worth noting that both Henry II*: Bak, *Henry and Edsel*, 266.

p. 57   *"Without anyone knowing my name*: NYT, March 9, 2014.

p. 58   *After old Henry came into the money*: Bak, *Henry and Edsel*, 64–65, 90–91.

p. 58   *They called it Gaukler Pointe*: Collier and Horowitz, *The Fords*, 138. On Oct. 13, 2023, I took a guided tour of the buildings and grounds. A popular tourist attraction officially known at the Edsel and Eleanor Ford House, the estate is now listed on the National Register of Historic Places and has been designated a National Historic Landmark.

p. 59   *There was never any doubt*: Ibid., 140–141.

p. 60   *The children were sent off*: Ibid., 138–139.

p. 60   *The sight of these wealthy provincials*: Ibid., 144–145.

p. 61   *Edsel took the boys to races*: Interview with William Clay Ford.

p. 62   *Henry Ford's father*: Collier and Horowitz, *The Fords*, 15–19.

p. 63   *The story of Henry Ford's rise*: Ibid., 18–54.

p. 64   *As Henry II quickly learned*: Nevins and Hill, *Ford: Decline and Rebirth*, 110–117, 252–269.

p. 65   *As the company came back from the grave*: Collier and Horowitz, *The Fords*, 279.

Blank Slates

p. 67   *Bill Ford was not going to make*: Interview with Dick Morris.

p. 68   *McNamara's nearly religious worship*: Ibid.

p. 68   *When McNamara arrived in Washington*: Reeves, *President Kennedy*, 25.

p. 69   *One Kennedy biographer*: Ibid., 14.

p. 70   *This was not lost on Joe Falls*: DFP, Jan. 2, 1967.

p. 71   *"Ford said Schmidt*: DFP, Jan. 12, 1967.

p. 71   *"Russ Thomas and Edwin Anderson*: Interview with Sam Williams.

p. 72   *The team had brought in one of the NFL's first*: NYT, April 30, 2008.

p. 73   *After Lane retired as a player*: MC, March 19, 1966.

p. 74   *"I don't think the coaches had anything*: Bak, *When Lions Were Kings*, 219.

The Motor City Is Burning

p. 75   *No less an authority*: Levine, *My Lost Poets*, 40.

p. 76   *Horton claims in his memoir*: Horton and White, 91.

p. 76   *Detroit has always been a musical town*: Levine, *My Lost Poets*, 57–76. Levine's essay "Detroit Jazz in the Late Forties and Early Fifties" is a scintillating reminder of how vibrant the city's jazz scene once was. As a college student and aspiring poet, Levine saw some of the greats, including Billie Holiday, Charlie Parker, Lester Young, and Art Tatum, plus a galaxy of homegrown stars, from Kenny Burrell to Pepper Adams, Yusef Lateef, and Paul Chambers. The venues ranged from high school gyms to dark dives (including "a toilet on Grand River"), the Flame Show Bar and the Paradise Theater. Those musicians taught the budding poet an invaluable lesson: "it was possible to be a kid from Detroit and an artist." See also: "From Hastings Street to the Bluebird: The Blues and Jazz Traditions in Detroit," by Lars Bjorn, MQR, Vol. 25, No. 2. A documentary called *Best of the Best: Jazz From Detroit* premiered at the 2024 Freep Film Festival. It was written and co-produced by former *Free Press* music critic Mark Stryker, author of the superb book, *Jazz From Detroit*. On the eve of the documentary's debut, Stryker told the paper that the history of the city's jazz scene mirrored the city's larger history. "Parts of it make you want to cheer," he said, "and other parts of the history make you want to weep. That's part of the Detroit experience."

p. 76   *The Motor City Is Burning*: by John Lee Hooker, Bluesway Records, 1967.

p. 77   *Detroiters are, in Philip Levine's words*: TPR, Summer 1988, 185.

p. 78   *In the fiery summer of 1967*: MQR, Vol. 25, No. 2.

p. 78   *Bill Ford's mansion on Lake Shore Road*: NYT, June 17, 1967.

p. 79   *He called Ford Motor Company and asked*: Collier and Horowitz, *The Fords*, 352.

p. 79   *A week after the last fires were extinguished*: AP, Aug. 6, 1967.

p. 80   *"I wanted to draft quarterback*: Vintage Detroit Collection, Dec. 2, 2014.

p. 80   *In another interview*: Interview with Carl Brettschneider.

p. 80   *"The head coach did not trust the general manager*: DN, April 27, 2022.

p. 81   *When the team, on Ford's orders*: Ibid.

Ball of Confusion

p. 82   *For the first time, Americans saw proof*: WP, May 25, 2018.

p. 82   *Ford's eldest child, Muffy*: Collier and Horowitz, *The Fords*, 354.

p. 83   *"Well, anybody who's against this war*: Ibid.

p. 83   *"I had a wonderful time*: Ibid., 354–355.

p. 83   *Four days after Johnson's shocker*: Molina, *Like a Fading Shadow*, 270–273. This re-creation of the assassin in action was inspired by the novel *Like a Fading Shadow*.

p. 84   *Yet Detroit, still reeling*: DFP, April 5, 1968.

p. 84   *Much of it was racially motivated*: Oates, *them*, 82.

p. 84   *A young writer named Joyce Carol Oates*: MQR, Vol. 25, No. 2.

p. 85   *Or, as the Temptations would cleverly depict*: "Ball of Confusion," Gordy Records, 1970.

p. 85   *Oates and her husband, Raymond Smith*: MQR, op. cit.

p. 85   *After winning the California Democratic primary*: *Time*, June 14, 1968.

p. 86   *The place was a typhoon*: I heard some of the noise firsthand and heard about a lot more of it secondhand from hearing-impaired Grande regulars.

p. 86   *The balm of baseball*: DFP, Sept. 9, 2018.

p. 87   *Russ Thomas had dealt the unloved*: DFP, May 2, 1968.

p. 87   *Computers were turning scouting*: CR, July 29, 2019.

p. 87   *Bill Ford once sat across the bargaining table*: Interview with William Clay Ford.

p. 88   *Back at the table, Gordy stumbled*: Maraniss, *When Pride Still Mattered*, 441.

p. 88   *Some owners wanted to bring in scab players*: Ibid., 442.

This Love Affair

p. 90   *"In years past*: SI, Sept. 16, 1968.

p. 90   *The movie version of George Plimpton's bestseller*: DFP, Oct. 4, 1968.

p. 91   *After a twenty-three-year absence:* I attended my only World Series game that Saturday afternoon, and I watched the Cardinals blast home runs, steal bases at will, and utterly deflate the Tigers and the sellout crowd in a runaway 8–3 win. With the Cardinals' intimidating Bob Gibson scheduled to pitch on

Sunday and the Tigers trailing two games to one, the mood in Detroit was gloomy.

p. 91   *Lost in the opening-night hoopla*: DFP, April 14, 2018.

p. 92   *Film critic Roger Ebert*: rogerebert.com, Dec. 10, 1968.

p. 93   *There was interracial dancing in the streets*: DFP, Sept. 7, 2018.

p. 93   *For the first time in his tenure as head coach*: DN, Oct. 21, 1968.

p. 93   *A day and a half of incessant rain*: https://rayonsports.com/nfl-throwback-thursday-thanksgiving-mud-bowl/.

p. 94   *In the next morning's paper*: DFP, Nov. 29, 1968.

p. 95   *"I think soccer-style kicking is a fad*: SI, Oct. 24, 2022.

A Lucky Man

p. 96   *As it turned out, Morris had a second act*: Interview with Dick Morris.

p. 96   *His face was now puffy and pink*: Collier and Horowitz, *The Fords*, 297.

p. 97   *In the executive dining room*: Iacocca and Novak, *Iacocca: An Autobiography*, 95–97. Henry II's provincial tastes in food were hardly unusual in the Midwest at that time. At Detroit's better restaurants, a popular entrée was "roast beef *au jus*," a slab of pink beef swimming in its bloody juices. A typical salad was a wedge of iceberg lettuce topped with "Thousand Island" dressing—half ketchup, half mayonnaise.

p. 97   *Anne McDonnell had married Henry II*: AAC, March 14, 2014; Collier and Horowitz, *The Fords*, 173.

p. 97   *Henry's jet-set crowds*: Lasky, *Never Complain, Never Explain*, 140–141.

p. 97   *As general managers came and went*: Interview with Dick Morris.

p. 100   *Having established his worth*: Sanders and Paladino, *Tales from the Detroit Lions*, 24.

p. 101   *As his duet partner Tammi Terrell*: George, *Where Did Our Love Go?*, 174–175.

p. 102   *In early October the* New York Times *wrote*: NYT, Oct. 7, 1970.

p. 103   *"I don't believe this,"*: youtube.com/watch?v=aEoG5pUdAsY.

p. 103   *Jack Saylor of the* Free Press: Interview with Joe Lapointe.

p. 104   *They locked the barroom doors*: DFP, Nov. 3, 2013.

p. 104   *"That plane flight did wonders for me,"*: Ibid.

p. 105   *In the week after the game*: Sanders and Paladino, *Tales from the Detroit Lions*, 154.

p. 105   *The Lions' defense kept Dallas out of the end zone*: DFP, Dec. 27, 1970.

p. 106   *Berry Gordy had balked at releasing*: George, *Where Did Our Love Go?*, 178.

Dodging the Ziggy

p. 107   *Joe Schmidt even coined a term*: DN, Nov. 7, 2015.

p. 107   *He still had a year left on his contract*: DFP, July 2, 1971.

p. 107   *Russ Thomas said the decision*: DN, Sept. 14, 1971.

p. 107   *As the teams were moving toward*: Maraniss, *When Pride Still Mattered*, 371.

p. 108   *Schmidt's decision to let him go*: Interview with Joe Schmidt.

p. 108   *In the sixth game of the season*: DFP, Jan. 3, 2013.

p. 109   *Veteran linebacker Wayne Walker put it*: DFP, Oct. 23, 2021.

p. 110   *"Being subjected to Bill Ford and Russ Thomas*: Interview with Joe Schmidt.

p. 110   *As both head coach and general manager*: Maraniss, *When Pride Still Mattered*, 200.

p. 111   *"He could even tell his players*: Interview with Joe Schmidt.

p. 112   *Schmidt has a theory*: Ibid.

p. 112   *Here's another theory*: This speculation is based on interviews and my reading of the history. Several people with longstanding connections to the Lions and the Fords agreed that it's plausible. They asked not to be quoted by name.

p. 112   *"The general manager has to know what's best*: Interview with Joe Schmidt.

p. 113   *Berry Gordy had been spending more*: George, *Where Did Our Love Go?*, 148–149.

p. 113   *Years after his retirement*: Sanders and Paladino, *Tales from the Detroit Lions*, 153.

p. 113   *Under the* Free Press *headline*: DFP, Dec. 13, 1972.

p. 114   *"When that negative stuff gets in the papers*: Interview with Joe Schmidt.

p. 114   *"I do not understand that team,"*: DFP, Jan. 14, 1973.

p. 115   *With Ford sitting to his right*: DFP, Jan. 13, 1973.

SECOND QUARTER: An Overkill of Mediocrity (1973–1989)

Twist This!

p. 119   *For years Bill Ford had dreamed*: DFP, Dec. 25, 1965.

p. 119   *That began to change in the 1960s*: https://www.vintagedetroit.com/the-birth-of-the-silverdome, Nov. 29, 2018.

p. 120   *By the late 1960s, Bill Ford had joined*: silverdome-architect.blogspot.com.

p. 120   *A separate committee was exploring*: DFP, Dec. 25, 1965.

p. 121   *"Babylonian ziggurat hotels,"*: Wolfe, *From Bauhaus to Our House*, 74.

p. 121   *To pay for such an insular fantasy*: NYT, Dec. 30, 2017.

p. 121   *"The logo of the Renaissance Center*: Lasky, *Never Complain, Never Explain*, 180–181.

p. 122   *"The message is clear,"*: TG, May 22, 2015.

p. 122   *"To understand the Renaissance Center*: Ibid.

p. 122   *It now houses*: DFP, April 15, 2024. In April 2024, General Motors announced that it planned to move its headquarters personnel from the RenCen to the skyscraper that was rising a few blocks to the north on the site of the former J.L. Hudson department store. The RenCen can't seem to win for losing.

p. 123   *Given the tenacity of his commitment*: This is speculation based on the well-documented sibling rivalries that festered between Henry II and both of his brothers.

p. 123   *In 1970 he signed a tentative agreement*: DN, March 5, 1970.

p. 123   *In early 1971, his deadline long past*: DN, Feb. 1, 1971.

p. 123   *"This," he crowed*: silverdome-architect.blogspot.com, Feb. 1, 1971.

p. 123   *"I think I ought to say something before*: DN, Feb. 1, 1971.

p. 124   *Bill Ford claimed that he preferred*: Ibid.

p. 124   *"This isn't an anti-Detroit move,"*: Ibid.

p. 124   *The $55.7 million cost would be covered*: http://football.ballparks.com/NFL/DetroitLions/index.htm, April 24, 2024.

p. 125   *Bill Ford was free to do as he pleased*: This speculation that Bill Ford derived pleasure
          from having the upper hand for a change comes from my personal experience of
          being the younger of two brothers—and therefore almost always the underdog.
p. 125   *"Bill's ass," as the historian*: Lacey, *Ford: The Men and the Machine*, 551.

Mayor Motherfucker
p. 126   *Two weeks after Schmidt's resignation*: AP, Jan. 26, 1973.
p. 126   *That fall, while the enclosed stadium*: NYT, Oct.7, 1973.
p. 127   *A month after the beginning of the Arab*: Young and Wheeler, *Hard Stuff*, 1–38.
p. 127   *In his first inaugural address*: Ibid., 200–201.
p. 128   *In his autobiography*: Ibid., 200.
p. 128   *The book's ghostwriter:* Interview with Lonnie Wheeler. Readers who wish
          to take a deeper dive into the fluorescent rhetoric of Coleman Young should
          read the compendium *Quotations from Mayor Coleman A. Young*, compiled by
          former *Free Press* reporter Bill McGraw. This delightful little red book owes
          an acknowledged debt to another world-class aphorist, Mao Zedong.
p. 129   *The following summer, on July 28*: AP, July 28, 1974.
p. 129   *The next day, Bill Ford reversed course*: AP, July 29, 1974.
p. 130   *"The coach would introduce him,"*: DFP, Sept. 10, 2023.

The Big Muffin
p. 131   *The house was not close to being full*: DFP, Aug. 23, 1975.
p. 131   *Now in its fifth season*: sportsmediawatch.com.
p. 132   *The sportscaster Howard Cosell*: DFP, Oct. 7, 1975.
p. 132   *It would soon become evident*: NYT, Aug. 21, 1996.
p. 133   *By the fourth quarter*: Interview with Dave Tremblay.
p. 133   *One* Free Press *reporter*: Interview with Bill McGraw.
p. 133   *The Lions' starting center that season*: Interview with Jon Morris.
p. 134   *When he approached Russ Thomas*: DN, May 22, 1975.
p. 134   *"He treated me like a dumb slave*: Ibid.
p. 134   *Bryant refused to leave a winner*: DN, July 26, 1975.
p. 134   *He filed a lawsuit*: DFP, July 30, 1975.
p. 135   *Rick Forzano announced that he didn't care*: DFP, Aug. 2, 1975.
p. 135   *After Rozelle awarded the Lions*: Ibid.
p. 135   *Rosenbloom claimed he had made*: Ibid.
p. 136   *When the Lions tried to persuade*: Interview with David Jackson.
p. 136   *Morris rarely lifted weights*: Interview with Jon Morris.
p. 138   *Even Bill Ford got in the spirit*: DFP, Dec. 22, 1975.
p. 138   *The last few years*: DN, Dec. 23, 1975.
p. 138   *"This is a great bunch of guys,"*: DFP, Dec. 22, 1975.

Yooperman and Yooperwoman
p. 139   *The team may have been locked forever*: DFP, Dec. 10, 1978.
p. 139   *For starters, Michigan is a state*: worldpopulationreview.com.

p. 140   *It could even be argued*: TPR, Summer 1988, 186.

p. 141   *Why did football bring me so to life?*: Exley, *A Fan's Notes*, 8.

p. 141   *"It is foolish and childish*: NYT, May 20, 2022.

p. 142   *It never went out of Donnie Stefanski's life*: DFP, Sept. 11, 2023.

p. 143   *In the closing days of 1975*: NYT, Dec. 31, 1975.

p. 143   *After that high courtroom drama:* DFP, Feb. 2, 1976.

On the Couch

p. 145   *One headline read*: DN, Aug. 26, 1976.

p. 146   *Nicknamed the Bird*: Epstein, *Stars and Strikes*, 128–31, 206–10.

p. 146   *The night turned into a horror*: DFP, Aug. 16, 1976.

p. 147   *"It happens everywhere,"*: AAS, Sept. 3, 1976.

p. 147   *"I jumped on Rick and Russ*: DN, Sept. 20, 1976.

p. 148   *After a 10*: DFP, Oct. 5, 1976.

p. 148   *"Those who know Ford and his relationship*: DFP, Oct. 6, 1976.

p. 149   *Jerry Green of the* News: DN, Oct. 5, 1976.

p. 149   *Later that day Ford proved*: NYT, Oct. 6, 1976.

p. 150   *Joe Falls of the* Free Press *opened*: DFP, Dec. 28, 1976.

p. 150   *Ford noted that he traveled all over*: TFN, Dec. 14, 1976.

Out-Ownered

p. 151   *Ford, who'd scoffed at the "ridiculous"*: DFP, Jan. 29, 1977.

p. 152   *Raised in Baltimore*: Izenberg, *Rozelle*, 166–167.

p. 152   *One veteran sportswriter*: Izenberg, *Rozelle*, 167.

p. 152   *The reason for Knox's openness*: DFP, Jan. 29, 1977.

p. 152   *"They have not sought permission*: DFP, Jan. 27, 1977.

p. 152   *So Bill Ford boarded a plane to Los Angeles*: DFP, Jan. 29, 1977.

p. 153   *"They think if a guy can walk*: DFP, Jan. 30, 1977.

p. 153   *Then Knox abruptly killed*: DN, Feb. 9, 1977.

p. 153   *Rosenbloom Beats Ford Again*: DFP, Feb. 10, 1977.

p. 153   *Joe Falls tarred Ford and Thomas*: DF, Feb. 4, 1977.

p. 153   *One headline said it all*: DFP, Feb. 10, 1977.

p. 153   *Red-faced and empty-handed*: Ibid.

p. 153   *The thought of three more years*: DN, Feb. 11, 1977.

p. 154   *So far, in fact, that a state legislator*: DFP, Nov. 20, 1977.

p. 154   *"The state of Michigan*: Ibid.

p. 154   *Meanwhile, a group in Grand Rapids*: DFP, Nov. 18, 1977.

p. 155   *"The Lions' offense is a joke*: DN, Dec. 6, 1977.

p. 155   *Jon Morris, who kept putting*: Interview with Jon Morris.

p. 156   *When he owned the Baltimore Colts*: SI, Dec. 13, 1965.

p. 156   *A longtime writer on the Lions beat*: Interview with Mike O'Hara.

p. 156   *Rosenbloom's displeasure went even deeper*: Izenberg, *Rozelle*, 169–176.

p. 157   *It appeared in most newspapers*: SI, Dec. 13, 1965.

p. 158   *More than 900 people attended*: ramsrule.com.

Detroit Chainsaw Massacre

p. 159   *He promptly announced the wholesale firing*: DFP, Jan. 10, 1978.

p. 159   *Two days after the mass firing*: DFP, Jan. 12, 1978.

p. 160   *"[Clark] will run the draft*: Ibid.

p. 160   *Which led Jerry Green*: DN, Jan. 12, 1978.

p. 160   *Ford gave a simple explanation*: DFP, Jan. 12, 1978.

p. 160   *"That's when things got out of control,"*: DN, Jan. 12, 1978.

p. 161   *In April he called in the veterans*: DN, July 12, 1978.

p. 161   *Then he started shuffling the deck*: DN, Aug. 24, 1978.

p. 161   *The day after his fourth game as a Lion*: DFP, Sept. 29, 1978.

p. 162   *As the stakes climbed ever higher*: thefootballodyssey.com, July 14, 2020.

p. 162   *"The best thing that happened to us*: DN, Dec. 21, 1978.

p. 163   *"We all believe we're right on track*: DFP, Oct. 18, 1978.

p. 163   *The Lions were getting their money's worth*: DN, July 17, 1979.

p. 163   *For years Henry II had been feuding*: Iacocca and Novak, *Iacocca: An Autobiography*, 126–129.

p. 164   *One headline asked the question*: DFP, March 10, 1978.

p. 165   *Two weeks after the outsider was ousted*: NYT, July 28, 1978.

p. 166   *In the introduction to his mid-season interview*: DN, Oct. 24, 1978.

p. 166   *At the age of thirty-two, Charlie*: DN, July 3, 1981; NYT, June 16, 1981.

p. 167   *His wife likened him*: Ibid.

p. 168   *On that day George Wilson*: DFP, Nov. 25, 1978.

The Charlie Brown of Detroit

p. 169   *The dreamy optimism that prevailed*: OP, July 16, 1979.

p. 169   *Meeting in Honolulu in March*: DFP, March 14, 1979.

p. 169   *When asked about potential problems*: Ibid.

p. 170   *Monte Clark called it a "disaster."*: DFP. Aug. 25, 1979.

p. 170   *When he went looking for a new No. 3*: DFP, Aug. 17, 1979.

p. 170   *Clark, desperate for another No. 3*: OP, Sept. 5, 1979.

p. 170   *Jerry Green speculated*: DN, Sept. 19, 1979.

p. 171   *"After yesterday's game,"*: OP, Oct. 1, 1979.

p. 171   *Gary Danielson, still recuperating*: OP, Oct. 22, 1979.

p. 171   *At a bar in suburban Rochester*: DFP, Dec. 7, 1979.

p. 172   *After the game several Eagles players*: DN. Dec. 3, 1979.

p. 172   *The only bright note*: DFP, Nov. 21, 1979.

p. 173   *As Ford Motor Company's board of directors*: Lacey, *Ford: The Men and the Machine*, 658–659.

The Savior (I)

p. 175   *A fledgling, content-starved cable TV operation*: TA, April 23, 2020.

p. 175   *All of which inspired the comedian George Carlin*: https://www.youtube.com /watch?v=v0X34YpEQVU.

p. 176   *Rather than work out a fair contract*: DN, Jan. 27, 1980.

p. 176   *Jerry Green repeated a common, if vague, rumor*: DN, Nov. 19, 1979.

p. 177   *Hours before the free agency deadline*: DN, Feb. 1, 1980.

p. 177   *Sims was next into the meat grinder*: OP, April 4, 1980.

p. 177   *Asked what it would take to get his signature*: DFP, April 30, 1980.

p. 177   *The* New York Times *sports columnist*: TA, April 23, 2020.

p. 178   *While the contract negotiations*: DFP, May 8, 1980.

p. 178   *Thomas and Argovitz slugged it out*: DFP, April 5, 1980; June 10, 1980.

p. 179   *One giddy fan hoisted a banner*: OP, Sept. 28, 1980.

p. 179   *By late September*: SI, Sept. 20, 1980.

p. 179   *After each win, the roof of the Silverdome*: DFP, Sept. 25, 1980.

p. 180   *In the latest Silverdome snafu*: OP, Sept. 21, 1980.

p. 180   *"The field is unbelievably bad,"*: DFP, July 23, 1981.

p. 180   *First, Al "Bubba"*: Baker: OP, Sept. 12, 1980.

p. 181   *The veteran defensive tackle*: DFP, Oct. 30. 1980.

p. 181   *The veteran placekicker Benny Ricardo*: DFP, Sept. 5, 1980.

p. 181   *"I just can't take it anymore,"*: DFP, Oct. 30, 1980.

p. 182   *"I think it's hurting our team,"*: DN, Nov. 3, 1980.

p. 182   *Thomas shot back*: FJ, Nov. 3, 1980.

p. 182   *Woodcock's agent, Howard Slusher*: FJ, Oct. 30, 1980.

p. 183   *When the team announced it would appeal*: NYT, June 16, 1981.

The Ayatollah's Hush Puppies

p. 184   *A* Sports Illustrated *reporter*: DFP, Jan. 22, 1982.

p. 185   *It was hard to argue with his central point*: DFP, Jan. 25, 1982.

p. 185   *After the game*: Ibid.

p. 185   *To add to the chill, Billy Sims announced*: DFP, April 4, 1982.

p. 186   *After the call from Ford he told reporters*: DFP, Aug. 25, 1982.

p. 186   *Or as Sims's agent, Jerry Argovitz*: Ibid.

p. 186   *Bill Ford responded*: DN, Aug. 23, 1982.

p. 186   *Under the settlement*: WP, Nov. 17, 1982.

p. 187   *"Management will never again*: WP, Dec. 9, 1982.

p. 187   *When they returned to action*: DN, Nov. 26, 1982.

p. 188   *After the game, Bill Ford said*: DN, Jan. 1, 1984.

p. 188   *Many of them were gone*: DN, Oct. 15, 1984.

p. 189   *Lying on the field, he recalled later*: DN, Oct. 21, 1984.

p. 189   *The Lions' tight end Rob Rubick*: DFP, Feb. 7, 2015.

p. 189   *Sims added, "It's not*: FJ, Oct. 22, 1984.

White Boy Rick

p. 190   *In Detroit, "the crack mecca of the Midwest,"*: Adler, *Land of Opportunity*, 4.

p. 190   *At their peak, the Chambers brothers*: Ibid. 136-140.

p. 191   *When the couple had a child*: The Atavist *Magazine*, No. 41, 2015.

p. 191   *Meanwhile, the Motor City was burning again*: Chafets, *Devil's Night*, 1–4.

p. 192   *Part of the reason was the announcement*: OP, July 23, 1986.

p. 192   *Two noteworthy lives were soon:* NYT, Dec. 2, 1986, Sept. 30, 1987.
p. 192   *A few nights after:* OP, Oct. 29, 1987.
p. 193   *After practice, when a reporter asked:* detroitlions.com, July 12, 2018.
p. 193   *By then Fontes had pleaded guilty:* DFP, Nov. 10, 1987.
p. 193   *After years of waffling, Bill Ford finally:* DN, July 29, 1987.

THIRD QUARTER: Rock Bottom (1989–2014)

The Savior (II)
p. 197   *One fan referred to him:* Author interview with anonymous source.
p. 198   *The top pick, Troy Aikman:* AP, Dec. 24, 1993.
p. 198   *C. Lamont Smith and David Ware had an added:* Interview with C. Lamont Smith.
p. 199   *"The difficulty for Blacks in sports management:* Ebony, August 1992.
p. 199   *When Barry announced his intention:* Sanders and McCormick, *Now You See Him*, 47.
p. 199   *When the elder Sanders agreed to meet:* Interview with C. Lamont Smith.
p. 200   *"He was a numbers guy:* Ibid.
p. 200   *Finally, three days before the season:* DFP, Sept. 8, 1989.
p. 200   *Three days later:* Interview with Mike O'Hara.
p. 201   *When Sanders jogged off the field:* DFP, Sept. 11, 1989.
p. 201   *After the Lions lost the game:* Ibid.
p. 202   *As far as Thomas was concerned:* Interview with Bill Keenist.
p. 202   *At the end of the season, Sanders gave:* Ibid., DFP, Dec. 2, 1989.

A Rollercoaster on Steroids
p. 203   *In the last weeks of his long career:* DN, Dec. 4, 1989.
p. 203   *He made it clear at his introductory:* DFP, Dec. 28, 1989.
p. 203   *Then, with a fist pump, he added:* Interview with Bill Keenist.
p. 204   *Five months after Schmidt's promotion:* CT, May 23, 1990.
p. 204   *Fontes hired him as assistant coach for tight ends:* 1989 Detroit Lions Media Guide.
p. 205   *While few tears were shed:* DFP, March 20, 1990.
p. 205   *The New York Times obituary:* NYT, March 21, 1990.
p. 206   *Linebacker Chris Spielman had a simple:* OP, Nov. 21, 1991.
p. 207   *"The goal is to win tomorrow,":* DFP, Jan. 30, 2024.
p. 207   *"Somewhere in the parking lot,":* DFP, Jan. 13, 1992.
p. 208   *As the tomb-like Lions team bus pulled away:* DFP, Nov. 3, 2013.

Another Sickening Thud
p. 209   *Quarterback Rodney Peete wondered:* SN, July 20, 1992.
p. 209   *That fall, after years of nasty legal wrangling:* AP, Sept. 11, 1992.
p. 209   *By the end of the year:* AP, Jan. 7, 1993.
p. 210   *"We're going to do whatever you can do:* DN, Jan. 24, 1993.
p. 210   *"I had a very matter-of-fact conversation:* Ibid.
p. 210   *Schmidt, able to spend more freely:* DFP, April 26, 1993.

p. 210   *"He backed up his talk,"*: OP, April 28, 1993.

p. 211   *The playoffs opened*: DFP, Jan. 9, 1994.

p. 211   *Bill Ford had started moonlighting*: DFP, May 20, 1993.

p. 212   *Sounding like a Vince Lombardi acolyte*: DFP, Nov. 1992.

p. 212   *That summer, an astonishing work of art*: DFP, June 4, 1994.

p. 212   *After the team got off to a*: DFP, Nov. 6, 1995.

p. 213   *One day Sanders walked into Moore's office*: TA, Aug. 30, 2023.

p. 213   *After the season*: Interview with Bill Keenist.

p. 214   *"When you see a guy*: DN, Nov. 10, 1995.

p. 214   *Bill Ford Jr. later acknowledged*: OP, March 2, 1996.

p. 214   *The free agent lineman was pursued*: OP, Feb. 29, 1996.

p. 215   *"They let a core group of guys go*: DN, Oct. 6, 1997.

Private People

p. 216   *In early 1995*: DFP, Feb. 16, 1995.

p. 217   *A Pontiac health inspector discovered a large pipe*: FJ, April 21, 1996.

p. 218   *The team hired the well-connected*: OP, June 17, 1996.

p. 218   *To this end he took fifty*: OP, May 15, 1996.

p. 218   *That summer, after talks with Silverdome*: DFP, Aug. 21, 1996.

p. 219   *After the Lions finished*: DN, Dec. 29, 1996.

p. 219   *In his autobiography*: Sanders and McCormick, *Now You See Him*, 97.

p. 219   *A compelling theory was put forward*: DN, Dec. 21, 1996.

p. 219   *Now, as if to rebut Bacon's critique*: AAN, Jan. 14, 1997.

p. 220   *Dean Howe offered this*: Ibid.

p. 220   *One observer noted*: DN, Jan. 14, 1997.

p. 220   *"The thing that sets this apart*: DN, July 21, 1997.

p. 220   *When some suggested that Sanders*: Ibid.

p. 221   *To commemorate the moment*: Interview with Bill Keenist.

p. 221   *The win over the Jets*: DFP, Dec. 22, 1997.

p. 222   *Now Glover, also disinclined*: DFP, Feb. 18, 1998.

p. 222   *But on that day something died*: Interview with Bill Keenist.

p. 222   *"I just sort of come here to work,"*: OP, Oct. 27, 1998.

p. 222   *A picture in the* Oakland Press: Ibid.

p. 223   *"The Jekyll-and-Hyde aspect,"*: Ibid.

p. 223   *Meanwhile, Lomas Brown was missing*: DN, Oct. 29, 1998.

p. 223   *"The agreement," MacCambridge wrote*: MacCambridge, *The Big Time*, 386.

p. 223   *"The Ford family are good people*: DFP, Sept. 9, 2017.

Sick of It

p. 225   *While the Lions were in San Francisco*: Interviews with Mike O'Hara, Bill Keenist.

p. 225   *A few days after the Lions returned*: OP, Jan. 4, 1999.

p. 225   *Millen's lack of management experience*: Ibid.

p. 225   *Bill Ford Jr., an ardent advocate*: DN, Jan. 6, 1999.

p. 226   *Millen played down his contact*: DFP, Jan. 4, 1999.

p. 226   *"Mr. Ford," Millen said*: SI, Dec. 2, 2013.

p. 226   *Sounding a lot like a man auditioning*: OP, Jan. 5, 1999.

p. 227   *One headline laid out the truth*: DN, Jan. 13, 1999.

p. 227   *Bill Ford Jr. was said to be livid*: Interview with Mike O'Hara.

p. 227   *"I think it's a shame,"*: DN, Jan. 13, 1999.

p. 227   *Barry Sanders observed*: Sanders and McCormick, *Now You See Him*, 99.

p. 227   *After one year with the Lions*: OP, Feb. 10, 1999.

p. 227   *"Pyne is typical of the decisions*: DFP, Jan. 12, 1999.

p. 228   *After Sanders failed to show up*: Interview with Mike O'Hara.

p. 228   *In the next day's*: DFP, May 7, 1999.

p. 229   *His son did not ask to be traded*: WE, July 28, 1999.

p. 229   *As he wrote in his autobiography*: Sanders and McCormick, *Now You See Him*, 120.

p. 230   *Then Sanders took a belated shot*: Ibid. 123.

p. 230   *Bill Keenist, the team's publicist*: Interview with Bill Keenist.

p. 230   *With his face red and his eyes ablaze*: NYT, Nov. 8, 2000.

p. 231   *The website Football Outsiders*: footballoutsiders.com, 2004.

p. 231   *The players looked indifferent*: DN, Nov. 6, 2000.

p. 231   *In the locker room after the game*: Ibid.

p. 231   *"He had nothing else to give,"*: USAT, Nov. 7, 2000.

p. 232   *When Drew Sharp of the* Free Press: DFP, Nov. 7, 2000.

The Wizard of Arrrgh

p. 233   *He was still devoted:* Collier and Horowitz, *The Fords*, 428.

p. 233   *It was there*: Interview with Dick Morris.

p. 234   *With the downtown stadium nearing completion*: Interview with Bill Keenist.

p. 234   *Despite Millen's lack of any front-office experience*: OP, Jan. 6, 2001.

p. 234   *"Let's not get carried away*: DFP, Jan. 5, 2001.

p. 235   *Then Millen tried to woo*: Interview with Matt Millen.

p. 235   *While the lawyers haggled*: DFP, Nov. 30, 2001.

p. 236   *Pete Rozelle had let the games go on*: Izenberg, *Rozelle*, 87.

p. 236   *Meanwhile, the Glass House was boiling*: DFP, Oct. 31, 2001.

p. 236   *That immaculate record had also caught*: DN, Dec. 26, 2001.

p. 237   *The settlement with the Silverdome*: OP, Nov. 29, 2001.

p. 237   *The players and fans reacted*: DN, Dec. 17, 2001.

p. 237   *The next night Leno jumped*: DFP, Dec. 18, 2001.

p. 237   *Morton soon found himself*: DFP, Dec. 19, 2001.

p. 237   *For the first time in a life*: Interview with Matt Millen.

p. 238   *"We played on some brutal fields,"*: DN, Aug. 19, 2002.

p. 238   *"This stadium makes you feel*: DFP, Aug. 26, 2002.

p. 239   *It was a case of he said, he said*: AAN, Feb. 15, 2005.

p. 239   *When Harrington stepped off the plane*: DFP, Nov. 24, 2020.

p. 240   *The two losses led the* News: DN, Sept. 16, 2002.

p. 240   Fire Millen Now: OP, Sept. 19, 2002.

p. 240   *"This was his first opportunity*: DFP, Nov. 19, 2002.

p. 240   *Though Harrington acknowledged*: DFP, Nov. 24, 2020.

p. 240   *Two months later*: OP, Oct. 18, 2002.

p. 240   *"It's derogatory toward the player*: Ibid.

p. 241   *The papers pounced*: DFP, Oct. 18, 2002.

p. 241   *It was also the end*: OP, Jan. 28, 2003.

This Culture of Losing

p. 242   *But by hiring a new head coach*: WP, July 25, 2003.

p. 243   *When he showed up for training camp*: Interview with Matt Millen.

p. 243   *"Straight up," Rogers admitted*: espngo.com, "Outside the Lines."

p. 243   *"I think teammates started*: DFP, Nov. 24, 2020.

p. 243   *"Joey had all the tools,"*: Interview with Matt Millen.

p. 244   *"Roy didn't like to work,"*: Ibid.

p. 244   *"Three years of coming close,"*: DFP, Nov. 24, 2020.

p. 244   *After Matt Millen compiled*: AP, Aug. 4, 2005.

p. 245   *"Dad," Matt Jr. roared*: Interview with Matt Millen.

p. 245   *He didn't work the job year-round*: Ibid.

p. 246   *"We're all at fault,"*: DFP, Nov. 29, 2005.

p. 247   *Marinelli was, in the words*: SI, Aug. 28, 2012.

p. 247   *"The confidence I had that was brimming*: DFP, Nov. 24, 2020.

p. 247   *Ford Jr. brought in his brother-in-law*: Hoffman, *American Icon*, 52.

p. 249   *Late that summer, Joe Cullen*: espn.com, Dec. 19, 2006; NYT, Nov. 1, 2007.

p. 249   *Newfangled things called websites*: DN, Dec. 15, 2005.

The Ghost of Grosse Pointe

p. 251   *A month earlier*: NYT, Sept. 24, 2008.

p. 252   *The blogger Sean Yuille*: https://www.prideofdetroit.com/2008/9/24/621319
          /matt-millen-leaves-the-lio.

p. 252   *After a typically lopsided*: espn.com, Dec. 22, 2008.

p. 252   *Marinelli didn't see the humor*: mlive.com, Dec. 22, 2008.

p. 252   *Managing editor Don Nauss*: DN, Dec. 23, 2008.

p. 253   *In the penultimate year of his life*: SI, Aug. 29, 2012.

p. 254   *Even Lomas Brown*: Brown and Isenberg, *If These Walls Could Talk*, 92.

p. 254   *After taking over the Lions' beat*: Interview with Dave Birkett.

p. 254   *In the summer of 2013*: NYT, July 18, 2013.

p. 255   *The obituaries were generally kind*: NYT, March 9, 2014.

p. 255   Automaker William Clay Ford Sr. couldn't: nfl.com, March 9, 2014.

FOURTH QUARTER: On the Road to Redemption (2014–2024)

Quinntricia

p. 259   *The obituaries noted*: DFP, March 10, 2014.

p. 259   *The day after Bill Ford died*: DFP, March 11, 2014.

p. 259   *With the Lions holding a narrow lead*: DFP, Jan. 5, 2015.

p. 260   *Martha Ford soon made it known*: DFP, Nov. 5, 2015.

p. 260   *"You got me on offense,"*: https://www.cbssports.com/nfl/news/calvin-johnson -opens-up-about-his-early-retirement-aaron-rodgers-recruitment-pitch -ongoing-rift-with-lions, Nov. 13, 2020.

p. 260   *Rod Wood, the team's new president*: DFP, Nov. 19, 2015.

p. 261   *His hiring by the Lions was rated "a coup"*: DFP, Nov. 25, 2015.

p. 261   *After the Lions had decamped*: TS, Nov. 24, 2009.

p. 262   *On Sunday, Dec. 3, 2017*: DFP, Dec. 4, 2017.

p. 262   *"Once again angry people leave*: npr.org, Dec. 3, 2017.

p. 262   *Thirteen minutes into*: https://www.detroitlions.com/video/matt-patricia -introductory-press-conference-20346410, June 30, 2018.

p. 262   *Before Patricia coached a game*: DN, May 9, 2018.

p. 263   *When the story broke in Detroit*: Ibid.

p. 263   *Seeking to assert himself*: Bleacher Report, Nov. 13, 2020.

p. 264   *While the players were cleaning out*: Ibid.

p. 264   *Fans now arrived at Ford Field*: si.com, Nov. 25, 2019.

p. 264   *"[Changing coaches] would have been*: DFP, Dec. 18, 2019.

p. 265   *In her first lengthy interaction*: Ibid.

p. 265   *When Bill's and Martha's kids*: Hoffman, 18.

p. 265   *Her interest in sports seeped into*: CDB, Nov. 8, 2021.

p. 265   *In a column, Smith dubbed Sheila*: NYT, Feb. 8, 1976.

p. 266   *Elena Ford, a granddaughter*: Hoffman, *American Icon*, 209.

p. 266   *And one of Bill Jr.'s daughters*: DFP, May 14, 2021.

p. 266   *Until Sheila's mother assumed*: This statement is based on the front office personnel listed in Detroit Lions Media Guides going back to 1966.

p. 266   *"In a family like the Fords,"*: Hoffman, *American Icon*, 203.

p. 267   *Signs of Sheila's rising influence*: DFP, Nov. 17, 2015.

p. 267   *After his introductory meeting*: Hoffman, *American Icon*, 70.

p. 267   *Ford Jr. admitted as much*: Ibid., 75.

p. 268   *Ford family watchers*: Three sources concurred with this assessment but declined to be quoted by name.

p. 268   *Two days later she fired Quinn and Patricia*: DFP, Nov. 28, 2020.

"We're Going to Bite a Kneecap Off"

p. 269   *Sheila Ford Hamp had a different idea.*: The account of the search for a new general manager and head coach comes largely from DFP, Sept. 3, 2003, and TA, Jan. 20, 2023; Sept. 4, 2003; Sept. 6, 2023.

p. 271   *When Spielman called Campbell's boss*: TA, Sept. 4, 2003.

p. 271   *The Lions announced the hiring*: DFP, Jan. 14, 2021.

p. 271   *At his ninety-minute introductory*: DFP, Jan. 22, 2021.

p. 273   *Holmes was in this for the long haul*: USAT, April 30, 2023.

p. 273   *The gifted but oft-injured receiver*: DFP, Nov. 18, 2022.

p. 273   *When the Lions' No. 7 pick*: TA, Sept. 2, 2023.

p. 274   *"There are clips that I see*: Ibid.

p. 276   *The halftime ceremony*: DFP, Sept. 26, 2021.

p. 276   *Some even expressed outrage*: thedenforum.com, Oct. 2021. On the eve of the 2024 NFL Draft, the Lions unveiled several tweaks to their uniforms. One noteworthy change was the removal of the WCF monogram from the left sleeve of the jerseys. The late owner's initials would now appear in a small decal affixed to the helmets. Weaselpuppy, surely, was pleased.

p. 276   *As Johnson recalled*: DFP, June 2, 2018.

p. 276   *When their franchise quarterback Andrew Luck*: IS, Aug. 25, 2019.

p. 277   *Barry Sanders, after paying back*: DN, July 20, 2017.

p. 277   *Before the Lions' Mike Disner*: DFP, Aug. 6, 2021.

p. 278   *When it was announced that he would be inducted*: DN, Feb. 22, 2023.

p. 278   *Holmes, though discouraged*: DFP, Sept. 3, 2023.

One Ass Cheek and Three Toes

p. 279   *The Lions' rocky 2021 season*: hbo.com/hard-knocks.

p. 280   *He elevated Ben Johnson*: DFP, Feb. 7, 2022.

p. 280   *"I know this is difficult,"*: DFP, Oct. 26, 2022.

p. 281   *She made a very Sloan-esque vow*: TA, Sept. 4, 2023.

p. 281   *"The film was talking to me*: TA, Sept. 6, 2023.

p. 282   *By Christmastime, the* New York Times: NYT, Dec. 14, 2022.

p. 283   *The victory at Lambeau Field*: DFP, Jan. 9, 2023.

A Joyous Din

p. 285   *In the locker room after the game*: DFP, Sept. 8, 2023.

p. 286   *I came upon a burly guy*: Interview with Dave Tremblay.

p. 287   *"I think they'll make the playoffs*: Interview with Dave Birkett.

p. 288   *Before they left town*: TA, Oct. 14, 2019.

p. 289   *It was on Page 1-D*: DFP, Nov. 4, 1963.

Baptism of a Fan

p. 290   *After a long-standing Lions bar*: Interview with Will Johnson.

p. 291   *"We're not used to having that volume*: BR, Dec. 7, 2023.

p. 292   *"Most of our away games*: DFP, Jan. 26, 2024.

p. 292   *Dan Campbell added*: mlive, Oct. 16, 2023.

p. 292   *But under Al Davis*: espn.com, June 14, 2023.

p. 293   *For this very reason, Robert Irsay*: Euchner, *Playing the Field*, 105–115.

p. 293   *Carroll Rosenbloom's widow*: AP, Jan. 12, 2016.

p. 293   *But no owner, born rich or self-made*: WP, April 15, 2023.

p. 293   *"We have to act,"*: espn.com, Oct. 18, 2022.

p. 293   *After Jim Irsay pleaded guilty*: TG, Nov. 22, 2023.

p. 294   *Rather than face possible banishment*: cbsnews.com, May 12, 2023. The math is staggering. Bill Ford paid the unheard-of sum of $6 million for the Lions in 1963, and Snyder pocketed $6 *billion* on the sale of the Washington team six decades later.

R-e-s-p-e-c-t

p. 296   *Detroiters were generally understanding*: TG, Feb. 9, 2022.

p. 296   *It was so different that one bar*: DFP, Jan. 12, 2024.

p. 297   *"It's just a beautiful piece of poetry*: DFP, Jan. 9, 2024.

p. 297   *The Lions-Rams game became the most expensive*: mlive.com, Jan. 10, 2024.

p. 297   *Dave Tremblay, the chili-cooking*: Interview with Dave Tremblay.

p. 297   *Ann Morris, a cousin*: Interview with Ann Morris.

p. 298   *Peter King, the veteran*: The Peter King Podcast, Jan. 16, 2024.

p. 298   *"I've been to a lot of sporting events in Detroit,"*: Interview with Mark Sutter.

p. 299   *On this day, his daughter Megan*: DFP, Jan. 14, 2024.

p. 300   *Now another witness to forty years*: Interview with Bill Keenist.

Like a Snowman in the Sahara

p. 301   *On page A-20*: DFP, Jan. 28, 2024.

p. 301   *Will Johnson knew Bailey's Corner Pub*: Interview with Will Johnson.

p. 302   *In a snub to the Dallas Cowboys*: NYP, Jan. 21, 2024.

p. 302   *A color-coded map*: DMT, Jan. 25, 2024.

p. 302   *Will Johnson's six-hour wait*: Interview with Will Johnson.

p. 303   *Through the thin walls in the Kezar Stadium*: DFP, Sept. 9, 2017.

p. 303   *"We were just pissed off,"*: USAT, Jan. 29, 2024.

p. 304   *When Aiyuk caught that pass*: Interview with Will Johnson.

p. 306   *"The mood in this city on Monday*: Interview with Bill Dow.

p. 308   *Shortly after the loss in San Francisco*: TA, Jan. 30, 2024.

p. 308   *In its power rankings*: TA, Feb. 13, 2024.

SOURCES

Books

Adler, William M. *Land of Opportunity: One Family's Quest for the American Dream in the Age of Crack*. New York: Atlantic Monthly Press, 1995.

Aldrich, Nelson W. *Old Money: The Mythology of Wealth in America*. New York: Alfred A. Knopf, 1988.

Angell, Roger. *Five Seasons*. New York: Simon & Schuster, 1977.

Bak, Richard. *When Lions Were Kings: The Detroit Lions and the Fabulous Fifties*. Detroit: Wayne State University Press, 2020.

———. *Henry and Edsel: The Creation of the Ford Empire*. New York: John Wiley & Sons, 2003.

Binelli, Mark. *Detroit City Is the Place to Be: The Afterlife of an American Metropolis*. New York: Metropolitan Books, 2012.

Brown, Lomas (with Mike Isenberg). *If These Walls Could Talk: Stories from the Detroit Lions' Sideline, Locker Room, and Press Box*. Chicago: Triumph Books, 2016.

Chafets, Ze'ev. *Devil's Night: And Other True Tales of Detroit*. New York: Random House, 1990.

Collier, Peter (and David Horowitz). *The Fords: An American Epic*. New York: Summit Books, 1987.

———. *The Kennedys: An American Drama*. New York, Summit Books, 1984.

Epstein, Dan. *Stars and Strikes: Baseball and America in the Bicentennial Summer of '76*. New York: St. Martin's Press, 2014.

Exley, Frederick. *A Fan's Notes*. New York: Harper & Row, 1968.

Fountain, Ben. *Billy Lynn's Long Halftime Walk*. New York: Ecco, 2012.

George, Nelson. *Where Did Our Love Go?: The Rise and Fall of the Motown Sound*. Urbana: University of Illinois Press, 1985.

Fussell, Paul. *Class: A Guide Through the American Status System*. New York: Summit Books, 1983.

Halberstam, David. *The Reckoning*. New York: William Morrow and Co., 1986.

———. *The Best and the Brightest*. New York: Random House, 1972.

———. *The Fifties*. New York: Random House, 1994.

Hornung, Paul. *Golden Boy*. New York: Simon & Schuster, 2004.

Horton, Willie (and Kevin Allen). *Willie Horton: 23: Detroit's Own Willie the Wonder, the Tigers' First Black Great*. Chicago, Triumph Books, 2022.

Iacocca, Lee (with William Novak). *Iacocca: An Autobiography*. New York: Bantam Books, 1984.

Izenberg, Jerry. *Rozelle: A Biography*. Lincoln: University of Nebraska Press, 2014.

Lasky, Victor. *Never Complain, Never Explain: The Story of Henry Ford II*. New York: Richard Marek Publishers, 1981.

Layne, Bobby (with Bob Drum). *Always on Sunday*. Englewood Cliffs, N.J.: Prentice-Hall, 1962.

Leibovich, Mark. *Big Game: The NFL in Dangerous Times*. New York: Penguin Books, 2018.

Levine, Philip. *My Lost Poets: A Life in Poetry* (ed. Edward Hirsch). New York: Alfred A. Knopf, 2016.

Lyons, Robert. *On Any Given Sunday: A Life of Bert Bell*. Philadelphia: Temple University Press, 2010.

MacCambridge, Michael. *The Big Time: How the 1970s Transformed Sports in America*. New York: Grand Central, 2023.

———. *America's Game: The Epic Story of How Pro Football Captured a Nation*. New York: Random House, 2004.

Maraniss, David. *When Pride Still Mattered: A Life of Vince Lombardi*. New York: Simon & Schuster, 1999.

McGraw, Bill. *The Quotations of Mayor Coleman A. Young*. Detroit: Wayne State University Press, 2005.

McNamara, Robert. *In Retrospect: The Tragedy and Lessons of Vietnam*. New York: Random House, 1995.

Moldea, Dan E. *Interference: How Organized Crime Influences Professional Football*. New York: William Morrow & Co., 1989.

Molina, Antonio Muñoz. *Like a Fading Shadow* (trans. Camilo A. Ramirez). New York: Farrar, Straus and Giroux, 2017.

Nevins, Allan (and Frank Ernest Hill). *Ford: Decline and Rebirth 1933–1962*. New York: Charles Scribner's Sons, 1963.

Oates, Joyce Carol. *them*. New York: Vanguard Press, 1969.

Plimpton, George. *Paper Lion*. New York: Harper & Row, 1965.

Reeves, Richard. *President Kennedy: Profile of Power*. New York: Simon & Schuster, 1993.

Sanders, Barry (with Mark E. McCormick). *Barry Sanders: Now You See Him: His Own Story in His Own Words*. Indianapolis, Emmis Books, 2003.

Sanders, Charlie (with Larry Paladino). *Tales From the Detroit Lions.* Champaign, Ill.: Sports Publishing, 2005.

Sloan, Alfred (with John McDonald). *My Years with General Motors.* New York: Doubleday & Co., 1964.

Wolfe, Tom. *From Bauhaus to Our House.* New York: Farrar, Straus and Giroux, 1981.

Young, Coleman A. (with Lonnie Wheeler). *Hard Stuff: The Autobiography of Mayor Coleman Young.* New York: Viking, 1994.

News Agency, Newspaper, Magazine, Journal, and Internet Articles

News Agency: the Associated Press.

Newspapers: *Detroit Free Press, Detroit News, Michigan Chronicle, Ann Arbor Sun, The Athletic, The Guardian, New York Times, New York Post, Flint Journal, Oakland Press, Pittsburgh Post-Gazette, Pittsburgh Press, Indianapolis Star, Washington Post, Wichita Eagle,* and *USA Today.*

Magazines: *Sports Illustrated, Ebony, Time, The Atavist, Fortune, Collectible Automobile, Hour Detroit, Belt Magazine,* and *Texas Monthly.*

Journals: *Michigan Quarterly Review, Sloan Management Review, Sports Business Journal,* and *The Paris Review.*

Archives: Burton Historical Collection at the Detroit Public Library; Automotive Oral Histories at the Benson Ford Research Center, Dearborn, Mich.; Detroit Lions Scrapbooks, Allen Park, Mich.; photographs at the Walter P. Reuther Library in Detroit.

Websites: Vintage Detroit, mLive, Mac's Motor City Garage, Deadline Detroit, Detroit Metro Times, Bleacher Report, Bridge Michigan, Pro Football Journal, detroitlions prideofdetroit, woodwardsports, hagerty, michiganadvance, deadspin, pbs, theweek, nbcsports, texasmonthly, footballoutsiders, stonegreasers, and youtube.

Interviews

Birkett, Dave (by author)

Bordinat, Gene (by Automotive Oral Histories, AOH)

Brettschneider, Carl (by Bill Dow)

Dow, Bill (by author)

Ford, William Clay, Sr. (by AOH)

Gregorie, Eugene T. (Bob) (by AOH)

Jackson, David (by author)

Johnson, Will (by author)

Keenist, Bill (by author)

McGraw, Bill (by author)

Millen, Matt (by author)
Morris, Ann (by author)
Morris, Jon (by author)
Morris, Richard "Dick" (by author)
O'Hara, Mike (by author)
Schmidt, Joe (by author)
Smith, C. Lamont (by author)
Sutter, Mark (by author)
Tremblay, Dave (by author)
Walker, George (by AOH)
Wheeler, Lonnie (by author)
Whitlow, Bob (by Bill Dow)
Williams, Sam (by Bill Dow)

ACKNOWLEDGMENTS

Like all books, this one was a team effort. Among the many people I want to thank are Joe Lapointe and Bill Dow, veteran Detroit journalists who were the first readers of my first draft. Their knowledge of the terrain and their critical acumen were invaluable. Bill also generously shared tapes of interviews he conducted with many retired Lions players, a rich, firsthand source of insights into the workings of a professional football team. Another Detroiter who offered his wisdom and support was former *Free Press* reporter Bill McGraw. As noted in the text, my late father, Richard Morris, produced the seed that grew into this book.

Eamonn Reynolds, the Lions' current director of football communications, diligently provided access to events and information, including an extensive file of newspaper clippings that opened a window into the team's turbulent, colorful history. Bill Keenist, who held Eamonn's job for many years, is every writer's dream: a man with deep knowledge of the history and personalities who was willing to share his memories, opinions,and insights. As a bonus, Bill is a peerless storyteller. The staff at the Burton Historical Collection at the Detroit Public Library pointed me to an array of gems, and the staff at the Benson Ford Research Center provided transcripts of interviews that helped put flesh on the bones of this story. The photo archives at the Walter P. Reuther Library are a gold mine.

People with varied connections to the Lions and Detroit also opened up to me. They include the former Lions player and head coach Joe Schmidt;

the former player Jon Morris; the former general manager Matt Millen; the reporters Dave Birkett, Mike O'Hara, and Lonnie Wheeler; the agent C. Lamont Smith; the fans Will Johnson, Dave Tremblay, Ann Morris, and Mark Sutter; and the former doorman at the Lindell AC, David Jackson.

Once again, I'm grateful to the dogged crew at Pegasus Books and especially to my editor Jessica Case, who believed in this book even before the Lions woke up. My agent, Alice Martell, is the still point of my turning world. And Marianne remains, always and forever, the love of my life. Thanks to all of you for making this book possible.

INDEX

ABOUT THE AUTHOR

Bill Morris is the author of the novels *Motor City Burning*, *All Souls' Day*, and *Motor City*, as well as the nonfiction books *The Age of Astonishment: John Morris in the Miracle Century—From the Civil War to the Cold War* and *American Berserk: A Cub Reporter, a Small-Town Daily, the Schizo '70s*. His writing has appeared in numerous publications, including the *New York Times*, *Granta*, *Washington Post Magazine*, *LA Weekly*, *Popular Mechanics*, *Daily Beast*, and *The Millions*. Bill grew up in Detroit during the 1950s and '60s and now lives in New York City.